GIVING LEADERSHIP

Costa Mitchell

1

VINEYARD INTERNATIONAL PUBLISHING
8 Golf Street, Ladysmith, South Africa
Tel: +27 (0)366311612; Email: admin@emoyenipublishing.com

The Bible: ISV – International Standard Version (1996-2010 THE ISV FOUNDATION) is the version of Scripture quoted most often. If another version is used, it is indicated as follows:

ASV	American Standard Version (Public Domain)
BBE	Bible in Basic English (1949-1964 Cambridge Press)
CEV	Contemporary English Version (1995 American Bible Society)
ERV	Easy to Read Version (1978-2008 World Bible Translation Center)
ESV	English Standard Version (2001 Crossway Bibles through Good News Publishers)
GNB	Good News Bible (1992 American Bible Society)
KJV	King James Version (1769 Public Domain)
LITV	Literal Translation of the Holy Bible (1976-2008 Copyright Jay P. Green Sr.)
MKJV	Modern King James Version (1962-1978 Copyright Jay P. Green Sr.)
MSG	*The Message* (2002 NavPress Copyright Eugene H. Peterson)
NIV	New International Version (2008, Zondervan Publishing)
NLT	New Living Translation (2007 Tyndale Charitable Trust)
NRSV	New Revised Standard Version (1989 National Council of the Churches of Christ)
RSV	Revised Standard Version (1971 National Council of the Churches of Christ)
RV	Revised Version (1881 Public Domain)
TLB	The Living Bible (1971 KNT Charitable Trust)

ISBN

CONTENTS

ACKNOWLEDGEMENTS

I owe thanks beyond my ability to describe, to so many people who have made this book possible:

My wife, Lorraine, who has been my pillar, my joy, my love and peace in the midst of every adventure of my adult life, and whose honesty and acceptance have shaped my thinking, discerned God's will with me and taught me the life lessons without which everything would be empty theory.

My children, the laboratory subjects for this parent in process to live, and learn, and laugh a lot, and ultimately make family work quite well!

My parents, who shaped my soul and believed much more of me than I could have imagined without them.

My mentors, whose names appear in these pages and who, though absent, are still present through their wisdom and influence.

My professors, Drs Coenie Burger, Frederick Marais, Ian Nell, Marius Nel and others, who designed and delivered the M.Th. program through the Faculty of Practical Theology at Stellenbosch University, giving me insights and experience of which I can never say enough, and which I will never forget.

My friends and colleagues in ministry, who have allowed me the privilege of leading with them and through their willingness to serve.

Those who have advised, and worked alongside, and read, and edited, and designed, what is now the final version of a book I have dreamed of for 20 years. Stephan Vosloo Sr, who gave time, energy and wisdom to the entire process of preparing and publishing.

My editors Judy Twycross and Rhonda Crouse, whose patience and grace made the straight path easier to find.

Kim Hough, who first called me "Papa"(!) and who did the DTP while under threat from the Southern Cape fires. Alexander Venter and Bob Fulton for their generous endorsements.

Stephen Vosloo Jr, for the cover design and other graphics. I am very grateful. It beautifully captures my favourite animal, in this case the matriarch of a breeding herd, giving leadership, taking her herd with her through dangers of every kind, to their destiny. You will see her footprints in the pages that follow.

The Church of Jesus Christ in all its forms, and especially in the Association of Vineyard Churches, which has, by its faith and love, allowed me to see reflected in its face the length, and breadth, and height and depth, and to know God's unknowable love.

To God, who knows me so well, and still lets me play at His house!

FOREWORD BY ALEXANDER F. VENTER

Leadership, leadership, leadership! Why yet another book on leadership?

Beside other good reasons, it is because we are in a failure of leadership globally and in Africa, in particular, as seen by those of us who live in Africa. We have not learned from the literally thousands of books on leadership available to us today. Rather, we have regressed into a crisis of immoral, post-truth, self-serving leadership. Most things stand or fall on the quality of leadership – or lack thereof – in each of us, in the home, in churches, organisations, societies and nations in general.

We have specialised in the technology of leadership, the "know-how" of techniques and skills to get things done, to get people to do what we believe they ought to do. But in the process, we have become bankrupt in the spirituality of leadership, in the true spirit and character of authentic leadership. That is why things are largely the way they are in our world. *Giving Leadership* addresses this and other issues in leadership, for the sake of our own integrity as leaders, and for the sake of our world.

But it's not just about another book on leadership, it's about a person, a model, a track record, a life. I have had the privilege of knowing Costa as a personal friend and ministry colleague for over 40 years. He has functioned in leadership, in various capacities and different contexts, ever since I first met him. Having been a practitioner and learner, both in organic life and formal education, he has developed and worked with the material in this book for many years. Now, in his succession plan to hand over structural leadership, toward the end of his formal leadership journey, Costa has put it all down in this book for our benefit. This probably will constitute (a record of) his primary legacy for the Vineyard churches and beyond. So, what you are holding in your hands is, once again, not just another book on leadership, but a lived life. And not just another life, but a life of diligent learning and persevering implementation, of hard-won experience and faithfulness to God and his people – with many battle scars to show for it!

What is different in, or the particular contribution of, *Giving Leadership*?

The book is centred in Kingdom leadership, what I earlier called the spirituality of leadership. Here Costa seeks to communicate the key spiritual dynamic of the motivation and mode of leadership – based on the teachings and models of *biblical* leadership – what he calls character-based, selfless-serving, effective leadership.

First we need to know the essential idea and notion of leadership that Costa works with. Leadership is the actual process of leading people to a preferred future. Hence, it is functionally *giving* leadership in a vulnerable self-*giving* manner, not firmly *holding* leadership (the appointment, position, title) in a self-serving way. And, therefore, it is leadership by *vision* – the preferred future – the key to leadership for Costa. And then buy-in, implementation and momentum.

The functional aspects of leadership – skill, style and process – make up the last section of the book. This is where rich practical experience comes through – a great resource for any leader, whether beginning your journey, or a seasoned warrior. Costa has been true to his training in Practical Theology, constantly reflecting on how it can all work in practice, while seeking consistency with biblical revelation and relevance to the particular context in which we exercise leadership.

I heartily commend this book for your learning and growth.

Alexander F. Venter

Team Leader of Following Jesus
Association of Vineyard Churches, South Africa

PREFACE

"Everything I've ever learned about leadership,
I learned from ..."

I could complete the sentence in a number of ways. For example, my father, my wife, my children, my mentors, about 400 books on the subject, a great Master's program, the schools of experience and hard knocks! And all of them would be accurate. That is why what you are about to read is a story with many strands: narrative, precept, revelation and lessons from life. It is drawn from the input of great people and leaders I have been privileged to know, and from the observation of ordinary people in the ebb and flow of their life and mine.

My wife, Lorraine, and I have often reflected that, before couples are entrusted with a child to raise, they should be allowed a "practice kid" on whom they can make their mistakes, because it is so unfair on the real child to be the laboratory specimen for our learning, by trial and error, how to be half-decent parents to our children! The same thing could probably be said about church leaders. I think of Lorraine and myself, both aged 22, with a brand-new baby in tow, planting our first church, and trying to lead a small group, which included some senior business executives, missionaries and other mature, experienced Christians, into becoming an effective church. Thank goodness I didn't realise the true immensity of the task; I would have quit before I started!

I hope that in this book I have successfully condensed my story and its lessons into a helpful resource. Let me begin by introducing myself, and then, after some disclaimers, define the scope of this book.

My background, and the traditions which inform me, are quite ecumenical. I was born to a Greek father and South African mother, baptised (but not very well discipled!) in the Greek Orthodox Church, and taught the Christian faith and the Bible in a Methodist Sunday school. From an early age, I wanted to be a veterinary surgeon, and began studying veterinary science immediately after completing high school. In my first year of studying, I embraced atheism, but was rudely interrupted out of that comfortable philosophy through the witness of an evangelical Presbyterian who introduced me to Jesus Christ and discipled me in faith and serving. I followed his example into youth ministry, and through him became involved with the Christian Brethren, where I was baptised and taught to love the Scriptures. A year later, I had an experience of being filled with the Holy Spirit, and through the remainder of that year experienced a growing sense of calling to the ministry. This culminated in my leaving veterinary studies and starting a ministry internship in the Norwood Assembly of God (International), where Doug Fischer was my pastor and mentor. He had brought a very gifted preacher/evangelist, Carl Cronjé, onto the Norwood ministry team. Carl also became a beloved mentor, taking us onto the streets of Hillbrow to do street evangelism, involving us in rehabilitation work with drug addicts through the Teen Challenge "Haven" in Johannesburg. I owe a huge debt to these two men, both of whom have since passed away, but who impacted hundreds of young men and women, dozens of whom went into ministry and significantly affected the

Body of Christ in South Africa in the 1970s and 1980s.

My initial studies were completed through the Assemblies of God International College of Theology (1970-1973) under the unforgettable teaching ministry of men and women like Bob and Marg Carlson (Principal), Don and Theola Phillips, William F. P. Burton, as well as Carl Cronjé, Doug Fischer and others. After planting our first church in 1973, Lorraine and I pastored three other churches between 1975 and 1981. In 1981, while pastoring our fourth Assembly of God church, I was introduced to materials produced by the Fuller Institute of Church Growth. Later that year, I met John Wimber. While launching the Vineyard movement internationally, John was lecturing at Fuller. That meeting changed my perception of church and ministry forever. John later guided and facilitated the planting of the first Vineyard church in South Africa in October 1982, with a team of two colleagues and myself. I have been involved in the launching and direction of the Association of Vineyard Churches (SA) since it was formally constituted in 1988, and since its formation have had responsibility to direct and co-ordinate its operations in South and sub-Saharan Africa. My perspective in things ecclesiastical has thus been shaped mostly by Evangelicalism, Pentecostalism and what Peter Wagner has called "Third Wave" theology and praxis.[1]

An eight-year-old boy called Ricky, when asked for his opinion on how love happens, said: "Love will find you whatever you do. I've been trying to run away from love for years, and it always finds me!" I have a sneaking suspicion that the same applies to leadership. Leadership "found" me at an early age, so that I was selected to captain sports teams at school, to be a school prefect and to be a leader of my Boy Scout troop. Whatever form it took

---

[1] C. Peter Wagner, *The Third Wave of the Holy Spirit* (Servant Publications, 1988) see also: Kevin Springer and John Wimber, *Riding the Third Wave: What Comes After Renewal?* (Harper Collins, 1987).

earlier, however, since becoming a church leader, the development of leaders and, eventually, the "pastoring of pastors" has been intrinsic to my sense of calling. I have lectured in several Bible colleges, including one which I founded in 1982,[2] and have always found the training environment, in both the church and business context, a fulfilling one. But the Church of Jesus Christ, its leaders, and their development and godly success are my primary ministry passion.

The title of this book conveys the major point I would like it to make. I call it *Giving Leadership* in a deliberate play on words. The word "Giving" is used here as both an adjective and a verb.

1. "Giving" is a verb, a word describing an action. I believe that leadership is something that is only discovered when it is *given*. There is an action required, of "putting out" what leadership is, before it will become what it is. It is not a badge you wear, but an action you "give". It is also going to cost you your life – which brings me to the second application of the word.

2. "Giving" is an adjective qualifying the *kind* of leadership in which I believe. It has a quality of "givingness", or "otherliness"; it involves a selfless attitude on the part of the leader. Its true nature and power will not be discovered by leaders who lead for their own benefit, but rather by those who do so to benefit those they lead. It is a gift given by God and affirmed by people you lead, but it is not for you; it is to be "passed on" if it is to have any real value.

I know that most teachers and authors in the sphere of church theology necessarily assert biblical authority in support of their point of view, and that such authority can be both abused and

---

[2]Christ for Africa Institute, a daughter school of the well-known Christ for the Nations Institute in Dallas, Texas. I started and led CFAI from February 1982 until it merged with the newly formed Africa School of Missions in White River, Mpumalanga, in 1986.

misapplied. I am also aware of the danger of textualism, or "proof-texting" (i.e. using a single text to support a doctrine), and will try to avoid that danger by ensuring that my major points are supported by more than one text, and then establish the grammatical and historical context against which the text should be viewed. My major textbook is, nonetheless, the Bible, which I will use various translations, depending on which one renders the text quoted in the clearest and most easily applicable way.

My approach to Scripture is Reformed and Evangelical. I believe the Scriptures, in their original form, to be substantively inerrant and authoritative for faith and practice, containing all we need to know for our salvation and maturing in Christ. I also approach Scripture from an integrationist perspective, believing that, while "everything in the Bible is true, not everything true is in the Bible". The integration of significant information from the social sciences with biblical truth is part of the toolbox employed by practitioners of Practical Theology. Thus, I will integrate biblical information with truth from other sources which, in my view, do not contradict, but help us better understand, describe and apply Scripture to our lives and ministries.

I believe that leadership is both inherited and developed, a product of both natural growth and divine gifting, both pragmatic and mysterious, both a godly calling and a reluctant desire. However, when we are talking about the spiritual gift of leadership, it is important to note at the outset that this is just what it says it is – a spiritual gift. Gifts of this kind, as we shall see later, are given by God, but grown by responsible stewardship. While their origins are "of grace", their ultimate effectiveness will be determined by how we manage not only the gift, but also the vehicle through which it is manifest. Here are some helpful definitions:

1. "Leadership is a gift given by those led, to a person leading them, in response to servanthood or benefit received from

the leader." (John Wimber)[3]

2. "Leadership is influence." (J. Oswald Sanders)[4]
3. "Leadership is getting people to do what they have to do." (Rudolf Giuliani)[5]
4. "Leadership is mobilising others toward a goal shared by the leader and followers." (Garry Wills)[6]
5. "Leadership is a gift that you are given, and that you, in turn, give to others ... Leadership is the achievement of a specific purpose through others." (Tony Manning)[7]
6. "Leadership is a journey of discovery. It is both a journey in search of yourself and a journey in which you help others search for their essence and possibilities." (Tony Manning)[8]
7. "To be a leader means ... having the opportunity to make a meaningful difference in the lives of those who permit leaders to lead." (Max de Pree)[9]

These definitions condense into a definition of leadership, especially of a "spiritual" nature, as a gift given by God, through people, to a person, who then gives it back to people for the sake of God. They also condense into certain non-negotiables or leadership essentials. From all the sources I have read, observed, studied and heard over these many years, I have distilled a list of common denominators of leadership. While one or the other may be more prominent in individual leaders, traces of all of them will

---

[3]John Wimber, *Seven Constants in Leadership Seminar* (Johannesburg, 1996).

[4]J. Oswald Sanders. Quoted by George Barna in *Leaders on Leadership* (Regal, 1997), p. 21.

[5]Rudolf W. Giuliani, *Leadership* (Little, Brown, 2002), pp. xii-xiii.

[6]Garry Wills, quoted by Barna in *Leaders on Leadership, op. cit.,* p. 21.

[7]Tony Manning, *Discovering the Essence of Leadership* (Zebra Press, 2002), p. 11.

[8]Manning, *op. cit.,* p. 25.

[9]Max de Pree, *Leadership Is an Art* (Dell, 1989), p. 22.

be observable in every leader. To describe this succinctly, I have coined a mnemonic that might seem a little forced in places, but it conveys the big picture in a hopefully memorable way. A teacher's gotta do what a teacher's gotta do!

LEADERSHIP is spelled:

L = Life quality – the essential character and exemplary nature of the leader

E = Envisioning – having, casting and inspiring *vision*-mindedness in people

A = Attraction – *influence* or "charisma"

D = Dividend – the benefit followers derive from a leader who serves them

E = Empowering – enabling others to discover, develop and deploy their gifts

R = Relationality – being a people person, building community

S = Servanthood – going up by going down

H = Hustle – the ability to create and sustain *momentum* or a sense of "going places"

I = Implementation – the ability to make vision practical and practicable

P = Potentiality – taking individuals and the organisation to their God-given destiny

The features of great leadership will be discussed in three parts:

Part One introduces the **Notion of Leadership**: what it is, its general qualities and those that are common to Christian usage of the idea of leadership. I believe it can be shown that three of the ten characteristics of leadership taken from the above mnemonic are common to all leaders, whether Christian or not. Those three are:

1. Attraction – what several authors have called "influence"
2. Envisioning – vision or future-focus; and
3. Hustle – the ability to generate momentum.

Part Two will cover the essentials of what we could call **Kingdom Leadership**, or leadership as it should be given in the context of the Church. In addition to the three traits described in Part One, the biblical texts, and especially the New Testament, paint a picture showing this kind of leadership to be about:

1. Life quality – it is character-based;
2. Servanthood – it is sacrificial and otherly in focus; and
3. Dividend – it realises actual benefit for others.

These qualities place self-aggrandisement, pride and the abuse of power off-limits for the godly leader. The spiritual gift of leadership may have many characteristics in common with secular forms and models of leadership, but it should always have a distinct character of its own, and be accountable to a different set of standards.

Part Three will investigate **Leadership Models and Styles.** Leadership is something that needs to be exercised, or given. It is located in a person and manifested through that person, usually "on purpose". Peter, in his first epistle, speaks about gifts – forms of the grace of God – needing to be "administered" or "stewarded", in the sense of management with accountability.[10] Administration of a gift, through a unique individual, will result in a specific style of leadership. The last four character traits of leadership, while existing in some measure in all spiritual leaders, will manifest in one of these more than others, resulting in styles or strengths of:

1. Empowering;
2. Relationality;
3. Implementation – or Administration; and
4. Potentiality.

We will look at these in detail, and conclude with a discussion of what I call "Process leadership", where leadership involves

---

[10] 1 Peter 4:10–11.

applying the right strength or style to the context of the organisation at any given time.

I believe that the Church, like postmodern society in general and African society in particular, is suffering from a dearth of healthy leadership, and an excess of unhealthy leadership. It seems as if leadership has become synonymous with pretentiousness, self-enrichment, corruption and the abuse of power. The place where this is most heartbreaking is the Church. These excesses have unique expressions in the Church in Africa, although they are not unique to Africa. I mention the African Church here because it has been the landscape of so much of my experience, and this is where I would dearly love to see a timely correction of the horrendous practices I mention, and the recovery of what is good.

The Church's leadership troubles began with episodes, in its early history, when leadership was abused, resulting in the spiritual disempowering of its members, especially in the context of heresy and heretical cults. Montanism and other "cult-like" practices[11] were signals of leadership going wrong. The Church's reaction to these was to establish the rule of monarchical bishops, and later, to make the Bishop of Rome the final authority in the Church.[12] What was a reaction for defence of the Church became a tool of abuse. Thus, the establishing of structural authority, the hierarchical separation of clergy and laity, and a tendency to a "my leader right or wrong" leadership culture, became norms in the Church universal, and particularly the Roman Catholic arm thereof. Many of the churches arising out of the Reformation simply followed this model, so that, while hierarchy may have changed its names and colours, its nature remained in place. Where the altar is the high and unapproachable place in "high church" contexts,

---

[11]Williston Walker, *A History of the Christian Church* (T&T Clark Ltd, 1976), p. 81.
[12]Walker, *op. cit.*, pp. 123-124.

in many Protestant churches, the preacher stands in the pulpit, as has been said, "six feet above contradiction"!

In later church history, especially in the missionary expressions of the past 100 years, pretentiousness in leaders has become a debilitating norm. Missionaries of every persuasion modelled self-importance and cultural imperialism in almost every context where they operated. Whether through physical and social separation between missionary and "objects of mission" inside "missionary compounds", or the reinforcing of a spiritual, figurative and literal gap between clergy and laity, or whether the cultural imperialism expressed through the importation of Western dress codes, musical styles and the English language, etc., the lesson conveyed was that leaders, and the external authority they represented, were more important in their own right than the people they were meant to be leading. Leadership was by status and rank, qualification and title. Ecclesial polity was, and remains, in many cases, an imported culture of its own.

I have experienced this in numerous situations, for example in the Transkei region of South Africa, where the predominant tribe is the Xhosa. In a particular area, many people still wear a red blanket as their clothing. On one visit, after walking many kilometres to visit a remote rural church that met in a hut, I was offered a Western-style tweed jacket to put on before preaching, with the explanation: "It is the jacket for the one who preaches God's Word." On politely enquiring why that was necessary, I was told: "It is our culture." "From whom did you obtain this culture?" I asked. "The missionaries," was the answer. What was in evidence, I discovered, was *not* Xhosa culture, but religious culture, which was, in turn, an importation of Western culture.

The Episcopal model is only one version of what, in general, establishes external authority – i.e. rank, status or "title and turf" – as the basis of leadership. In the "post-missionary" Church scene in Africa, such cultural imperialism continues to be propagated through the preponderance of certain religious television ministries, which are often the only "free" television channels available to the populace. Televangelists and preachers in megachurch pulpits broadcasting on these channels are characterised by ostentatious dress, jewellery, flashy cars, furniture and other tokens of prosperity and superior status. In some parts of the contemporary Church, as in some African and other examples of political leadership, those in authority are learning to be position-conscious, pretentious and self-serving. The multiplication-by-division of so many African Independent Churches in the cities of Africa can be traced most often to rivalry and the view that leadership of one's own "church" will give one power, status and a means of income. But far worse than these alarming signals of deviancy is the frequent exercise of spiritual abuse, with church members being shamed, verbally harangued and even physically abused for what the sole leader sees as insubordination.[13]

In other church contexts, the same hierarchical style of leadership is manifest in a corporate model, with the leader as "CEO", an "A-type" leader, strong, autocratic, hands-on and insistent on having the last word about everything. The "buck" starts and ends on his desk.[14] He calls himself – and is called by his followers – "The Man of God", "God's anointed", or other titles reflecting

---

[13]As reported by several leaders and church members I have interviewed in Zambia, Kenya and Burundi (2009–2011).

[14]"The buck stops here" is a phrase that was popularised by US President Harry S. Truman, who kept a sign with that phrase on his desk in the Oval Office. The expression is said to have originated with the game of poker, in which a marker or counter (frequently in frontier days, a knife with a buck-horn handle), was used to indicate the person whose turn it was to deal. If the player did not wish to deal, he could pass the responsibility by passing the "buck", as the counter came to be called, to the next player. He was thus describing his role as leader as having the responsibility or accountability of making things work (en.wikipaedia.org).

elevated status. Additionally, the view is that he and only he has "the Word of the Lord", and the content of his teaching, as well as his decisions, may not be questioned.[15]

I have often heard both critics and supporters of the abovementioned model quote African tribal culture, with a strong, autocratic "chief" in a feudal lord-like position of dictatorial leadership, as its basis. Those who quote this model are referring to an assumed expression of African tribal culture which elevates the role and status of the tribal chief. The chief is regarded as untouchably superior in power and status, which ostensibly gives his followers a vicarious lift in status. While his people may be living in poverty, they will be pacified and even be extremely proud of having a chief who is stronger, wealthier and has the best house in the district by comparison with other Chiefs. Many African political leaders can be seen to embody this model of leadership.[16] The same model is often incorporated into church structure in the form of autocratic and pretentious titles for leaders in churches. Terms like "Father", "Pastor", and "Reverend" are not seen to be important enough, and have been superseded by increasingly important-sounding, self-assigned titles, like "Bishop", "Apostle", "Prophet" and more.

Respected authors on the subject, however, do not share the above view of traditional tribal leadership culture unanimously. It can be argued that the leadership model in African culture is much closer to a "servant leader" model.[17] Dr Reuel Khoza, a well-known

---

[15]If a leader in this model is criticised, he will usually quote 1 Samuel 26:9 (ESV): "Who can raise his hand against the LORD's anointed and be guiltless?"

[16]A prime recent example of this is seen in what has become known as "Nkandlagate" in South Africa, where our President had improvements worth R250 million made to his tribal home/estate at taxpayers' expense. The people of the nearby town defend his right to do so, despite themselves having inadequate services and an 80% unemployment rate.

[17]Article by Bruce E. Winston (Regent University) and Barry Ryan (Argosy

economist, a successful leader in the South African banking industry and commentator on leadership from an African humanist perspective, has written eloquently about *Ubuntu* in leadership as a major ethic regulating how leaders should lead.[18] In his preface to Khoza's book, Barney Mthombothi makes the point that post-colonial Africa has not done as well as post-colonial Asia, and that "leadership has to be the key distinguishing factor".[19] Ubuntu in leadership means: "The wellbeing of the people you lead must be your absolute priority."[20] In his second preface, Khoza notes: "As is common in Africa, the chief does not so much rule as assess the opinions that are expressed in an open forum, by ordinary people … Decisions are not taken by majority vote but by consensus when there is sufficient unanimity for *the chief to speak with the voice of the people.*"[21] Later he adds: "A leadership that is not vested in the vital interests of its followers in this manner is not leadership at all, but a perversion of authority."[22] Both Western and African nations, he believes, "are adrift in a leaderless world – or rather a world led by self-interested politicians, economists and intellectuals who have lost touch with community and can no longer grasp the ethical and spiritual core of humanism".[23] What he proposes as "attuned leadership" is the acknowledgement that "people make the best leaders when they act in harmony with the

---

University), "Servant Leadership is more Global than Western" in *International Journal of Leadership Studies*, Vol. 3 Iss. 2, 2008, pp. 212-222 © 2008 School of Global Leadership & Entrepreneurship, Regent University ISSN 1554-3145, www.regent.edu/ijls.

[18] Reuel J. Khoza, *Attuned Leadership – African Humanism as Compass* (Penguin, 2011).

[19] *Ibid.*, p. xvi.

[20] *Ibid.*, p. xix.

[21] *Ibid.*, pp xxiii-xxiv (emphasis mine).

[22] *Ibid.*, p. xxxii.

[23] *Ibid.*, p. xxxiii.

spirit of the group",[24] and that "[t]he chief cannot rule against the people; he can only rule with them".[25] He sums up attuned leadership thus: "Listen, deliberate, reflect, respond to the followership, be compassionate towards suffering, be humble in leadership, seek to be effective, expand your personhood through relationships, and above all, be ethical."[26]

The authors of the article quoted above believe, in agreement with Khoza, that the concept of "Ubuntu" lies at the heart of African leadership praxis. "Although the concept of Ubuntu focuses on the person, it stresses supportiveness, sharing, listening, building community, and cooperation …"[27] This model is well applied in the process of "indaba", where the chief calls together not only elders, but everyone who has an interest in a particular matter, and listens to the voice of every person at the gathering. Having heard the opinion of everyone around the room, the chief might then have to make a leadership call, but his goal would be to have the group reach consensus.[28]

One of my purposes with this book is to attempt to "redeem", in both semantic and practical terms, the use of the names of "the five-fold" offices. All five – or four, depending on your hermeneutic – are, in my view, not titles to be put before your name on a business card. Instead, they are job descriptions, intended by Jesus to operate interdependently in His Church until the end of the age, and always subject to principles of humility, servant-heartedness and accountability. This will be the topic of my final two chapters.

Models are not just illustrative; they are also formative. They form what they communicate, creating a template against which

---

[24] *Ibid.*, p. 150.

[25] *Ibid.*, p. 273.

[26] *Ibid.*, p. 392.

[27] Winston and Ryan, *op. cit.*, p. 6.

[28] See Khoza, *op. cit.*, p. 150.

we consciously or unconsciously measure reality, and thus they end up creating things after their image. The models of church and leadership by which we measure our roles and praxis are, therefore, more powerful than we think. Once a "model" leader is defined, and especially if that model is seen to be successful – or if there are no alternative models – aspiring leaders will sacrifice their own identity to emulate that model. In the unlikeliest of places, such as a small schoolroom or tin shack, with a congregation of ten people, I have seen "wannabe" replicas of televangelists, wearing a three-piece suit with scarlet handkerchief protruding from the top pocket, striking a theatrical pose with microphone in hand, and preaching in a loud voice. The essential tools of a pastor's trade are deemed to be a PA system – with the volume turned up to distortion levels – and an electric piano keyboard. While the congregation may lack food to eat and Bibles to read, the presence of the former items are seen to be essential to claims of being a real "church".

The effects of the model run exactly counter to the ideals of the New Testament Church, which I will list briefly from Paul's letter to the Ephesians chapter 4. It is, and has been, a key text for me with regard to the Church and leadership for some 40 years. David Watson taught from this text at a conference in 1978 in Cape Town. That teaching opened my eyes to the nature of the Church, and consequently, Ecumenism became a non-negotiable for me as a minister. The text resonates through my personal story, as it does through church history, as an encyclopaedic elucidation by the apostle Paul of God's ideal for the Church: the Church as it is in heaven, and should be becoming on earth:

> [1]*I therefore, the prisoner in the Lord, beg you to lead a life worthy of the calling to which you have been called, [2]with all humility and gentleness, with patience, bearing with one another in love, [3]making every effort to maintain the unity*

of the Spirit in the bond of peace. ⁴*There is one body and one Spirit, just as you were called to the one hope of your calling,* ⁵*one Lord, one faith, one baptism,* ⁶*one God and Father of all, who is above all and through all and in all.* ⁷*But each of us was given grace according to the measure of Christ's gift.* ⁸*Therefore it is said, "When he ascended on high he made captivity itself a captive; he gave gifts to his people."…* ¹¹*The gifts he gave were that some would be apostles, some prophets, some evangelists, some pastors and teachers,* ¹²*to equip the saints for the work of ministry, for building up the body of Christ,* ¹³*until all of us come to the unity of the faith and of the knowledge of the Son of God, to maturity, to the measure of the full stature of Christ.* ¹⁴*We must no longer be children, tossed to and fro and blown about by every wind of doctrine, by people's trickery, by their craftiness in deceitful scheming.* ¹⁵*But speaking the truth in love, we must grow up in every way into him who is the head, into Christ,* ¹⁶*from whom the whole body, joined and knit together by every ligament with which it is equipped, as each part is working properly, promotes the body's growth in building itself up in love.* (Ephesians 4:1–8, 11–16 NRSV)

Here are a few principles that emerge from the text:

1. The model for all believers is humility and selflessness (verses 1–2).
2. The goal of the Church is deep-spirited unity and peace, *shalom* (verses 3–6).
3. That unity of spirit exists in the context of diversity of gifting (verses 7–8).
4. Leaders are required to give their gifts into this context (verses 11–12).
5. The leader's task is to work himself out of a job (verse 12a).
6. This involves equipping each member to fulfil his or her

potential (verse 13).

7. Teaching secures the foundation of people's faith (verse 14).
8. Pastors build loving, honest community (verse 15).
9. The evidence of Kingdom health in the Church is qualitative and quantitative growth through the maximum mobilisation of the "laity" (verse 16).

On the other hand, the effects of the leadership models observed and cited above, are not humility but pride; not freedom but control; not potentiality but dependency; not interdependent unity but rivalry; not maximum mobilisation/participation but spectatorism; not growth to maturity but keeping members ignorant and immature.

The result will not be a Church "grown up into Christ", but rather one shrunk into irrelevance.

The topic and the problem

One of the marks of a missional[29] church is what I call "maximum mobilisation". A missional church, as defined by Lois Barrett, "is a community where all members are involved in a process of learning to become disciples of Jesus".[30] The questions I am asking are: "Does this definition have any resonance in the modern Church? If so, where and how? If not, why not?" I believe that the demonstrable failure of segments of the Church to make disciples out of church members can be ascribed, in large part, to a failure of leadership. Leaders who fail to empower their followers will

---

[29]I use the word advisedly, taking its definition from its first usage by Darrell L. Guder in *Missional Church: A Vision for the Sending of the Church in North America*, in *The Gospel and Our Culture* series (Eerdmans, 1998). Guder's meaning had to do with seeing the church as an outward-looking organism joining God in His Mission.

[30]Lois Barrett et al., *Treasure in Clay Jars: Patterns in Missional Faithfulness* (Eerdmans, 2004), pp. xii-xiv.

perpetuate dependency, weakness and lack of genuine transformation of character in those followers. It seems as if the office/role of leader has been distorted by the religious culture described above, in many expressions of the Church in the West, as much as in Africa. As you follow the chapters to come, my hope is that you will allow your concept and model of leadership to be formed, focused and, if necessary, re-formed by the model of servant leadership to which Jesus calls His Church in Matthew 20:25–28:

> *But Jesus called them to him and said, "You know that the rulers of the Gentiles lord it over them, and their great ones are tyrants over them. It will not be so among you; but whoever wishes to be great among you must be your servant, and whoever wishes to be first among you must be your slave; just as the Son of Man came not to be served but to serve, and to give his life a ransom for many."* (NRSV)

In the light of this unequivocal statement, and the even stronger expression of the admonition in Matthew 23:1–12, we have to decide which will win the argument: the prevailing religious culture or the culture of the humble Kingdom? The Church needs to recover a healthy vision for what the spiritual gift of leadership is, and how it works, in God's economy. The core of that discovery is a deliberate embracing of the attitude which Paul says was "in Christ Jesus", i.e. the attitude of servanthood.[31] I further hope that the embracing of this attitude, and the practices that follow it, will inevitably produce the outcome for which all ministers should strive: the cultivation of grace-motivated followers of Jesus Christ, free in heart, empowered in gifts, humble in mind and obedient in works.

---

[31] Philippians 2:5ff.

PART ONE

THE NOTION OF LEADERSHIP

One of my aunts on the Greek side of our family was, like any Greek woman of her generation, a great cook. She was also notorious among her siblings and sisters-in-law for passing on a recipe which omitted one ingredient, so that the user would not be able to produce a result to rival her own!

Leadership is a multi-faceted and broad concept, and is expressed in diverse ways by millions of people in every sphere of society, at every socio-economic level, and in every kind and size of organisation, from the nuclear family to the multinational corporation. There are common denominators, standard dynamics and processes contained in all these advocates of leadership. While this book has been conceived and developed in the context of leadership in the Church, we will see in this section how these commonalities combine to make anyone into a leader.

I believe that leadership is a power, a force that flows outward from its source toward individuals or a group, sweeping them up and carrying them toward the achievement of their *raison d'être*, their goals, their destiny. It has, as we shall see, several components or ingredients, which work together to produce that end. And if any of them were to be omitted, that end would not be achieved. The three qualities that are common to leaders everywhere and of every persuasion, are *attraction, envisioning* and *hustle*.

CHAPTER 1

Attraction or Influence: The Quiet Power of a Leader

"Leadership is influence – nothing more, nothing less."
John Maxwell[32]

The one-liner above constitutes an extreme statement. While I may disagree with it in its extreme form (I would agree with the first part without adding the second, as I believe leadership is more than, though not less than, influence), it nevertheless strongly informs our discussion of leadership. Leadership requires a capacity – in word and deed – to influence people by eliciting their emotional investment. Henry Ward Beecher, the erudite American statesman, said: "He is greatest whose strength carries up the most hearts by the attraction of its own."[33]

In my LEADERSHIP mnemonic, the "A" is for "Attraction",

---

[32]John Maxwell, *The 21 Irrefutable Laws of Leadership* (Thomas Nelson, 1998), p. 17.
[33]Henry Ward Beecher on "Influence" on www.cybernation.com website quotation centre.

another word for Influence. The word "influence" is derived from the Latin words *in* (into) and *fluere* (to flow). It speaks of the unseen ways in which someone exerts personal power on others, subtly causing their thoughts, beliefs and actions to bend toward their will. It involves what the root words suggest: flowing into the lives of those who are being led, with the purpose of moving them toward purpose. Dictionaries define it as follows:

1. To move by moral power; to act on and affect, as the mind or will, in persuading or dissuading; to induce. Men are influenced by motives of interest or pleasure.
2. To lead or direct.[34]
3. The effect a person or thing has on another ... [with] moral ascendancy or power.[35]

I define influence by using a phrase an early mentor of mine used, namely "quiet power". Some leaders induce change in the behaviour of others by manipulation or intimidation, using fear or guilt, badgering or threat. Their co-operation, if thus gained, is called compliance, and is not really co-operation "from the inside out". It requires nothing more than a kind of external authority, or force, and engages action without actually leading the "hearts" of people. However, to induce a change in *attitude* – to persuade change from within – requires influence. The true leader will be content with nothing less than this. He or she will seek to be *a person of influence* before seeking to *influence persons*. It is, then, an earned right to speak with effect into the thoughts, beliefs, lives and actions of others, to cause decisions to be made and action to be taken in a direction you wish to see something go.

Andrew Clarke, writing on the contextual connection between the *ekklesia* (civic forum of governance) and the early church,

---

[34]Noah Webster's *1828 Dictionary of American English*, E-Sword edition, www.e-Sword.com.
[35]*The Concise Oxford Dictionary* (Clarendon Press, 1990), p. 607.

writes: "Considerable influence was accorded to those within the secular '*Ekklesia*' who had the ability to persuade by means of oratory."[36] He cites the Corinthians, who were critical of Paul's seeming lack of oratory, saying: "It is clear that these early Christians were ... operating with the expectation that the characteristics of leadership in the Christian *ekklesia* should parallel those characteristics of leadership in the civic *ekklesia*."[37]

In a novel set during World War I, Robert H. Pilpel describes the real, historical character, Admiral of the British Dreadnought Battle Group "Silent Jack" Jellicoe, as having "about him an air of compelling galvanic energy of stored up magnetic force flowing outward in carefully measured waves. The net impression he gave was one of purposeful vitality and high intelligence, tempered by remarkable patience and self-restraint".[38] This is somewhat reminiscent of the statement Jesus makes after the woman with a haemorrhage is healed by touching the edge of His robe. He notices it because, in His words, "*virtue* [power] has gone out of me".[39] When Jesus speaks of the power of the Holy Spirit that will equip His followers after His ascension, He uses the analogy of a "river of living [flowing] water" that will quench their own thirst and that of others.[40]

Pilpel writes further that the result of Silent Jack Jellicoe's influence on his personnel was "a sense of missionary zeal in the

---

[36]Andrew D. Clarke, *Serve the Community of the Church: Christians as Leaders and Ministers* (Eerdmans, 2000), p. 152.

[37]Clarke, *op. cit.*, p. 152.

[38]Robert H. Pilpel, *To the Honour of the Fleet* (Chaucer, 1979), pp. 218-219.

[39]Luke 8:46 KJV cf. ISV.

[40]When saying this, Jesus specifically references "as the Scripture has said ...". The text that seems to best convey this thought is found in Isaiah 32:1–2, which suggests that, when God's King rules, His "viceregents" or rulers "will rule with justice. Each one will be ... like streams of water in the desert". The text speaks of the redemptive and restorative function of those God redeems, which of course includes the function of leadership.

air, of total dedication to the work at hand". Jellicoe's men were, in his words, like "a conclave of disciples".[41] Influence is thus an intangible, but real, power that radiates from an individual and causes a response of curiosity, attention, attraction and ultimately, loyal following, on the part of others. We will examine these results later in the chapter. It may also be true of influence that its major effect is noticed more after a leader has left the scene, than when he is in it. Iain MacLeod said: "The influence of individual character extends from generation to generation."[42]

Paul, in the context in which he uses the word "leadership" for the one and only time in the New Testament (Romans 12), introduces his discussion of spiritual gifts in general with the phrase, "by the grace given to me" (verse 3). He goes on to urge the Roman believers to function "by the grace given to [them]" (verse 6). I believe that grace is, among other things, a force, a dynamic that works inwardly to change our motivations, and outwardly to affect the motivations of others. In Paul's thinking, therefore, the influence, i.e. the force or moral power in him is appealing to the same influence operating in them, reminding them that spiritual effectiveness requires each one to operate in keeping with what is "flowing" out of them.

Influence, in my view, has at least six ingredients. The first of these is *attention*. A leader is someone toward whom people's eyes turn in expectation. It has been said of leaders like Nelson Mandela that, whenever he entered, his presence "commanded" or "filled the room". He carried "weight" or "gravitas". When Jesus went to the synagogue in Capernaum, He drew the people's attention: "The eyes of everyone in the synagogue were fixed on Him" (Luke 4:20). The apostle Peter, preaching on the day of Pentecost, calls

---

[41] Pilpel, *op. cit.*, p. 218.
[42] Iain MacLeod on "Influence" on www.cybernation.com, website quotation centre.

the group to "pay close attention to my words" (Acts 2:14). The leader is given attention.

But secondly, influence compels what I have called *attraction*. Beecher's definition refers to this quality. For real influence to occur, the potential "followers" need to *like* what they see. In most contexts of secular and even church leadership, this is obtained by physical impressiveness, "power dressing", charm, charisma or eloquence. It is also frequently true that such attraction is offered as an alternative to genuine authority. Obviously, they are not always mutually exclusive: a person may be beautiful as well as being a good leader! However, when this is placed in the context of the Church and the Kingdom of God, a leader should not depend on external symbols as a source of, or a substitute for, real authority.

A third ingredient of influence is *representativity*, which is given to the leader by the group he or she leads. The group is able to defer to them when its opinion is asked for. When the leader speaks, others in the group nod their agreement. Without needing to vote, there is a sense that the leader speaks on their behalf. The reason many leaders became part of the Vineyard movement in the 1980s was the shared sense in which John Wimber spoke "for" them, articulating what was in their hearts and minds. The person exercising the spiritual gift of leadership will often cause a feeling of "he's reading my mail" or "… but that's *my* song!" His followers see him as an embodiment of the vision toward which they strive. When the Jerusalem Council met to discuss the admission of Gentiles to the church, James stood up, seemingly without being voted into the job, and spoke for them all. His "judgement" becomes the representative view of the leadership, and ends up being "what seems good to the Holy Spirit and to us" (Acts 15:13–29). Of course, this represents a moment of unusual inspiration by the Holy Spirit. But the principle of representativity by a leader, as an ingredient of influence, nevertheless applies.

A leader will seek to hear God's heart on behalf of the group they lead, and cause followers to own the view delivered as theirs.

The fourth element of influence goes further. It extends representativity to the point of *empathy*. You will most readily give leadership to someone you feel walks in your shoes, who knows and articulates your pain, your aspirations, your feelings and your external vision for your future. Jesus exemplifies this most perfectly in the incarnation. He identifies with humanity, takes on our pain and becomes acquainted with our grief. I believe this is a key reason why we are told that the common people "heard Him gladly" (Mark 12:37 KJV).[43] Understanding and identification increases credibility and influence, and is a vital quality for a leader. This characteristic of "Emotional Intelligence",[44] coined by Daniel Goleman, could quite well be summarised by the word empathy.

A fifth element of Influence is *competence*. A person has influence to the measure they demonstrably know what to do and how to do it. This is not merely with regard to the *theory*, but also the *practice* of competency. The leader not only knows what is to be done and how to do it, but can "lead from the front", by exemplifying and embodying what they are calling their followers to be and do. The influential leader is involved in a constant process of "show and tell". This ingredient continues where empathy leaves off. It builds on credibility and is what inspires confidence and security in the follower. In the New Testament, "signs and wonders" were biblical markers of Kingdom competence. Jesus attracted large crowds when He dealt with their sicknesses and demonic oppressions. They followed Him in numbers, having seen that He spoke with authority, that sicknesses were healed by Him, and

---

[43]Greek *hēdeōs* means "pleasurably" or "with delight".

[44]A concept popularised by Daniel Goleman in his book *Emotional Intelligence: Why It Can Matter More Than IQ* (Bloomsbury Publishing, 1996).

that demons fled when He spoke (Mark 1:23–39, etc.). On a few occasions, Jesus makes the point that the works themselves were His credentials of Sonship with the Father, and of His Kingship.[45] Paul quotes this kind of supernatural gifting as an essential qualification for apostolic leadership.[46] However, this is not the only area in which competence attracts a following. Leaders are to be good at what they advertise. They are to be practitioners of the obedience and effectiveness to which they call others. We make disciples by what we do, to the point that, if what we do contradicts what we say, people will reject what we say in favour of what we do. So, says Paul, a leader who calls people to excellence in the knowledge of Scripture, will need to "handle the word of truth with precision" himself, and by living by the truth he teaches, draw people to obey it (2 Timothy 2:15, 22–25).

A final element of influence is *complementarity*. The followers of a leader see a range of characteristics that are lacking in themselves. For example, people who are not well-informed will love the stabilising effect of the knowledge they receive from a teacher-leader. Those who are perhaps jaded and bored with their lives, will be attracted to an inspirational, or "prophetic" leader, and so on. The old adage about marriage partners said: "Opposites attract." It is true in marriage, and also in leadership, that people are fascinated by, and attracted to, uniqueness, and the recognition of what we lack in evidence in another. We fall in love with the mystery of the "otherness of the other". Qualities of uniqueness may similarly become stimulants of leadership when people see them at work in the leader, and when they are stretched to renewed growth by those qualities.

Influence is achieved in people's lives by bringing them some

---

[45] John 5:20–36; 10:25–38; 14:10–14 and Luke 11:15–20
[46] 2 Corinthians 12:12: "The signs of an apostle were performed among you with utmost patience – signs, wonders, and powerful actions."

benefit. Benefit means that those who receive the input, or the service, of the leader experience, as a result, an improvement of their condition. So says Peter, the apostles would not leave Jesus, because He "[had] the words of eternal life" (John 6:68). If a leader is a teacher-leader, they will be better informed and equipped; if an administrator-leader, they will be secure and organised; if a pioneer, or catalytic leader, they will have advanced toward a mutually desirable goal in new "territory". If the leader is pastoral, they will feel loved, embraced and empowered. They will feel a gratitude and loyalty toward the leader, and give him or her greater authority or permission to lead them further. They will find in the leader a safe place, a source of help, warmth, dignity and growth. This, again, is what will stimulate a following. Relationships begin and are sustained when people spend time with one another and add value to one another's lives. In the case of a leader, she or he adds more value to a follower than vice versa.

A group exists to make a difference, to touch the world, to achieve a vision. It needs internal coherence, or a substantiated belief system, which is provided by sound teaching. It also needs the security of solid relationships, a sense of belonging and care. And then, it needs to be enjoyable or entertaining. Its meetings need, as Bill Hybels says, to be memorable.[47] These elements are the essence of group cohesion; their presence at appropriate times in the group's life determines the reason why individuals become, and stay, involved. They are the benefits for which people "sign up". The result of this sense of benefit is influence.

John Maxwell said, in a talk he gave on the subject of the dynamics of influence, that it is like change in the leader's pocket.[48] His view is that every time a leader brings benefit to a person or

---

[47]In a talk called "These Things We Must Do", the Global Leadership Summit, October 2005.

[48]From a story he tells in the video "The Law of Influence", https://www. youtube.com/watch?v=MmwdqDOeAbA.

a group, the recipients of that benefit put money in the leader's pocket. The leader can build up the amount of change in his pocket over time, and bring it out when it is needed to influence a decision or course of action. John Wimber used the term "equity" to describe the same thing. You earn it by showing the characteristics mentioned. You prove it is the real thing by walking alongside people and benefiting them with your gifts. You invest it by spending time with the people you are walking with. You spend it by giving leadership in the ways you are uniquely gifted to do so. Let us explore this process.

A leader with a compelling vision will get alongside people and win their confidence by articulating it. He or she will need to meet them in their world, and inspire them with words and actions that show the reliability and relevance of the vision to their lives. There is no substitute for spending time with those you lead. It shows them that you want from them not just what they offer you or the organisation, but relationship with them. Influence does not happen by remote control, or by public proclamation from a distance, but by personal investment of time and interest in the lives of warm-blooded human beings. This opens the "bank account" of influence with those you lead.

Meaningful contact with people will also require that the leader listens to them, takes their concerns seriously, and seeks to enable them to discover their sense of purpose, gifting and passion. This is the point at which the people you lead begin to give you some of the change in their pockets. It is entrusted to you as the leader as you listen with empathy and enthusiasm. Your balance grows.

As a leader, every time you benefit people, you gain equity. When you make decisions that take the group forward, when the experiences they share under your leadership are meaningful and inspiring, you gain equity. You spend yourself as you extend care, love and effort toward them. They repay you by showing that your opinion, your input and serving is valuable to them. Thus, your balance increases even more.

In the life of any group, occasions of challenge, stress and opposition will arise. They may originate from within or without, from obstructive people or difficult circumstances, or deferred or failed vision. They may involve a discovery that the leader has made mistakes. She may have made decisions that did not produce what she promised they would. He may have "hit the wall" and experienced frailty of a physical, emotional or spiritual nature.

This is when you will discover whether you have equity with those you lead. You, as the leader, may have to make decisions in the situation, some of which may not be popular. If you have failed, you may need to humble yourself and ask for forgiveness. When you are vulnerable, and ask people to trust you, forgive you, or indulge you, you will find that those with whom you really have influence, will rise to the occasion. You will take some of the change out of your own pocket, and find them receiving the currency you offer ungrudgingly. You will also find out that some will not be so generous. They will give either a grudging response, or perhaps refuse altogether. You will have found out that you have none of their particular change in your pocket.

When I experienced an episode like this, where my own mistakes made when I was in a state of emotional exhaustion had impacted on the church's wellbeing, I was dismayed to encounter all of the above reactions. It was disillusioning to discover that some whose respect I thought I had, were unable to forgive me, even for years afterward. I had no equity with them, or at least not enough to carry our relationship over that particular hole in the road. Others surprised me in the opposite way, showing me a generosity of heart when I expected them to walk away. Some of those people are among my dearest friends to this day. In such times, it is easy to surrender to despair, and feel disqualified. The fact is, however, that we as leaders are not qualified to lead by our perfection; therefore, we are not disqualified from leadership by our failures. Influence transcends our failures, and can even be enhanced by it, if we handle it in appropriate ways. As painful as all this may be, it is actually a good thing to discover who you "have", and who you never "had" as a follower. Our role as leaders is to turn away from our disappointment and abandonment, and give ourselves to those with whom we still have influence. In the episode in Paul and Barnabas's lives described by the following text, this is how they handled rejection:

> *The next Sabbath almost the whole town gathered to hear the word of the Lord. But when the Jews saw the crowds, they were filled with jealousy and began to object to the statements made by Paul and even to abuse him. Then Paul and Barnabas boldly declared, "We had to speak God's word to you first, but since you reject it and consider yourselves unworthy of eternal life, we are now going to turn to the gentiles. For that is what the Lord ordered us to do: 'I have made you a light to the gentiles to be the means of salvation to the very ends of the earth.'" When the gentiles heard this, they began rejoicing and glorifying the word of the Lord. Meanwhile, all who had been destined to eternal life believed, and the word of the Lord began to spread throughout the whole region.*
> (Acts 13:44–49)

If your spiritual gift is leadership, it will not abandon you when some, or even many, stop following you. Leadership is not a popularity contest; in fact, a real leader will often offend people as they exercise their gift. You will sometimes need, like Paul, to pick it up, take it with you, step over the offence, and lead onward. Like him, you may find that it leads to the discovery of your true mission.

The spiritual gift of leadership, which contains at least a large component of influence, needs, like all gifts, to be *given*. Find it within you, believe in its intrinsic worth, invest it where you are called to serve, and give it away without fear.

We will return to some of these concepts when discussing spiritual gifts later. But, suffice it to say here that leaders are those with the confidence to put forth a quiet power called influence among others, which will, in turn, carry them "upward and onward" toward a purpose he or she can see before it becomes obvious to others. And this introduces the subject of my next chapter.

CHAPTER 2

Vision: The Key to Leadership

"Those who have a 'why' to live, can bear with almost any 'how'." Viktor E. Frankl[49]

The key to leadership, in my view, is *vision*. It is the one component of leadership common to every book I have read on the subject. The very idea of leadership contains vision at its core, because a leader is someone who moves a group from where they are to a preferable future. A leader, therefore, needs to "see" that preferable future in their mind's eye, and to articulate and exemplify that vision in their life and function as a leader. It is this trait that unlocks the picture contained in the hearts and lives of others, and causes them to follow. I will speak in a later chapter about different styles of leadership, among which is the leader who is truly, or primarily, a visionary. That is a specialised leadership style, "poise" or "wiring" that some leaders have. However, I want to emphasise the point here that, at a certain level, *all leadership is visionary*, in that every leader will *see* a "mind picture" of a preferable future,

---

[49]Viktor E. Frankl, *Man's Search for Meaning* (Beacon Press, 1959).

feel a creative discontent with the present in comparison to that future, *articulate* a vision and *move* intentionally at the head of the group or individual he leads, towards that vision.

Where there is no vision, the people are unrestrained. But blessed is he, the one keeping the law. (Proverbs 29:18 LITV)

The above text uses the word "vision" (Hebrew *chazone*), to describe a prophetic insight, or an oracle. Although the parallelism in the text points to the "law", or the written word, I believe the text can be taken to refer to vision in the meaning most people give it. God's Word puts vision and leadership together by saying that without vision, the people "cast off restraint", disintegrate or fall apart. This happens to us as individuals: we become confused, frenetic, disintegrated, like the cowboy I heard about who ran into the corral, jumped on a horse, and rode off in all directions! It happens to a person without a personal vision for their lives. One piece of research in the 1980s found that 85% of people living and working in a large urban environment (Johannesburg) wished they were living somewhere else and doing something else for a living. Someone summed up this phenomenon with the expression: "If you don't know where you're going, *anywhere* will do!" The result of a directionless, purposeless existence is living a life without meaning, which psychologists and philosophers have long identified as the primary reason for stress, as well as depression. It expresses the exact opposite of the way of thinking expressed in the quote by Victor Frankl at the head of the chapter. It is a series of "hows" without the "why". Eventually, the "anywhere" that has seemed good enough, will cease to be so. Disintegration and low self-esteem are the result.

The same thing also happens to us communally. Without the cohesive power of vision, everyone goes in his or her own direction, or drifts around without any direction, focus, meaning or purpose at all. The word picture painted by Proverbs 29:18 is of a cattle "funnel" fence – the use of which, in the ancient Middle East, is well supported by archaeological evidence – such as you would find at a cattle dip. The animals come off a vehicle, or out of the veld, and are directed by the "funnel" of fencing into the dip tank. Diagram 1 is an example:[50]

Diagram 1: The Cattle Funnel

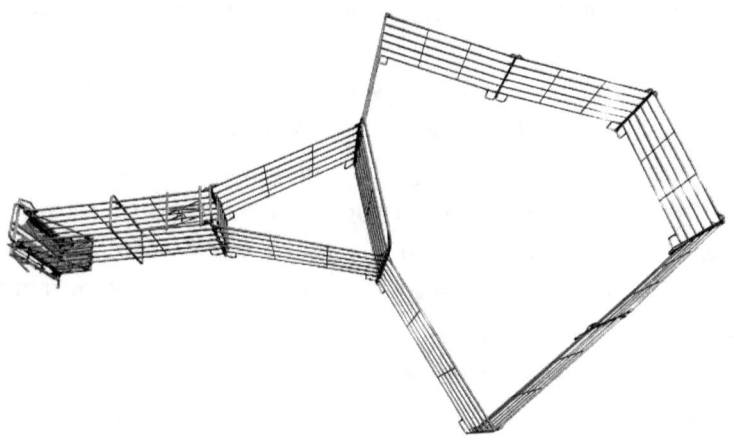

The funnel becomes progressively narrower as it gets closer to the tank, until only one animal at a time can go through it. The fence determines the direction for each animal in turn. The cattle are united in pursuit of this common direction and momentum. That is, in Solomon's mind, the effect of vision on a group, or a "people". It "funnels" them toward obedience in pursuit of the goal. The way God does that is through His Word, whether by the written Law or the proclamation of a prophetic message. It involves

---

[50]Based on the cattle or sheep "funnels" built in fields to direct and control a flock toward a specific point, for the purpose of, e.g. capturing them or bringing them into a corral. You can see pictures of ancient stone walls in this shape (called desert kites) at www:http://archive.archaeology.org/blog/a-fatal-illusion/ and related internet sites. This one is from https://www.priefert.com.

engaging the people in a common, intelligent allegiance to God and His purpose, and the effect is focus, direction, cohesion and unity of purpose. The opposite is disintegration, loss of energy, and failure to achieve anything.

Vision focuses a leader, and, through that leader, focuses a group on where they want to go, what they want to achieve and who they want to become. In a later chapter, I will discuss the necessity of discerning vision, among other things, in community and not as a "lone ranger" type leader. However, once discerned, it is the responsibility of whoever is leading the group, to crystallise, articulate and continually inspire allegiance to the group's God-given vision. Walter Wright puts it as follows: "A gifted leader is also needed to serve the team: to see that the mission is pursued, the people are cared for, and the decisions are made."[51]

Vision defined

The text from the Proverbs speaks of vision in the form of the revelation of God's Word, the instruction of His Law and the inspirational call of His prophets. But, in modern usage, what does the word "vision" mean? Here are a few quotes about vision and definitions of the concept:

- "Vision is the art of seeing the invisible." (Jonathan Swift)
- Vision is "seeing possibilities before they become obvious". (John Sculley)
- "I saw the angel in the marble and carved until I set him free." (Michelangelo Buonarroti)
- "The greater danger for most of us is not that our aim is too high and we miss it, but that it is too low and we reach it." (Michelangelo Buonarroti)

---

[51]Walter C. Wright, *Relational Leadership: A Biblical Model for Influence and Service* (Paternoster Publishing, 2009), Kindle edition, loc 886.

- "If you want to build a ship, don't herd people together to collect wood and don't assign them tasks and work, but rather teach them to long for the endless immensity of the sea." (Antoine de Saint-Exupéry)
- "The greatest tragedy is not to be born with no sight. The most pathetic person in the world is someone who has sight, but has no vision." (Helen Keller)
- "Ah, but a man's reach should exceed his grasp, or what's a heaven for?" (Robert Browning)

George Barna calls it "a clear mental portrait of a preferable future that is imparted by God to His chosen servant-leaders, based on an accurate understanding of God, self and circumstances".[52]

Vision is the essential ingredient of change, or even the hope of change. It motivates by inspiring hope. It makes the difference between mere interest and focused passion. It increases frustration tolerance in the short term, and thus provides the "why" for living, which Viktor Frankl said enables us to cope with almost any "how".[53] It is the means of shaping the future. Without it, the future takes its own shape and we have to fit into that. That scenario results in people burning out because, as I alluded to earlier, burnout is not the result of hard work, but of work without meaning.

What is the difference between *vision* and *mission*? In a nutshell, while mission encapsulates your job description, vision describes what you will become when you have fulfilled it. George Barna once shared a list of differences between vision and mission, which are represented in the following chart:[54]

---

[52]Barna, *ibid.*, p. 47.
[53]Frankl, *op. cit.*
[54]George Barna, in a talk given at a conference in Randburg, South Africa, August 1994.

MISSION	VISION
Broad and general	Specific and detailed
Macro-activity	Micro-activity
Why you are here	What to do with your life
Rules of the game	Position you play in
Philosophic	Strategic
Conceptual	Practical
Call to servanthood	Empowers for service
Static	Evolving
Stabilising, securing	Exciting, compelling
Makes us alike, builds community	Makes you unique, builds momentum

A mission statement is a clear description of what you exist to *do*, and *how*. It determines your uniqueness, as an individual or an organisation, and is oriented to the present with regard to action, and to the future with regard to short and medium-term goals. Thus, it enables you to measure success or stagnation, effectiveness or failure.

A vision statement, on the other hand, describes who you want to become in the long-term future. It does this in vivid and tangible terms, including what you will look like, and what flavours and fragrances, colours and dimensions will spell success. In other words, where a mission statement is practical and mundane, a vision statement is inspiring and memorable. Where the first engages to action, the second inspires qualities, values, and sustainable energy.

Both mission and vision are necessary. They do different jobs in the creation, development and sustaining of an organisation. We will learn more about this in the final chapter. But it is important to know the difference between the two, and to allow vision to set the direction for the organisation you lead. In my experience, the lack of vision, or the confusing of vision with mission, has been a major cause of organisational failure.

Essentially, it is vision that makes the difference between *maintenance* and *momentum*, between *management* and *leadership*. A manager is someone who maintains and operates within a system or set of operating principles that are at work in the organisation. He or she does not need to create them or even grow them; they are given and must merely be maintained with a regular report back to the CEO. Lee Iacocca, the former CEO of Chrysler, suggested that "a manager is like a little boy with a big dog on a leash, waiting to see where the dog wants to go so he can take him there"[55]

Vision is what Steven Covey is referring to when he lists the second of his seven habits of highly effective people as "Start with the End in Mind".[56] To illustrate the difference between management and leadership, Covey uses the metaphor of a team of people whose task was to create a road through a forest. He describes the various functions within the team: those who cut the bush down with machetes and chainsaws; those who maintain and sharpen the axes and chainsaws; those who provide food and other supplies for the workers; the transport drivers who drive the trucks to carry away the rubble; the surveyors who draw the operational boundary lines through the forest, etc. All of these are *management* functions. As we look at this picture of industry and enterprise, where is the leader? Covey describes him as the person who has climbed the tallest tree in the forest, so that he can get a perspective on where the road was to go. Sometimes, in the middle of all of the hard work and "management" functions going

---

[55]Quoted by John Maxwell, *op. cit.*, p. 14.
[56]*The 7 Habits of Highly Effective People* (Free Press, 1989).

on, the leader at the top of the tree might be heard to shout to the workers below: "Wrong forest!"[57] He is not interested in how well everyone is doing his or her management tasks. He is more interested in them applying those tasks in the right context, with the right outcome.

Leaders, then, do not need maps; they draw their own. They are not interested as much in detail as they are on focusing on overall tasks and outcomes. This does not mean that a leader is someone who will subjugate the means in favour of the end. Rather, they will integrate the members of a group, together with their knowledge, skills and other resources into a cohesive organism by the power of the vision toward which they are leading. Just as groups and individuals disintegrate without vision, so a compelling vision will cause them to integrate like nothing else can.

Vision, especially as we place it in the context of the Kingdom of God, is made up of three ingredients: *calling*, *purpose* and *values*. Every great leader, in Scripture and Church history, started out with a *calling* from God. The calling on a leader will determine the *what* of her or his life, providing a job description; in other words, it will determine your mission as well as your unique place in it. Here are some examples of calling from the stories of men and women of the Bible:

- Noah: The Lord said: "Build an ark – like this!" (Genesis 6:13)
- Abraham: The Lord said: "Leave Ur and go to a place I will show you." (Genesis 12:1)
- Isaac: The Lord appeared and said: "Carry on your father's work." (Genesis 26:24)
- Joseph: Given dreams to lead and deliver Israel (Genesis 37)
- Moses: God spoke from a burning bush: "Go and deliver

---

[57]Covey, *op. cit.*

my people from oppression." (Exodus 3:10)

- Joshua: The Lord said: "Take the people into the promised land." (Joshua 1:2)
- Deborah: Called to be a ruling judge in Israel. (Judges 4)
- Samson: Dedicated from his mother's womb to deliver Israel. (Judges 13:3–5)
- Samuel: Dedicated from his mother's womb to prophesy to Israel. (1 Samuel 1:11)
- David: Identified by prophecy to rule Israel. (1 Samuel 16:12–13)
- Isaiah: A priest who saw the Lord, called to prophesy to Israel. (Isaiah 6:1–9)
- Jeremiah: Called from his mother's womb to "pluck up, break down, build and plant". (Jeremiah 1:4–10)
- Daniel: Endowed with knowledge, grew in resolution and gifting to prophesy to a pagan king. (Daniel 1:17)
- Most of the "minor prophets": The word of the Lord/vision came to them.
- Elizabeth: Called by an angel at a late age to bear a son who would prepare the way for Christ. (Luke 1:24–25)
- Mary, the mother of Jesus: Called by an angel to conceive, carry, give birth to and raise the Messiah. (Luke 1:26–38)
- The apostles: Jesus called them to Himself and gave them authority to preach and cast out demons. (Mark 3:13–15)
- Paul: Knocked off his horse, saw the Lord, details given by a prophetic church leader. (Acts 9:3–6, 15–16)
- Timothy: Prophetic word given through an apostle and elders when they laid hands on him. (1 Timothy 1:18; 4:14)

Some are more dramatic than others. Some required mere availability; others were called despite their non-availability! Some saw things; others heard things. Some received their calling while they were sleeping; others while they were awake. Some heard the call through other human beings; others from a direct encounter with an angel or God Himself.

Calling, then, is a product of *crisis* and *process*. The crisis may be quite mundane (a king died, an army invaded) or profound (wickedness, idolatry, drought, oppression). They might be internal (dreams, prayers) or external (visions and angelic visitations). The process, similarly, can be, and was, a mixture of natural growth and obedience and of deliberate preparation and training in relationship with God. Calling will be recognised by other godly people when it is real, and confirmed prophetically and/or pragmatically. Calling is the factor that puts "the end in view".[58] It "fills in the blanks" about your ultimate reason for being here, the reason why Jesus stopped you, arrested you and changed the course of your life. It is future-focused, while at the same time defining your present practice. Many wise people, including my father, have said: "When you are doing what you are called to do, you will never work a day in your life." In other words, a person working by vocation will work effortlessly. I think that is what Jesus meant when He said: "Take my yoke upon you, and learn from me, for I am gentle and lowly in heart, and you will find rest for your souls. For my yoke is easy, and my burden is light."[59] He is conveying the idea that working (carrying a yoke) in partnership and rhythm with Him, will be "restful work".

In my opinion, every Christian is called. Whether it is a general calling to follow Jesus, or to the particular career you pursue, all of it is covered by God's plan for your life, which is revealed to you by His call. The following list gives the uses of the word "called" in the New Testament. We are called to:

- salvation (Romans 8:28ff; Hebrews 9:15; 1 Peter 2:9);
- sonship (1 John 3:1);

---

[58]Covey, *op. cit.*
[59]Matthew 11:29–30 ESV.

- eternal life (1 Timothy 6:12);
- sainthood (Romans 1:6);
- fellowship with Christ (1 Corinthians 1:9);
- freedom (Galatians 5:13);
- hope (Ephesians 4:4);
- eternal glory (1 Peter 5:10);
- justification (Romans 8:30);
- belonging (1 Corinthians 1:26);
- holiness (Romans 1:7; 1 Corinthians 1:2);
- a worthy life (Ephesians 4:1);
- gifting (Romans 11:29);
- service (Galatians 5:13);
- peace (Colossians 3:15);
- marriage (or singleness) (1 Corinthians 7:17ff);
- career (1 Corinthians 7:17–24);
- blessing (1 Peter 3:9);
- suffer ("some" – 1 Peter 2:21);
- preach (Galatians 1:15);
- the work (Acts 13:2); and
- apostleship (Romans 1:1).

All of the above references, except for the last three, use the plural pronoun "you" or "we", inferring that they pertain to every Christian. The reference to "suffering" (1 Peter 2:21) implies that it is a calling for some, perhaps even most. The last three use the personal pronouns "I" or "me", and refer to Paul's personal calling to preach, to engage in "the work", and to apostleship. The implication is that every Christian's life, gifting, marital and career status, as well as our journey to wholeness and righteous living, is the object of a calling. There are "general" callings for every believer, and there are specific callings that help us know our unique role in God's plan. For example, all Christians are called to discipleship, but not all are meant to be teachers of the Word. All are called to be witnesses or missionaries wherever we are, but not all are called to become a missionary in a foreign culture. A Christian woman or man called to be a dentist is as called (and, therefore, mandated and accountable for that calling) as is one called to be a pastor. Our place of involvement in the world is always a mission field. God wants us to serve Him and extend His Kingdom wherever He places us, whether in the business environment or a church pulpit. Those who preach are no more "called" than any other person. Their calling is not "greater" or "higher" or more "holy"; it is merely *different.*

Here is the essential thing: You cannot lead anything unless you are called. Without a calling to a particular ministry, you will fail and drop out of it, or you will burn out in it. Calling gives you the resolve, the reason why and the "what" for your existence. So, before you go on, answer these questions:

1. Has God spoken to you specifically about your ministry and life purpose?
2. How has He spoken? When and where? Through what and whom?
3. What have those you serve said about your ministry function and gifting?
4. What do people most often thank you for doing for them?
5. What have your leaders said about the above?
6. What has your spouse or family said?
7. What would you like your epitaph to say in summary of your life?

It is a helpful exercise to reflect on your answers to the above questions, and condense them into a written statement of calling, if one has emerged from all this.

From your calling comes a sense of *purpose*, both in the sense of resolve, commitment or compulsion, as well as "design" (as in the purpose for which a building will be built). It adds the *where* and *who* to the previously given *what* of ministry. It identifies a target group, a people or peer group, a nation, city, etc., that will motivate you, draw you toward them, give you dreams while you are awake, and stir your heart with unusual passion and compassion. Like Paul who, after the Macedonian man appeared to him in a night-time vision, was immediately captured with a sense of purpose toward that place and people group. As Luke says: "As soon as Paul had this vision, we got ready to leave for Macedonia ..." (Acts 16:9–10).

Noah is called to his family and the animals! Isaiah and Jeremiah were called to Israel and Judah, Daniel to the king of Babylon, and Paul to the Gentiles and their leaders. And from then on, they could think of nothing else! They were consumed with purpose. Purpose produces an urgency of will that drives the called leader to do this and nothing else, as Paul, who says of himself: "For if I preach the gospel, that gives me no ground for boasting. For necessity is laid upon me. Woe to me if I do not preach the gospel!" (1 Corinthians 9:16 ESV).

Noah had to *build an ark*; it took him a long time. He was mocked and derided for it. Abraham had to *go*, and keep going until he reached the city God had built, pushing through danger, wars, some distractions in the form of alternative settling points, opposition and divisions within his "team". Samuel, Isaiah and Jeremiah had to *prophesy* against fearful persecution and opposition. Daniel had to *interpret dreams* in a way that did not make him very popular with the king he served. And as for the apostles, including Paul, they had to *preach* in a hostile environment, to a point that it cost them their lives (as it did Jeremiah and most other prophets). Without calling, their sense of purpose would have wavered, their focus would have become blurred, the price would have been too high to pay. It is purpose that creates compulsion and commitment, enables risk-taking, and raises our pain threshold.

The third aspect of vision is *values*. The leader, or visionary, needs to be a person who understands and is able to articulate values, and keep everyone on track concerning these values. Values are the ingredients of vision that give it meaning and flavour. They provide "the *why* for the *how* of the *what*". That is, they make us *want* to do *what* we are doing *the way* we are doing it. Without meaning, the achievement of vision, or tasks, is often both hollow and ultimately damaging to all participants. I believe that people will only experience depression and a loss of ego integrity in their work to the extent that they lose their sense of meaning in what they are doing. We will study the book of Nehemiah in more detail in chapter 8, but at this point I want to make reference to his role as leader. Nehemiah was a guardian, not only of a task, but also of the values and morals that governed the life of the community engaged in the task. If he and his fellow workers had succeeded in building the walls of Jerusalem, but had not honoured God in how they did the building, or in the lives that they lived within the boundaries of the walls they built, all would have been in vain for Nehemiah. For him it was not just about restoring a city, but providing for the worship of God within it. The Temple, the feasts, the Sabbath, all aspects of honouring and worshipping God were, for Nehemiah, the bottom line. He was as interested in the "why" and the "how" as he was in the "what".[60]

Where and how do you get vision? What is the difference between vision and an overstimulated imagination? Is vision the same as idealism, or is it more "sacred" than that? Perhaps the most prominent and well-known story of a person receiving a vision is that of Isaiah:

> *In the year that King Uzziah died, I saw the Lord. He was sitting on his throne, high and exalted, and his robe filled the whole Temple. Around him flaming creatures were standing,*

---

[60]Another of Covey's seven habits is articulated as "putting first things first" (i.e. knowing and engaging with your priorities, in order of priority!).

each of which had six wings. Each creature covered its face with two wings, and its body with two, and used the other two for flying. They were calling out to each other: "Holy, holy, holy! The LORD Almighty is holy! His glory fills the world." The sound of their voices made the foundation of the Temple shake, and the Temple itself became filled with smoke. I said, "There is no hope for me! I am doomed because every word that passes my lips is sinful, and I live among a people whose every word is sinful. And yet, with my own eyes I have seen the King, the LORD Almighty." Then one of the creatures flew down to me, carrying a burning coal that he had taken from the altar with a pair of tongs. He touched my lips with the burning coal and said, "This has touched your lips, and now your guilt is gone, and your sins are forgiven." Then I heard the Lord say, "Whom shall I send? Who will be our messenger?" I answered, "I will go! Send me!" So he told me to go and give the people this message: "No matter how much you listen, you will not understand. No matter how much you look, you will not know what is happening." Then he said to me, "Make the minds of these people dull, their ears deaf, and their eyes blind, so that they cannot see or hear or understand. If they did, they might turn to me and be healed." (Isaiah 6:1–10 GNB)

Isaiah saw three things in the process of receiving his vision, each of which is an essential ingredient of the vision of any godly leader. First, he *saw the Lord:* He became intensely aware of God's sovereignty, holiness and glory. He saw him and his realm as the defining reality for the universe, and the ruler of all He had made, whether the universe knew it or not. He saw Him as the One before whom everyone, including himself, was accountable. Second, he *saw himself:* as a person in need of forgiveness and cleansing. He was brought to a place of humility in the light of the presence and perfection of God. This is the only place any of us discovers true humility, and where we may keep our sense of vision and calling in perspective. Our vision, calling and ministry do not make us in any way great. They are simply gifts given into the heart and mind of an unworthy person. Isaiah was very aware of this. Third, he *saw his people*. He saw them as being in need of the God he had encountered, and desperate for salvation. His awareness of their sin, alongside his own, stimulates not revulsion, but rather a strong sense of compassion for the people who are thus exposed. For this reason, there is an immediate response when the Lord asks the question: "Whom shall I send?" As these three ingredients combine, Isaiah is left with a message and a responsibility. He is left with a promise, not of wine and roses, but of pain in the midst of purpose: the purpose that makes pain, disappointment and rejection bearable, and mission sustainable. The picture of the outcome of his ministry is one not many would have signed up for. Read verses 9–10 again! His church would not grow, but be a collection of spiritual ignoramuses. He would not heal, or help, or inform anyone, but only make them spiritually worse off! His truth would fall on deaf ears. But Isaiah is gripped by the power of it. He is motivated by a vision which contains values. He receives a sense of driving determination and purpose, which he would never be able to deny, and which would carry him through the opposition he would face for the rest of his life, as well as his own reluctance and, ultimately, martyrdom.[61] Like Jeremiah, he had a message that burned like fire in his bones:

---

[61] Legend has it, and most commentators believe, that Isaiah died by being placed inside a hollow log and sawn in half (Hebrews 11:37). If so, he certainly needed the high pain threshold that only a clear sense of purpose gives!

> *LORD … You are stronger than I am, and you have over-*
> *powered me. Everyone makes fun of me; they laugh at me*
> *all day long. Whenever I speak, I have to cry out and shout,*
> *"Violence! Destruction!" LORD, I am ridiculed and scorned*
> *all the time because I proclaim your message. But when I say,*
> *"I will forget the LORD and no longer speak in his name,"*
> *then your message is like a fire burning deep within me. I*
> *try my best to hold it in, but can no longer keep it back.*
> (Jeremiah 20:7–9)

Paul's experience is rather similar (Acts 9:1–20; Philippians 3:2–15). Paul *sees the Lord* whom he has been persecuting. He sees a light so bright as to literally blind him to everything else, hears a voice so challenging as to cause an instant change of life direction. The vision is given content through a leader in the Damascus church. Through Ananias, his eyes are opened to a new realm. He sees and receives a sense of calling to the Gentiles, kings and governors. He knows that, from then on, his life is to make a difference to the entire Gentile world. And, in the same tone as Isaiah, the vision contains as much "negative" promise as positive expectation: "… for I will show him how much he must suffer for the sake of my name" (Acts 9:16). It all receives its meaning from the vision of Jesus. That face makes everything else comprehensible, and worthwhile. As Paul puts it in the Philippians passage:

> *But whatever gain I had, I counted as loss for the sake of*
> *Christ. Indeed I count everything as loss because of the sur-*
> *passing worth of knowing Christ Jesus my Lord. For his sake*
> *I have suffered the loss of all things, and count them as refuse,*
> *in order that I may gain Christ.* (Philippians 4:7–8)

Paul *sees himself* and all his pedigree and qualifications as rubbish in the light of this God who reveals himself to him. Comfort, respectability, status, even achievement, is not worth comparing to Paul's "one thing". It makes everything else "fair exchange", and causes his knowledge, his religious observance and his social standing to become "dung"[62] by comparison. It is this sense of purpose or vision that drives Paul from that time forward, so that he concludes the description of the purpose of his life with the words: "One thing I do, forgetting what lies behind and straining forward to what lies ahead, I press on towards the goal for the prize for which God has called me heavenward in Christ Jesus." The goal is his vision, the prize is the reason why he is pursuing it, namely the approval of God over his life and the fruit of his ministry. He will live, and serve, suffer and die before an Audience of One. That is a compelling, sustainable sense of purpose.

In the context of the vision, and its explanation when he is with Ananias, Paul *sees his people*. He receives a mandate of evangelism to "Gentiles and kings, and the sons of Israel" (Acts 9:15). The vision unfolds and has details added to it over the years. But it remains a "one thing" for which he is prepared to count all else as loss. He is intensely, passionately ambitious for the one thing that he is meant to do, yet he is constantly aware that "it is not I but the grace of God which was with me"[63] that enables him to accomplish this.

So, in answer to the question: "Where do you get your vision?", you get it from your encounter with God Himself. I am talking here about the special, arresting, life-changing God-encounter that involves a sense of having been "undone",[64] or of being under new management. It sometimes comes in "serial" form, unfolding gradually in a series of visions. In my case, while I was happily pursuing my veterinary studies, God arrested me through a "word of knowledge" from a person who did not know me. A year

---

[62]Philippians 3:8 KJV.

[63]1 Corinthians 15:10.

[64]The rendering in English (KJV, RV) of Isaiah's response to seeing the LORD in Isaiah 6:5.

later, He spoke again through a powerful encounter with the Holy Spirit; six months after that through what seemed like an audible voice; followed finally by a text that leapt off the page during my daily reading of Scripture that placed all the other prompts into context; which brought me to a decision God confirmed to be right by giving me a profound sense of peace.[65]

This kind of "primary" encounter with God has content to it in most cases. There will be words spoken in your spirit; this may come in the form of reading Scripture, or hearing a sermon, or receiving a prophetic word. It may come from dreams and visions that you might know were supernatural in origin and intention. Vision might also be derived from what I have often called "sanctified desires". That is, the desires that arise within you when you are in God's presence, worshipping him and submitting yourself to his rule in your life. Psalm 37:4 says: "Delight yourself in the Lord and he will give you [i.e. he will cause, assign, originate and inspire] the desires of your heart." He causes desires to arise in your heart, and then gives you the means and the gifts to pursue those desires. The way that grace-motivation works is by God giving us a taste of what could be, of a preferable future in its many forms, with an element of desire for the full enjoyment of what He has offered. In this covenant of grace, God does not motivate us with fear or threat, duty or pain. We do not *have to* do things to please Him – we *get to* do them! The genius of God is that He makes us *want to* do His will!

The point of the above examples, from Scripture and personal experience, is to illustrate the fact that the *how* of calling does not matter – the *fact* of calling does. Calling is a non-negotiable for anyone contemplating ministry.

So, take some time to record your reflections on these things.

---

[65] The final confirmation of any directive being from God is "the peace that comes from Christ ruling [i.e. arbitrating] in your hearts" (Colossians 3:15).

Write down any words that you have received in your times of encounter with God. Write down any sanctified desires that arise as you spend time in his presence. Crystallise these around the values that have grown in your heart as you have served God and learned from Him. Then condense all of these thoughts into a vision statement. What do you want your life to accomplish? What footprints do you want to leave in the world? If you could be remembered for something, what would that something be? What would you like your epitaph to say? What would you give almost anything to be able to accomplish or achieve? Write out a vision statement for both what you wish to become as well as what you wish to accomplish.

Vision, as we saw in Barna's definition, is given by God. It does not belong to the leader. Once given, it may not be tampered with, compromised or adjusted. Some people are like the archer who, rather than identifying his target and then firing the arrow at it, thought he would save himself embarrassment by simply firing the arrow into the blank wall, and then painting the bull's eye around it afterwards! There are people who operate without a strong sense of vision, so that when you ask them what they see as the preferable future for their lives or the church they lead, will tell you: "I'll know when I get there." True leaders know when they have arrived, because they started out with a picture of the destination in their minds. Here is the song of the visionary, as sung by the writer of the letter to the Hebrews:

> *[Abraham] looked forward to the city which has foundations, whose builder and maker is God ... These all died in faith, not having received what was promised, but having seen it and greeted it from afar, and having acknowledged that they were strangers and exiles on the earth. For people who speak thus make it clear that they are seeking a homeland. If they had been thinking of that land from which they had gone*

out, they would have had opportunity to return. But as it is, they desire a better country, that is, a heavenly one. There-fore, God is not ashamed to be called their God, for he has prepared for them a city. (Hebrews 11:10–16)

Abraham saw a city with heavenly origins, shape and significance. He, and the people who followed him, would not stop in their search, or settle for less than the vision they had seen. If they had not seen that vision, the writer tells us, they would have stopped short of it, or quit and returned home when the going got tough.[66] The job of the leader is to paint the visionary picture so vividly, that those who follow you can "see" it through your eyes, hear its song through your ears, and believe it is available and attainable because of your words. The vision of the heavenly city Abraham painted for them was so powerful as to change their way of think-ing! They did not even *think* of the place they had left. Their imag-ination had been captivated by something they saw, and greeted from afar. The job of the leader is not just to receive vision, but to "cast" it; that is, to articulate it, communicate it, refine it, and to engage the senses of those he leads, so that they can smell its fragrance, thrill at its colours, feel its warmth on their faces, enjoy its textures. Once you have done that with the group you lead, they will run through brick walls with you to get to where you are going.

More than that, a leader needs to discover that he or she does not see the complete picture alone. They will seek to draw "all the saints"[67] into a constant process of discernment and refinement, hearing their dreams, seeing Jesus and His Church through their eyes, smelling the fragrances and tasting the flavours of their ideal world, and having everyone participate in "colouring in" the big picture to which they were first attracted. We only comprehend

---

[66]Hebrews 11:15. They would have found it opportune *(Kairos)* to go back.
[67]Ephesians 3:18.

God's love "together with all the saints". I suspect that it may be the same for comprehending God's dream for the Church.

How many of us stop short of God's ideals for our lives or ministries? Some quit because they run out of courage or energy; others because they do not take the time or trouble to find out what their city looks like. I heard a story about a man who arrived in heaven and was being taken on a guided tour by Jesus. While showing him the glories of the city, Jesus pointed to a man and remarked, "There is the greatest leader who ever lived." The man who was being given the tour said incredulously, "But I know that man! He was just an ordinary guy. A good enough person, but he didn't seem to lead anything significant, in my experience of him." Jesus replied, "Yes, but he was the greatest leader who ever lived – if only he had realised it!"[68]

The leader is not only a person who must *have* vision. As we saw earlier from Hebrews 11, he must be an effective, inspiring, non-stop *communicator* of vision. This is a leadership skill we call "envisioning", and "re-envisioning". Something we can learn from the tower of Babel, apart from the obvious warning it contains against idolatry or self-salvation, is that poor communication will shut down the best project! So, how do you cast vision, and develop it into the culture and lifeblood of the organisation you lead? Here are five steps:

1. Write your vision

    What's God going to say to my questions? I'm braced for the worst. I'll climb to the lookout tower and scan the horizon. I'll wait to see what God says, how he'll answer my complaint. And then GOD answered: "Write this. Write what you see. Write it out in big block letters so that it can be read on the run. This vision-message is a witness pointing to

---

[68]Quoted by Simon van Niekerk, late founding pastor of City Vineyard Church, Cape Town, in a sermon in 2005.

what's coming. It aches for the coming – it can hardly wait!
And it doesn't lie. If it seems slow in coming, wait. It's on its
way. It will come right on time. (Habakkuk 2:1–3 MSG)

Notice that the vision was just what the word itself says it is: *visual.*
Habakkuk waited to "see" how God would answer. When vision
comes, it is encoded in a form that the recipient can decode. It
should not be obscure, vague or irrelevant to the recipients. Then
God tells him to *write* it. Make it plain, and accessible, "so that
it can be read on the run". (Have you ever been frustrated when
trying to read the small print on a lamp-post poster, as you drive
by? That constitutes bad advertising practice!) It should be able
to be read "on the run"; i.e. understandable and easily retained.
Crystallise your vision statement into a few "bullets" that people
can remember easily, and that carry the ability to evoke emotion,
inspiration, motivation and commitment.

2. Communicate it all the time

The five elements of effective communication are *persuasion, in-*
spiration, desire, internalisation and *visualisation.* People have only
absorbed vision when they are persuaded it is true, when they
want what it promises, when they believe that they can have, or
achieve it, when it is repeated so often that it is part of their belief system, and when they can see it, smell it, taste it, hear its
music, and feel its texture. What this calls for from the leader is
creativity, poetic feel, humour and the involvement of as many
senses as possible in communicating. Have your vision statement
on every piece of stationery you give out; display it on your walls
and screen; symbolise it in a song; sloganise it and use the slogans
often; have contests for your leaders to be able to memorise it and
say it back to you ... There are many ways to communicate vision,
and there is no such thing as too much vision talk!

3. Strategise it

More will be said about implementation in a later chapter, but here I want to say that the work of the leader involves constantly matching suggested action to vision attainment. When you are teaching, training and preaching, you should show constantly how the action you are calling people to will lead to the achievement of the vision in a specific, measurable way. Likewise, when you address problems that might have arisen, including lack of money, link the remedy to vision. Vision, and not need, attracts resources of every kind, whether people, money, or anything else. Show people how every job in the organisation relates to the vision.

4. Celebrate it

When you reach milestones, make everyone aware of it, applaud those responsible, have a party! However, in doing this, make things clear. Let everyone know what has been achieved; show pictures of it, if possible. Let the communication of achievement be precise and believable. But by all means, keep the "fun factor" high!

5. Be single-minded about it yourself

Nothing communicates more effectively than modelling. You, as a leader, need to be the living example of a visionary fanatic. I worked for a man who had a note taped to his telephone. It said: "Is this telephone call, or whatever else I am about to do, taking me closer to the achievement of my vision?" One of the major distractions successful leaders have to avoid, is the proliferation of *other people's visions* that they will constantly put on your desk, ask you to endorse or help them with, or even become responsible for.

My mentor, Bob Fulton, used a great illustration about this. He pictured the overall vision of a church as a large patio umbrella. Under it, other leaders raise their own umbrellas, which may be the equivalent of golf umbrellas, parasols, foldaway umbrellas, etc. This is to be encouraged by the overall leader. But, the question the leader needs to always be asking, concerning every contributing vision people in his church tell him about, is: Does this fit under my big umbrella? Is this vision adding colour and texture to the big picture? If it is, let it add to your picture of the church's "what" and "how". Promote it, celebrate it as part of what God is doing through your group.

If not, as good as those mini visions may seem, you cannot give them time or energy. In some cases, you can endorse them, or pray for them. In still others, you have to say: "You go and do your thing. I can bless you as you go, but I can't 'lay hands on it'," i.e. give it time, energy or money. It may even seem divisive or parochial of you, but you need to be discerning and firm in making decisions about your umbrella and its range, and even about who else is supposed or not supposed to share your umbrella. As Nehemiah said to Sanballat, when faced with the subtle temptation of compromise: "You can keep your nose out of it. You get no say in this. Jerusalem's none of your business!"[69]

Diagram 2: The Vision Umbrella

---

[69]Nehemiah 2:20 MSG.

After the children of Israel were delivered from Egypt, they embarked on a three-day journey to the Promised Land. And the journey ended up taking them 40 years! As the saying goes: "It took God 24 hours to get Israel out of Egypt, but 40 years to get Egypt out of Israel!" The problem for all of us is conveyed by the expression: "Wherever you go, there you are!" That means you take yourself with you where you go: your habits, your mindset, your attitudes, your beliefs, your sinful patterns. All conspire to hold back change. The mercy of God saves us, but then, as Paul says, we need to respond to it with mind renewal:

> *I therefore urge you, brothers, in view of God's mercies, to offer your bodies as living sacrifices that are holy and pleasing to God, for this is the reasonable way for you to worship. Do not be conformed to this world, but continually be transformed by the renewing of your minds so that you may be able to determine what God's will is – what is proper, pleasing, and perfect.* (Romans 12:1–2)

Think about those children of Israel. Some of them were longing for the garlic, the leeks and the onions of Egypt after a very short diet of manna.[70] They enjoyed Egypt much more in retrospect than in real time. Then, when faced with the prospect of fighting their way into the Promised Land, they preferred the wilderness they had been complaining about.[71] So, many of them got their wish. They got the wilderness as a permanent abode – in the form of a gravesite! In every group, there will be those who are emotionally in the Egypt they supposedly left, those who are putting down roots in the wilderness, and the Calebs and Joshuas, whose eyes and hearts are firmly set on the vision of the Promised Land. A leader is there not only to love them as they are, but also to love them too much to leave them as they are.

---

[70]Numbers 11:4–6.
[71]Numbers 13.

Every person you lead, and the group itself, is somewhere on a scale of change from old ways of thinking, being, and doing, to the way you as a leader have seen in the vision God has given you. Every person, as well as the group itself, needs to be *led* into change. I am wary of leaders who give up on groups or individuals with dismissive statements like, "These people won't change" or "This is an old wineskin – I'm not pouring new wine into that!" I think statements like these are cop-outs devised by a fatigued leader, and they are often untrue. It is a leadership issue. A visionary leader will take responsibility to draw everyone entrusted to them into the new vision. John Wimber, speaking in a different context (about learning to heal the sick), said: "Pray for 100 people. If none of them is healed or improved, you can quit – but only then!"

Jesus, in one of the most poignant and intimate moments of His earthly ministry, prays the following in what is called His High Priestly prayer, and in so doing displays this quality of visionary resilience as a leader:

> *As long as I was with them, I guarded them. In the pursuit of the life you gave through me; I even posted a night watch. And not one of them got away, except for the rebel bent on destruction ... Now I'm returning to you. I'm saying these things in the world's hearing, so my people can experience my joy completed in them. In the same way that you gave me a mission in the world, I give them a mission in the world. Father, I want those you gave me to be with me, right where I am, so they can see my glory, the splendor you gave me ...* (John 17:12–24 MSG)

In a very helpful evangelism seminar I attended in the 1980s, we were introduced to the "Engel Scale",[72] which arranged every per-

---

[72]This model was first suggested by Viggo Sogaard while he was a student in the Wheaton Graduate School. It later was revised by James F. Engel and Wilbert Norton, and published in such sources as Church Growth Bul-

son you encounter on a scale from -10 (no knowledge of Christ) to +10 (fully committed, functioning disciple). James Engel, the deviser of the scale, proposed that evangelism consists of any and every action that helps to move someone up the scale, even if that action has not yet brought them to a point of "commitment". There is probably an equivalent "scale" for people going through vision transition. On the journey from -10 (no awareness of change required) to +10 (fully functional participant and proponent of the new deal), they will have moments of acceptance, reversed later by old, resistant patterns and comfort zones. They will experience the "anything for peace" syndrome, showing outward compliance while being a functional saboteur; and they will "sign up" emotionally long before they do so practically. From defiance, through regret, to curiosity, through exploration, to enjoyment and, finally, commitment, can be a short hop, a paradigm transplant, a Damascus road experience, or a long process of osmosis.

Here's one of those "How many … does it take to change a light bulb?" stories, as it applies to Church denominations. How many …

- *Pentecostals:* 10, one to change the bulb, and nine to pray against the spirit of darkness.
- *Calvinists:* None. Calvinists do not change light bulbs. They simply read the instructions and pray that the light bulb has been chosen to be changed.
- *Neo-orthodox theologians:* No one knows; they can't tell the difference between light and darkness.
- *TV evangelists:* One, but for the message of light to continue, send in your $100 today!

---

letin and elsewhere during 1973. Since that time, modifications have been introduced as others have made suggestions. Particularly helpful comments have been advanced by Richard Senzig of the Communications Faculty at the Wheaton Graduate School and Professors C. Peter Wagner and Charles Kraft of the Fuller School of World Mission (from *What's Gone Wrong with the Harvest*, Zondervan, 1975, p. 45).

- *Independent fundamentalists:* Only one, because any more might require too much co-operation.
- *Catholics:* Not required. They use candles.
- *Nazarenes:* Six. One woman to change the bulb while five men review church lighting policy.
- Members of an established, *Bible-believing church* that is over 40 years old: One to actually change the bulb, and nine to say how much they preferred the old one.
- *Interfaith ministers:* This statement was issued: "We choose not to make a statement either in favour of or against the need for a light bulb. However, if in your own journey you have found that a light bulb works for you, that is fine. You are invited to write a poem or compose a modern dance about your personal relationship with your light bulb (or light source, or non-dark resource), and present it next month at our annual light bulb Sunday service, in which we will explore a number of light bulb traditions, including incandescent, fluorescent, three-way, long-life, and tinted – all of which are equally valid paths to luminescence."
- *Baptist elders:* "CHANGE???"
- *Vineyardites:* About five, three to pray and "lay hands on" the old bulb, one to stand by in case it falls over, and one to pass the tissues while the light bulb gently weeps its way to renewal.
- *Amish:* "What is a light bulb?"[73]

Resistance notwithstanding, one of the jobs of a leader is to look for the gaps between people, the vision and himself, and live, work, and communicate the growth path. He or she is to find the route markers which are thought to be important, and help everyone see them clearly. The Sanballats and Tobiahs must be identified in the system: Who is resisting? Who is opposing? Who

---

[73]Author unknown, except for the "Vineyardites" clause, which I wrote!

is influencing others against change? They may need to be won over, rather than run over! Who are the permission givers and influencers, for you or against you? Your job is to listen to and influence them. Also identify your Ezras and Hananis – see Nehemiah – those who will help you rebuild the walls. One of the pieces of Nehemiah's genius was his capacity to involve others in planning and then reaching the group's goals. We will discuss this more in another chapter, but let us constantly keep in mind that the job of a leader is to give away his job! Your vision is yours, but if it stays only yours, it dies with you. A true leader is someone who passes it on before they die. Pass it on, then. Give away who you are, what you are passionate about, what God has entrusted to you. That is what it means to finish well.

CHAPTER 3

Hustle: Leadership Going Places

"All good things come to those who hustle while they wait."
Thomas Edison

Romans 12:8 is translated variously as:

"If it is leadership, lead enthusiastically." (GW)
"If it is leading, lead enthusiastically." (ISV)
"… the one taking the lead, in diligence." (LITV)
"If it is leadership, let him govern diligently." (NIV)

Leadership is a common theme, sometimes explicit and sometimes implicit, throughout the Scriptural account of the *Missio Dei*.[74] When God acted in history, it was most often through the agency of leaders called and equipped for their particular task. Secular history, too, could be, and often is, summed up by the leaders who made things happen, whether good or bad, and the philosophies or "visions" that drove them. But what, if anything,

---

[74]A term used by missiologists to describe "the Mission of God", which in turn defines our mandate and mission as the Church, namely "to join our intrinsically missionary God in His Mission".

was the distinguishing feature, the common denominator, of all those leaders?

Leadership, especially in churches, is often seen as synonymous with the word "charismatic" in both its meanings, namely: "of, relating to, or constituting *charismata* or spiritual gifts", and "having, exhibiting, or based on a personality or social style which has 'charisma' or emotional dynamism". Many confuse the second with the first, or see the second as a non-negotiable requirement for leaders, even in the absence of the first. In most circles, both ecclesiastical and commercial, the common wisdom says that leaders need to be extroverted, dynamic, decisive personalities. In church leadership roles, additionally, they must exhibit dramatic, sensational spiritual gifts of the clearly "supernatural" kind to qualify as leaders. How valid is this, and if it is at all valid, does it mean you either have it or you don't? In other words, are leaders born or made?

I said earlier that this part of the book discusses leadership as it is seen in action across the broadest of spectrums, from politics to business to charitable causes to military enterprise, as well as in structured church leadership. In other words, *all* leaders will show the elements of influence, vision and ability, and use them to lead whatever they lead. The areas of overlap, and the differences between leadership as a spiritual, rather than a natural gift, will emerge in this chapter. However, I think those differences are more about the *dynamics* than the *mechanics* of what a leader does. They are about what motivates, empowers and receives the benefit of the actions of a leader. A leader in any field will be a person who initiates things, who confidently steps forward and carries a group forward by the power of their vision, influence and ability. When this is done out of godly, Christ-centred, Holy Spirit-inspired motivation and ability that transcend natural abilities, we are seeing the spiritual gift of leadership at work.

Spiritual gifts in the New Testament

In the various passages of the New Testament where spiritual gifts are discussed, there are a few common themes. The first is that, while gifts are diverse, the greater good of the Body is their setting and goal. The second is that diversity is not arranged as a hierarchy (most important to least important), but rather on a spectrum (all equal, but different). There is great diversity, but all are equal – our individual gifts make us different, not superior or inferior, to others. The third is that gifts are given, not to make the practitioner famous, but to equip, empower and edify the functioning, multi-faceted Body. Joseph Allen, an Orthodox scholar, says it well:

> ... this *"work of ministry which builds up (edifices) the Body"* is a ministry which is of the entire Church; the charismata are given to the Body at large, and they are to function according to the discernment of that entire Church. ... If the shepherd is to lead, he is to lead the Body in such a way that these gifts (charismata), varied as they are, are brought forth and offered; shepherds are to help these gifts flourish ... in short, these shepherds, vis-à-vis the ministry of the laity, are to guide (for what else does a shepherd do?) all charismata to their proper service in the church, and for the world ... there is no *"first team"* and *"second team"*, that is, one ministry that is *"better"* than the other ... They belong together, and in a sense, explain each other within the one Body.[75]

---

[75]Joseph J. Allen, *The Ministry of the Church: The Image of Pastoral Care* (St. Vladimir's Seminary Press, 1986), pp. 62-63.

The textual passages

The three main texts where spiritual gifts appear as the subject are 1 Corinthians 12:4–31; Romans 12:3–18 and Ephesians 4:4–16.[76]

The background to Paul's writing of these letters varies considerably. The Corinthian letters (*c.* 55–56 AD, from Ephesus) are written to a church of which Paul had been the resident pastor for 18 months, and where, after his departure, some major division, disorder, false doctrine and malpractice had arisen, which he addresses in a series of "answers to questions".[77] He had similarly been the pastor at Ephesus (*c.* 60–61 AD, from Rome), but writes the Ephesian letter not to answer questions or deal with "issues", but as a kind of "Magna Carta" of salvation, doctrine and good order in Christian and Church life.[78] He writes to the Romans (*c.* 58 AD, from Corinth)[79] as a church he had not visited, though he had met some of its leaders. Once again, he provides his understanding of the gospel and its implications,[80] in order to "present his credentials" in advance of arriving there.

---

[76]While some NT scholars dispute Pauline authorship of Ephesians, evangelical scholars such as Robert H. Gundry, *Commentary on Ephesians* (Baker Academic, 2011) and Donald Guthrie, *New Testament Introduction* (Apollos/IVP, 1990) have made an equally strong case in its favour. I agree with them.

[77]Leon Morris, *The First Epistle of Paul to the Corinthians: An Introduction and Commentary* (Tyndale Press, 1969).

[78]D. A. Carson and Douglas J. Moo, *An Introduction to the New Testament* (Zondervan, 2005), pp.490-495; H. Chadwick, "Introduction and Commentary on Ephesians", in *Peake's Commentary on the Bible*, ed. Matthew Black (Thomas Nelson and Sons, 1967).

[79]Guthrie, *op. cit.*, p. 406; T. W. Manson, "Introduction and Commentary on Romans" in *Peake's Commentary on the Bible, op. cit.*

[80]Romans 12 starts with "Therefore", and begins a section of the letter containing the implications of justification by grace through faith, on moral/ethical choices in a Christian community.

The three letters which deal with spiritual gifts, while addressing churches which may not have seen the letters written to the other churches, have these factors in common:

- Paul had been the pastor of both the Corinthians and Ephesus; and
- he had, in all likelihood, taught the Corinthians what he writes about to the Ephesians and Romans, and vice versa.

The latter likelihood, together with a belief in the unity of Scripture,[81] brings me to believe that the three texts can be seen to build on one another, to form a total picture of spiritual gifts, functions, ministries and offices which were in evidence in the early Church. In my view, furthermore, the reason for the differences in the lists of spiritual gifts in these passages suggests that they should not be treated as an exhaustive "operations manual" – i.e. these and only these gifts, in this and only this manner – so much as a descriptive and suggestive text giving the range of possibilities of gifting that may arise when the Spirit is at work in the Church.

The *charismata* or *phanerosis*

Now there are varieties of gifts, but the same Spirit; and there are varieties of services, but the same Lord; and there are

---

[81]This view holds that, although the books of the Bible were written over a period of 1 600 years, by 40 authors of varied levels of education and even cultural bias, it is not a loose library but a unified message – virtually "one book", with God's overall Authorship and a common thought-thread expressed through human authors. See Henry C. Thiessen, *Lectures in Systematic Theology* (Eerdmans, 1990), p. 46. G. C. Berkouwer, *Holy Scripture in Studies in Dogmatics* series (Eerdmans, 1982), says of Scripture: "For the very words are God-breathed and point to the centrality of Scripture … In the doctrine of Scripture we are to be increasingly concerned with … this centrality of the one witness of Scripture" (pp. 166-167).

varieties of activities, but it is the same God who activates all of them in everyone. To each is given the manifestation of the Spirit for the common good. To one is given through the Spirit the utterance of wisdom, and to another the utterance of knowledge according to the same Spirit, to another faith by the same Spirit, to another gifts of healing by the one Spirit, to another the working of miracles, to another prophecy, to another the discernment of spirits, to another various kinds of tongues, to another the interpretation of tongues. All these are activated by one and the same Spirit, who allots to each one individually just as the Spirit chooses. (1 Corinthians 12:4–11)

The context in which this passage was written, is a church where division and jealousy were rife. At least three reasons for division are dealt with, namely competitiveness in the context of individual spiritual "giftedness", doctrinal disputes, and allegiance to different apostolic leaders. Paul addresses their divisions in the first three chapters. His first reference to spiritual giftedness and authority has him defending his right to direct them as an apostle (chapter 4; cf. chapter 9), and to warn them not to ignore his direction, citing the destruction of the Israelite nation for ignoring Moses as a parallel (chapter 10). Chapter 11 sets the scene of God's ideal for a united church, engaging in the Eucharist in the spirit of unity as a "love feast".[82] In chapter 12, he expounds on one of his key themes: the Church as the one body of Christ. Its functionality is dependent on the acknowledgement that the same Spirit unites them, the same Head rules them, and that the motivation for their being together should therefore be to seek

---

[82]Between chapters 4 and 9, Paul addresses various other manifestations of spiritual immaturity, such as lawsuits between them, as well as licentious behaviour (incest, using prostitutes, devaluation of marriage, factionalism and arguments over codes of legalism).

the building up and wellbeing of the whole, using their spiritual gifts to do so.

Paul is here dealing not only with the issue of division over spiritual gifts, but also with a general ignorance about "things spiritual".[83] Thus, I believe he is addressing not only answers to questions unique to the Corinthians, but timeless principles of operation in the "spiritual" realm, where God's life intersects with human agency. The result is spiritual gifts or, more correctly, "spirituals" (*pneumatikon*, i.e. things of the Spirit), which, when activated, are the evidence on earth of the presence of the God of heaven. Their expression brings the Trinity near, in that they are the "graces" (*charismata*) of the Spirit, the "servings" (*diakonia*) of the Lord Jesus, and the "effects" (*energemata*) of the Heavenly Father (verses 4–6).[84] The one who exercises them should pause and reflect: the "gifts" are not yours, but God's. When operating in spiritual gifts you, like the apostle, do not represent yourself, but God.[85]

There is an interesting paradox at work here concerning qualification and performance versus grace and accountability. Paul is writing to a church with noticeable problems caused by immaturity and poor character. At the same time, he commends them for "not lacking in any spiritual gift" (1 Corinthians 1:7), and

---

[83]His introductory phrase says: "Now concerning spiritual gifts, brothers, I don't want you to be ignorant." The word is *pneumatikos*, which is better translated "things spiritual".

[84]Richard B. Hays, *First Corinthians* (John Knox Press, 1997), p. 210. It seems obvious, as pointed out by Hays and also Anthony Thiselton, *1 Corinthians: A Shorter Exegetical & Pastoral Commentary* (Wm. B. Eerdmans, 2006), that Paul is speaking here of the Trinity's involvement in the enabling of every believer to manifest God's life. The verses, in Thiselton's words, "provide a kind of 'ground plan' of *trinitarian theology* … Paul's emphasis upon unity-in-diversity is grounded in the nature of the one God, who is holy Trinity" (p. 197).

[85]See chapter 4:1–6.

encourages them "all" to exercise gifts, and "especially to prophesy" (12:7; 14:5). For the exercise of *charismata*, neither character nor maturity are qualifications. Richard Hays states: "The possession of any gift is therefore not a matter of individual merit or worthiness but of the sheer free grace of God."[86] You are, however, accountable for your motivations and the outcomes of the gifting you employ, as for all else, before the *Bema* seat of Christ (Romans 14:10; 2 Corinthians 5:10).[87] The same God who graced you will ask you to account for that grace's deployment and its consequences.

Spiritual gifts, then, are the currency of our usefulness in the church and the world. They are the ways in which God gives us away, or spends us, for the benefit of others. They enable us to make a difference and, in turn, can make us different.[88] The list in this passage is a "snapshot" of the kinds of things God may manifest through members of the Body. Again, in my opinion, this is not an exhaustive but rather a suggestive and representative list,[89] covering "kinds of gifts" which display God's *thoughts*, God's *words* and God's *works* in the Church and the world.[90] They are called *charismata* ("grace-expressions") or, to use a term

---

[86]Hays, *op. cit.*, p. 213.

[87]The seat in which the governor or Emperor sat in judgment in the capital cities of the Roman Empire, and before which Paul stood (Acts 18; 25). Paul uses this as a picture of Christ's evaluation of His workers at the last day (see chapter 3:10–17, cf. 2 Corinthians 5:10).

[88]See the promise made to King Saul in 1 Samuel 10:6: "Then the LORD'S Spirit will come on you with great power. You will be changed. You will be like a different man. You will begin to prophesy with these prophets" (ERV).

[89]See Gordon D. Fee, *The First Epistle to the Corinthians* (Eerdmans, 1987), p. 585, as well as Thiselton, *op. cit.*, p. 197.

[90]I believe, with Robertson and Plummer, *A Critical and Exegetical Commentary on First Corinthians* (T&T Clark, 1953), p. 265, that "the gifts listed form three classes … the first is connected with the intellect, the second with faith (or Power), and the third with (the Tongue)". See also Fee, p. 590.

coined by Professor Russell Spittler and quoted by John Wimber, "gracelets".[91] Later in verse 7, Paul speaks of them as manifestations (Greek *phanerosis*), a word which means the "shining forth" from inside out of a particular attribute or grace of God the Holy Spirit.[92] Paul is emphasising the fact that these "charisms" are ways in which the Holy Spirit may express God's life and power in any particular gathering of the church. Gordon Fee says: "… thus, each gift is a manifestation, a disclosure of the Spirit's activity in their midst,"[93] and that believers may expect that, at any time, the Holy Spirit may use anyone ("to each is given", verse 7) in any of these ways, in any specific gathering of the church. The gift is not owned by the person thus "manifesting" it, but is rather given to the person in need, or to the entire Body, for its benefit, *through* that person. To express this idea, Miroslav Volf writes:

> *Luther used the image of the conduit: We are channels of God's gifts to our neighbors. The image is good, except that a conduit merely conveys goods and does not benefit from them. We, on the other hand, benefit from the goods, as well as bestow them on others. Which is to say that we do not just receive the gifts, but we are constituted and changed by them.*[94]

The *charismata* occur occasionally, are not subject to qualification, and "all" believers in a gathering of the church may seek and expect one or more to operate at any time the Holy Spirit wills

---

[91]John Wimber and Kevin Springer, *Power Healing* (HarperCollins Publishing, 1991), p. 239, where gracelets are defined as "occasional manifestations or anointings of gifts for specific purposes and for the good of the congregation".

[92]Hays says: "[T]he word 'manifestation' is employed as the generic category that includes 'spiritual gifts' in the narrower sense as well as other activities inspired by God in the church" *op. cit.*, p. 210.

[93]Hays' footnote adds: "the concern is not with the gifts, but with the manifestation of the Spirit through the gifts".

[94]Miroslav Volf, *Free of Charge* (Zondervan, 2009) Kindle edition, loc 723.

it. They are what Selwyn Hughes has called "the gifts we seek".[95]

A further list

> [27] *Now you are the body of Christ and individually members of it.* [28] *And God has appointed in the church first apostles, second prophets, third teachers; then deeds of power, then gifts of healing, forms of assistance, forms of leadership, various kinds of tongues.* [29] *Are all apostles? Are all prophets? Are all teachers? Do all work miracles?* [30] *Do all possess gifts of healing? Do all speak in tongues? Do all interpret?* [31] *But strive for the greater gifts. And I will show you a still more excellent way.* (1 Corinthians 12:27–31)

Here, Paul suddenly seems to put various gifts he has been discussing into the same "box", so that apostles are placed side by side with speakers in tongues. Is this to remove any distinction between them? I believe rather that the text is an emphatic restatement by Paul of the unity and equality of the *worth* of all gifts, in the context of their wide diversity. His closing set of rhetorical questions (assuming the answer "No!") in verses 29 to 30, exhorts every member of the Church to a celebration of individual uniqueness in oneself and others, and leads to an introduction of the "ruling virtue" of love as an overarching motivation and guide in all exercise of the *pneumatikon*. In my view, and contrary to several commentators of cessationist persuasion who use Paul's perceived contrasting of spiritual gifts and love (one replacing the other), love is not a gift, or something to be set in contradistinction to the gifts, but rather the motivating, divine character trait that qualifies any and every gift we seek to offer to the church, as coming from God through a Christlike, loving heart.

---

[95] Selwyn Hughes, *Discovering Your Place in the Body of Christ* (Marshall Pickering, 1982), p. 12.

Thus, we are introduced and invited to operate, imperfect as we are, with the realisation that no matter our "rank" or "office", we do so in a spirit of humility and interdependence, and without envy or rivalry. However, the text in itself does not blur the distinction between ranks of gifting. The evidence that offices, or leadership-orientated gifts, are different in Paul's mind, is that, while all gifts are placed together here, only those which are later called "offices" are numbered first, second and third (see verse 28). Thus, Gordon Fee says:

> *Hans Von Campenhausen suggests that the first three gifts in this list [that is, those of being apostles, prophets, and teachers – the gifts indicated by the ordinals first, second and third] seem to be more office-like while the rest of the list is more function-like ...*[96]

Hans Conzelmann makes the same point, for the same reason: "The three outstanding [chief forms of service] are thrown into relief by the use of ordinal numbers ... [they are] ... offices common to the church as a whole, whose bearers wander from community to community."[97] Hays and Thiselton suggest that the enumeration of the first three gifts here may be purely suggestive of the chronological sequence in which they do their work: "The itinerant apostle comes first and founds the church, while prophets and teachers follow to continue the work of constructing and instructing the community."[98] I think this is an excellent analysis, on which I will say much more in chapter 8, "Process Leadership".

---

[96]Fee, *op. cit.*, p. 49, quoting Hans von Campenhausen, *Ecclesiastical Authority and Spiritual Power in the Church of the First Three Centuries*, trans J. A. Baker (Adam and Charles Black, 1969).

[97]Hans Conzelmann, *1 Corinthians,* trans. James W. Leitch (Augsburg Fortress, 1988), p. 215.

[98]Hays, *op. cit.*, p. 217. Thiselton puts it: "... they are **first** through the **agency** by means of which their witness makes the gospel ... transparent" (p. 213).

In my opinion, Gordon Fee captures an essential distinction in his comment on this text, saying: "In any case, the word *charisma* is probably too narrow to embrace the great variety of things mentioned in this argument. Apostles and prophets, for example, would better be described as 'ministries', whereas 'prophecy' itself is a *charisma*."[99] David Bartlett seems to agree with this:

> *Paul sandwiches his picture of the church as the body of Christ between two more general discussions of spiritual gifts in the church. In the first discussion, the gifts seem to represent different functions within the community; in the second discussion, they hint more at a development towards offices.*[100]

Nowhere in this epistle does Paul shy away from leadership in the interests of egalitarian considerations. Equality for him does not mean that apostles, for instance, do not have a decisive role in ordering the Church's life, and may even "pull rank" on occasion when they feel it necessary to good order. Bartlett, discussing apostolic authority in 1 Corinthians 5:1–5, expresses this:

> *… the congregation performs the judgment the apostle announces. There is no room here for advice and consent. There is room only for obedience. Many times Paul exhorts, begs, as a kind of elder brother in Christ. Here he commands as a stern father.*[101]

Distinction between the different "levels" of gifting is taken further in Ephesians 4:7, which lists the *domata*, or ministry gifts of Christ, or what some have referred to as offices or established ministries in the global church. Selwyn Hughes called these "the

---

[99]Fee, *op. cit.*, p. 587.

[100]David Lyon Bartlett, *Ministry in the New Testament* (Augsburg Fortress, 1993), p. 46.

[101]*Ibid.*, p. 35.

gifts some become".[102] I will discuss the relevant text pertaining to these gifts, or offices, later. Suffice it to say here that the "weight" of the *domata* is qualitatively as distinct from *charismata*, in the mind of the apostle, as the mason is from the stones he uses to build (1 Corinthians 3:9–10, cf. Ephesians 2:19–22).

Charismata, however, do seem to be the building blocks, the "ABC" of how believers may partner with God in expressing heaven's will on earth. That is why Paul encourages "all" to use them, desire them more and more, and seek to excel in their use. He also exhorts believers to practise what many seem to regard as an entry-level gift (tongues), but to move beyond that to the more comprehensible gift (prophecy); i.e. to start with what builds up the individual and move to gifts that build up the congregation.[103]

How spiritual gifts operate

Jesus, while exhorting Nicodemus to seek a new or spiritual birth, explains something about the workings of the Holy Spirit in these words: "The wind blows where it wants to. You *hear its sound*, but you don't know where it comes from or where it is going. That's the way it is with everyone who is born of the Spirit" (John 3:8, italics mine). Using this phrase in its broadest application, I am going to suggest that the work of the Holy Spirit is noticed by its *effects*, rather than by its *methodology*. When the Holy Spirit is operative, Jesus says you will "hear a sound". You may "see" the wind by the fact that the branches of the tree are moving. What does it sound like? What does the moving tree look like? What does it make people feel? When something truly spiritual takes place, these may be some of the expected effects on all concerned:

---

[102]Hughes, *op. cit.,* p. 12.
[103]1 Corinthians 14:1–5.

1. People will be drawn "upward"; that is, to God. They will become aware of Him, will want to honour Him, will see His Nature, hear His words, and be motivated to follow Him. In another place, Jesus had urged His disciples to test "ministers" by their "fruits".[104] The fruit, or substance, of spiritual ministry is God-awareness. John Wimber, in his teaching on signs and wonders, or spiritual gifts,[105] spoke of their effect as "[introducing] the *numinous* of God".[106] As Allen puts it: "… in whatever form this gift of [lay] ministry is lived, St. Paul reminds us of the condition which makes it, in fact, a 'ministry': it is Christ we proclaim … (Colossians 2:28 KJV)."[107]

2. People will become aware of and be drawn to Kingdom values which were the driving motives of Jesus' life and ministry, such as mercy, purity, peace and goodness (Matthew 5:1–10), as well as the humility of the servant, a heart for the least and the lost, a desire for redemption, and the manifestation of positive personal change or healing. Additionally, these positive values will be balanced by aversion to the things Jesus hated, like self-righteousness, religiousness, "majoring on minors", pretentiousness and playing games with God's truth. (Read, for example, Matthew 23.)

3. People will focus on eternal rather than temporal outcomes. While many things are meant simply to be enjoyed in the moment, and God is "in" every moment of our lives, true

---

[104]Matthew 7:15–20.

[105]Seminar notes, *Signs and Wonders and Church Growth* (Vineyard Ministries International, 1987), p. 7.

[106]The word "numinous" ("otherness") was popularised in the early 20th century by the German theologian, Rudolf Otto, in his influential 1917 book, *Das Heilige*, which appeared in English as *The Idea of the Holy* in 1923 (adapted from a Wikipedia entry on "Numinous").

[107]Allen, *op. cit.*, p. 65.

spirituality requires a healthy dose of "deferred compensation", of refusing to settle for easy, short-term solutions to pain in favour of the dilemma of enduring pain for long-term (eternal) benefit (Matthew 4:1–11; 2 Corinthians 4:7–18). Allen reminds us that to minister is to sacrifice: "'Sacrifice' is the term that best describes [this] ministry, for the Church is itself a sacrifice."[108]

4. The operator will be drawn to a felt need, whether in an individual or a group, and is motivated to meet it, even at personal cost. Care, compassion and love are essential character traits of an operator of a true "charisma" of God (Matthew 9:36–38; 1 Corinthians 13:1–3).

5. The operator will be aware that, while he or she had to co-operate in the manifesting of the gift, the Initiator of both the gift and its effect, was always God (see 1 Corinthians 15:10). When the Holy Spirit was poured out on the Church on the day of Pentecost, one of the noticeable effects was that they "began to speak in other tongues as the Spirit gave them utterance" (Acts 2:4 KJV, RV). In the text, the Greek word for "speak", *lalein*, is in the "middle voice" of the verb, denoting that they were both active (speaking) and passive (being given utterance) in the exercising of the gift of tongues. Thus it is with any spiritual gift. The answer to the question: "God, is this me or is this You?" is *"It's both of us!"*

Summarising the above, Allen defines ministry as "doing something for the advent of the Kingdom, expressed in public and realised in such forms as witnessing, celebrating, guiding and teaching; given in behalf of the community as a gift (*charisma*)"[109]

As pointed out earlier, *charismata*, or *phanerosis* (manifestations),

---

[108]Allen, *op. cit.,* p. 67.
[109]*Ibid.,* p. 16.

are "entry-level" spiritual gifts, which we are encouraged to use, to desire, to perfect and to seek to excel in giving away. In so doing, both the gift itself, our ability to recognise it and the effects it has on others, will grow and bear fruit at all the increasingly significant levels of which Jesus speaks in John 15:1–8: fruit, more fruit, much fruit, and fruit that remains.

Motivational gifts

Taking the idea of the growth of spiritual gifts further, brings us to the Romans 12:3–8 text on the subject:

> ³*For by the grace given to me I say to everyone among you not to think of yourself more highly than you ought to think, but to think with sober judgment, each according to the measure of faith that God has assigned.* ⁴*For as in one body we have many members, and not all the members have the same function,* ⁵*so we, who are many, are one body in Christ, and individually we are members one of another.* ⁶*We have gifts that differ according to the grace given to us: prophecy, in proportion to faith;* ⁷*ministry, in ministering; the teacher, in teaching;* ⁸*the exhorter, in exhortation; the giver, in generosity; the leader, in diligence; the compassionate, in cheerfulness.* (NRSV)

Paul uses different words for "gifts" in this passage: *charismata* (verse 6), to describe the operation of individual gifts, but *praxis*[110] to describe how the gift has created a more dependable "function". His language seems to suggest that members of a body grow into not merely an "occasional" manifestation, but rather a practice or settled function, which operates so regularly through a

---

[110]*Praxis* is an adverbial form of *prasso*, "to practise", from which the idea of a practice (a noun – as in something conducted by a medical practitioner) is derived.

particular person that it becomes a predisposition, an expectation or a motivation in that person's life. Hughes calls these "the gifts we have".[111]

Paul uses several phrases which enlarge on one another:

1. He himself, in teaching, is operating by "the grace" (*chari-tos*) given to him (verse 3a). The "grace" that authorised Paul to speak as he did, is believed by most commentators to refer to his apostolic office. Thus, John Murray states: "In thinking about the grace given him he could not be unmindful of the grace by which he was saved … But he is thinking specifically of the grace bestowed upon him in his apostolic commission."[112] For Hodge, it "probably includes all the *favour* of God towards him, not merely in conferring on him the office of an apostle, but in bestowing all the gifts of the Spirit, ordinary and extraordinary, which qualified him for his duties, and gave authority to his instructions".[113]

2. He urges his hearers to think of themselves according to the "measure of faith" given by God (verse 3b). Paul is referring in the context to the grace which empowers function, so that the person being addressed is urged to believe what God has "said" about them, to renew their thinking about their relative value and potential (cf. verse 2). Moo's comment here is that "many … think that the faith Paul refers to is, or relates especially to, the differing capacities God gives to people for their service of the community".[114] I believe

---

[111]Hughes, *op. cit.,* p. 12.

[112]John Murray, *The Epistle to the Romans,* in *The New International Commentary on the New Testament* (Eerdmans,1977), p. 117.

[113]Charles Hodge, *A Commentary on Romans* in *The Geneva Series of Commentaries* (Banner of Truth, 1972), p. 386.

[114]Douglas Moo, "The Book of Romans" in *The New International Commentary on the New Testament* (Eerdmans, 1996), p. 761.

the context supports this view. Hodge continues: "*Faith* ... may be taken for that which is confided to any, and be equivalent to gift. The sense given then is, 'Let everyone think of himself according to the nature or character of the gifts which he has received.'"[115] Thus, no gift or function in the realm of God's work in and through the church is exercised apart from faith, and if any did exercise a gift in that way, it would be devoid of God's life and power. It is faith and grace that make the difference between leadership in general and the spiritual gift of leadership.

3. He reminds them that each one is gifted "according to the grace given" (verse 6). Paul begins an enumeration of the ways in which believers will function, with a reminder that, as he is exhorting them by the *charitos* given to *him*, each should function in keeping with, and consistently with, the *charis* given to *them*. He has both *proportion* – linking it to the last phrase in the verse – and *integrity* in mind, so as to say "don't overreach yourself, and don't distort or misuse the gift". The "grace" here is the gift that empowers function, just as it was for Paul himself: "... the fellowship of the godly exists only when each one is content with his own measure, and imparts to his brethren the gifts which he has received ..."[116]

4. Each of them will have a different, ongoing, vital "function" (verse 4). Various commentators render the word *praxis*

---

[115]Hodge, *op. cit.,* p. 387.

[116]John Calvin, *Commentary on Romans,* trans. Ross MacKenzie (Eerdmans, 1980): "The safety of the Church is preserved by this most excellent order and symmetry, when every individual of himself imparts to the common good what he has received from the Lord without preventing others from doing so. To invert this order is to fight with God, by whose ordination it was appointed" (p. 268).

differently. Calvin translates it "power(s)";[117] others use "duty"; yet others "office"[118] or "action", but most use "function". The word itself contrasts with the previous words used, *charismata* and *phanerosis*, which both carry the thought of a moment of arrival, a delightful opportunity taken, to allow the Holy Spirit's life to be seen in and through an individual. *Praxis*, however, suggests permanence of both ability and expectancy, much as a person would be "appointed" to do something because they have a proven track record of effectiveness, and then are expected to do that thing by virtue of the appointment. The occasional gift has become a regular function, or *ministry*. Paul's emphasis on the Church as the Body of Christ makes the point that the endowment of a human body with many and varied "parts" or members is the basis of each of them having a specific function, design and arrangement to facilitate dependable function. John Murray states: "… diversity of gift and office exercised according to the measure of faith in the harmony of mutual esteem and recognized interdependence, determines the mode of expression".[119]

Putting these phrases into a dynamic sequence: *faith* exercised toward spiritual effectiveness will manifest in *grace* received and expressed in a *gift* given, leading to an effect or *function* in a local church. Some persons who "have" such a function will *regularly and consistently* practise this particular gift, no matter where they are and no matter what the context (a *ministry*).

The gifts or functions listed in Romans 12 have become known as the "motivational gifts". The term was first used by Bill Gothard

---

[117]Calvin, *op. cit.,* p. 268.
[118]Hodge, *op. cit.,* p. 387.
[119]Murray, *op. cit.,* p. 120.

of the Institute of Basic Life Principles, in California.[120] It was taken up and developed as a teaching series by Don Pickerill of the L.I.F.E. Bible School, Los Angeles, in the early 1970s.[121] What these teachers were seeking to convey, was that such gifts indicate their presence in our lives by motivating us. We "see" any situation through the lens of the needs that gain our interest, and that motivate us to meet them. For example, when someone is looking to buy a new car, his or her constant interest is in cars, even while they are doing other things. They will have a "poise" or orientation that sees specific cars where others only see a road, or "traffic". Motivational gifts are an orientation, a predisposition, a "wiring" that will prod us toward a natural response to specific needs. Bartlett puts it like this: "They are not really offices, [but] they are not simply functions either."[122]

Although we should avoid a "watertight" compartmentalising of the gifts listed in Corinthians and Romans, we can see differences, both semantic and pragmatic. A picture emerges wherein the *regular* way ("praxis") in which someone is motivated to serve in the Church, becomes a kind of "DNA" of spiritual effect, so that the individual will "leave evidence" of him or herself at every scene in which they were involved, and be remembered for the effect they left behind. It creates a sense of focus, poise or purpose in a given situation, toward particular kinds of people and specific needs they have.

The difference between "charisma" and "praxis", then, is subtle but real. It has to do with an increasing level of convergence or integration of the person and the effect she or he has on others. A "word of wisdom", for instance, or an encouraging "prophetic" insight, may typically be offered by one church member to another,

---

[120]Quoted in *Discover Your Gifts,* a course taught at Churchlands Christian Fellowship, Perth, Australia, 1992, p. 3.

[121]*Discover Your Gifts,* p. 3.

[122]Bartlett, *op. cit.,* p. 52.

whether in the service itself, in the parking lot outside the church or in a telephone call through the week, without the person concerned being recognised thereafter as a "prophet" or "sage", nor with the expectation that every such exchange in the future will have the same effect. It was, in either case, an occasional "manifestation" of God's love to the person receiving it. On the other hand, when a person *regularly* has insights and is motivated by the needs they see in the church, for administrative help, or direction, or service of some kind, the result, in the context of churches like the Vineyard, will often be that the person will be invited into a structured group where the church's direction and functions are discussed. They will be "recognised" as the prophetic encourager, diaconal server, wise counsellor or spiritual leader they have become. The gift is now expected to be given through the same person, on a regular basis, and placed in a functional structure in which it may benefit the Body. The *charisma* has become a *praxis*.

When Jesus was challenged about His claims to some kind of "partnership" (i.e. Sonship) with Yahweh, He says, in effect, that the claim is validated by the fruit it bears: "Truly, I tell all of you with certainty, the Son can do nothing on his own accord, but only what he sees the Father doing, What the Father does, the Son does likewise."[123] He goes on to explain that His ministry is effective in Kingdom terms because He "sees" or discerns what Yahweh is doing and joins Him in His *mission*. One of the ways we may discern what God is doing, is by the desires or motivations that arise within us as we live worshipfully and consciously as vessels of God's presence.[124] A person operating in their motiva-

---

[123]John 5:19.

[124]Psalm 37:4, which can be read as a causative phrase, meaning that God's response to a worshipper includes causing desires to arise in her/his heart. The word "give" used here is the Hebrew word *Nawthan*, which includes, among its shades of meaning: "to pull, put (forth), render, requite, restore, send (out), set (forth) or shoot forth (up)". Compare Jesus' promise, in the

tion or grace from God, will be inspired and inspiring. They will be "at rest"[125] and experience the joy of bearing fruit, rather than the fatigue following hard "work". They will be "a square peg in a square hole"; they will be hitting the ball of involvement out of their "sweet spot"; they will not need to strive for place or success, but rather bear fruit from peacefully "abiding" in the flow of God's life, which in turn leads to joyful serving and "abundant" fruitfulness (John 15:4–11).

Bartlett makes the point, in discussing Romans 12, that:

> *What does seem clear is that the gifts are defined more in terms of function rather than in terms of office. Paul speaks of "prophecy" "not prophets". The one who "teaches" (as in the RSV) is really a better translation of Paul's terms than "teachers".* (Footnote: "On the whole the RSV captures better than the NRSV the fact that these descriptions are participial phrases, not titles of offices.")[126]

However, the point must be made that a *praxis* is a more settled, consistent function in a local church; *"a function, implying sustained activity and/or responsibility ..."*[127]

The seven motivational gifts, as they are listed for us in Romans 12:6–8, are:

---

context of calling and ministry fruit, in John 15:16, which suggests that those who "abide in my Word" will find different "desires" coming into play.

[125]See the "restful work" into which Jesus invites His followers to be "yoked together" with Him (Matthew 11:28–30). Eugene Peterson's rendering of this is particularly poignant when he has Jesus inviting us to "learn from me the unforced rhythms of grace".

[126]Bartlett, *op. cit.*, p. 51.

[127]J. P. Louw and Eugene Albert Nida, *Greek Lexicon of the New Testament* (United Bible Societies, 1989), 42.5 (italics mine), who continue: "In some languages one may express the meaning of this phrase in Ro 12:4 as 'all these parts help in different ways' or 'all these parts have different *work to do.*'"

- prophecy or insight *(prophetes)*;
- serving or facilitating *(diakonia)*;
- teaching or giving instruction *(didasko)*;
- exhorting or encouraging *(paraklesis)*;
- contributing, giving or sharing *(metadidomi)*;
- leading – to stand before, take forward *(proistamenos)*; and
- showing mercy, or active love *(eleeo)*.

I believe that every follower of Christ has something of all of these "wirings", because they summarise the elements of the *Missio Dei,* in which we are all called to participate. God wills to be known as Love manifested as wisdom, service, truth, encouragement, generosity, mercy and direction. Therefore, the love of God "poured out" into our hearts (Romans 5:5) will shine through each believer in some measure of the ways listed above. But one of those ways will predominate in each of us, setting off dreams and visions, desires and goals, and form a kind of "comfort (and discomfort!) zone" of operation. The way of being motivated will determine not whether, but *how* each applies their energies to the given situation, or role. In Romans 12:1–8, Paul is talking about these areas of ministry function in the context of the "Body"; that is, the gathered, functioning congregation. They describe how we serve primarily within the Church, but will also overflow in the ways we affect the "marketplace":

> *The ministry of the laity can certainly manifest itself in mission, in teaching, in service within the Body, in philanthropic works of the Church, etc. Furthermore, even in teaching mathematics, or working in industry or politics ... the mother teaching her children ...*[128]

Therefore, understanding that "having" a motivational gift does not make an office, and also noting that all gifts have equal value,

---

[128]Allen, *op. cit.,* p. 65.

we may ask ourselves: What "flicks my switches"? What needs grab me with compassion? Am I motivated to understand or know *why* a person, or a church, is in crisis? To organise them? To give them relief aid? To help them practically into a better place? Or to "take charge", step to the fore and give the whole group vision for the way to get all of the above done? If someone most often, most naturally and most effectively does the latter, then it is likely that his or her motivational gift is *leadership*.

Defining leadership biblically

To repeat what we have discovered thus far: Leadership is a form of ministry to God and others, rather than a title, a position or a right. "The exercise of leadership in the church is as truly a spiritual gift as any of the other [gifts] mentioned."[129] This is an important "stake in the ground" which I want to put in place on this massive subject. Let me describe the stake, and the ground in which it stands, as follows:

- If it is a gift, it is to be *given,* rather than *taken*.
- It is by grace that anyone receives the privilege of leading others.
- That also means it is for the benefit of those others, not the leader.
- A gift has to be *exercised* in order to become visible. A leader is a leader because he or she leads, i.e. goes somewhere *on purpose* which, in turn, means having a sense of initiative, responsibility and determination. It will involve faith which, as John Wimber famously said, is spelled: R-I-S-K!

Recalling what we discovered earlier concerning effectiveness of ministry, no ministry that does not actively engage with

---

[129] F. F. Bruce, *Romans: An Introduction and Commentary* in *The Tyndale New Testament Commentaries* series (Intervarsity Press, 1974), p. 228.

God's story will be sustainable and effective in Kingdom terms. Evidently Jesus lived a life in constant three-way dialogue, between Himself, people in His community, and His Heavenly Father. He heard and saw what the Father was saying and doing, not only in times of prayer and retreat, but also in the conduct of ordinary, daily life. He lived and led in a way that was naturally supernatural, and supernaturally natural. And, when He "sent" His apostles, His mandate was: "Go and do it as I have done it" (John 20:21).

All true ministry, therefore, links the divine story with the human story, in the form of one person, or one group, connecting with God's nature as it is made known through the person serving them as a minister of God. Allen continues: "God's ministry is nothing less than to 'reveal and reconcile' via 'theology', i.e. a word about God. Thus, theology is truly the handmaid of ministry … born out of God's ministry …"[130] However, its true task is to reveal, not *things about* God, but the *nature* of God, and our response to that nature. The job of the minister, to use another metaphor, is to represent Christ in His three-fold offices of Prophet, Priest and King. "He or she does this by exercising the Christlike virtues, in his or her leadership role, of faith (the King), hope (the Prophet), and love (the Priest)."[131]

---

[130]Allen, *op. cit.,* p. 17.

[131]I will say more about this theme later. However, it is pursued as a basic model for ministry in Richard R. Osmer, *Practical Theology* (Eerdmans, 2008), pp. 28-29, and Dr Coenie Burger, in five articles titled, *Die Predikantsamp* (2004), published on the website academic.sun.ac.za. I am grateful to both of them for the frame of reference.

The Offices and Functions of Christ and His Leaders

KING	FAITH
PROPHET	HOPE
PRIEST	LOVE

The gift of leadership is therefore one of the "ministries" or ways of serving this revelation of God. Paul here uses *proistemi* for "leadership". Some English translations of the New Testament render this with relatively innocuous words like "facilitate", "supervise", "manage", etc. The NKJV translates it "rule", while other translations use "lead". Its literal meaning is derived from two other words that translate, "to stand at the head, or in front of", and form the basis for the English word "priest". In fact, Allen, quoting St Basil, makes the two words almost synonymous: "In order to understand how St. Basil views the role of the shepherd, one must focus upon the one word which he himself uses to describe that role: (*proestos* = leader)."[132] The word itself is evocative, and infers willingness, ability, authority (the right to lead) and direction (the destination to which he or she leads others). A derivation of *proistemi* is *proistamenos*, which joins the idea of "standing forward/to the front" with that of "carrying", and is translated "chief", "head" or "leader". Thus, *a leader is someone who steps forward, taking initiative and setting an example, with determination to carry a group to a goal.*

In the English translations of the Old Testament, the words "lead", "leader" or "leadership" are taken from a range of sometimes poetic Hebrew words that paint a picture of someone who knows where they are going, either running, flowing (like a river) or plodding forward, guiding, and even carrying with them, the people they lead.

These nine Hebrew words, in their various applications, refer

---

[132]Allen, quoting St Basil, p. 86.

to Yahweh's leadership of Israel, as well as to the role of God-appointed leaders such as the Patriarchs, Moses, David, etc.:

1. *Ashar* (16 times) means to be straight, level and to go forward. It essentially refers to leading from the front, as a guide showing the way by walking on it first. (See Isaiah 3:12.)

2. *Nâhal* (10 times) means to run with a "sparkle" or to flow, hence (transitively) to conduct or lead gently or lead on. It is a word which is a metaphor in itself, revealing the gentle determination of the shepherd who walks ahead of his flock, yet watches their progress and carries the weak if necessary (thus Isaiah 40:11).

3. *Nâchâh* (39 times) also carries the meaning of "to guide" or "to lead forth". It also, like *Ashar*, carries strongly the idea of being goal-focused, of guiding people to a destination. In various texts it is also applied to: God himself (Exodus 13:21; Deuteronomy 32:12); God's Word (Psalm 43:3); God's Wisdom (Proverbs 6:22), and Moses as a leader under God (Exodus 32:34).

4. *Dârâk* (63 times) is a word for tread or walk, and also refers to stringing a bow by treading on it and bending it. It evokes images of strong intentionality or decisiveness, of bending others to one's will with firm resolve. Applied to God's leadership of His people, it reveals strength of purpose and loving power so, for example: "Lead me into your truth and teach me" (Psalm 25:5), and: "I [Yahweh] will lead them in paths that they have not known" (Isaiah 42:16).

5. *Hâlâk* (1 545 times) is the most frequently used word in this list, although not often translated by "to lead". It means, like *Dârâk*, to walk or to move oneself, so it once again carries a meaning of determination and visionary momentum.

In the texts where it is translated lead, therefore, it adds to the picture of a determined, goal-focused person stepping forward with intention to take others somewhere. Thus, Wisdom is described by this word, and can be seen to be a leader in this way (Proverbs 8:20).

6. *Nâhâg* (31 times) is a strong, intense, effort-laden version of the foregoing concept. It means "to drive forth" or "to lead or carry away". It conveys the idea of expelled breath, as in panting with effort or passion, or sighing with the same. It is used in texts describing God's leading or scattering of Israel among the nations (Deuteronomy 4:27; 28:37); the lover leading her suitor to her mother's house (Song 8:2); God's saving leadership of Israel out of exile (Isaiah 49:10; 63:14); and the leadership given by a little child in the consummated Kingdom (Isaiah 11:6).

7. *Rôsh* (547 times) means to shake the head, and is used mostly to mean top (of a mountain) or head (of a tribe or clan). When used with reference to leadership, it specifically means to rise up by rank. The word picture is one of stirring oneself to act decisively, of taking responsibility for something. It conveys the sense of rising into a calling, or behaving in a manner befitting one's badge of rank.

8. *Yâbal* (18 times) means "to flow" or "to bring or lead forth". It carries the idea of triumphal procession, carrying a trophy to reveal it publicly (thus Jeremiah 31:9).

9. *Yâtsâ'* (1 068 times) means to go, or to bring, out. It is used in describing the calling, or task, of Moses (Exodus 3:10ff) and of Yahweh's salvific promise (Exodus 6:6ff; 7:4ff). It is the grace-basis of God's right to impose the law on Israel (Exodus 20:2). Because God has delivered Israel, He has the right to impose obligations. (This is the normal shape of a covenant relationship.) When used of a human leader,

it describes something similar. From serving comes benefit; from benefit comes influence; and influence generates followership. This kind of leader earns the authority to lead, by his/her commitment to the wellbeing of the flock under their care. A key text, possibly of the entire subject in the OT, and one in which this word is used, is Numbers 27:17, where Moses asks God to appoint a leader for the congregation of the Lord. God's reply is that Moses should charge Joshua, and put some of his honour – another word for authority or influence – upon him, so that the people would be obedient to him.

I list them in the full realisation that we should not put too much store on the fine shading of meaning between words in the biblical languages. That does not mean we cannot gain insights from those nuances of meaning. We may seek overall trends and commonalities between them, and even then, hold those lightly. We are to learn more from the narrative and example offered by leaders in the Bible, than from semantic minutiae, although semantics can illustrate the principles we learn from the story. I invite you to meditate on these evocative words, and to ask how they are being reflected in your leadership style, and how you might embrace aspects not yet evident.

An interesting word derived from *proistemi* in the Greek New Testament, and which is used only once, is *prostatis* (see Romans 16:2), a feminine derivative which is often translated by an old English word "succourer" (meaning "supporter" or "promoter") and in more modern English by "helper". It carries the meaning of walking alongside and "holding upright" the one being thus "led".

Spiritual gifts and the Kingdom of God

The Kingdom (dynamic rule) of God is a manifestation of God's power, will and desire that breaks into human affairs, bringing a taste and sign of the perfected future into the present. For example, when Jesus taught His disciples to pray, He instructed that they should ask God to "[let] your kingdom come. [Let] your will be done, on earth as it is in heaven". The arrival of God's Kingdom is equated with the doing of God's will, demonstrated in forgiveness, providence and deliverance from evil, and perfect harmony between "heaven and earth". The question, for the Church, has always been: "When will this occur?" Has the Kingdom already come? Is it coming? Will it only come at the end of the age? I have found the answer which most satisfies my reading of Scripture is that provided by the writings of George Eldon Ladd,[133] who demonstrates, in summary, that the Kingdom of God is both "already" and "not yet". In Jesus' life and ministry, God brought the future age into the present, in the form of forgiveness, provision, deliverance, healing, wisdom and even resurrections. Yet, those things were neither universal nor formulaic. In the Church age, we may expect more of the same: the Kingdom fulfilled but not consummated, the "already" and "not yet". Because it is "already", we may expect deliveries of supernatural provision "from heaven to earth" at any time "as He wills".[134] But, because it is "not yet", we may not demand such provision, or take ownership of either the means or the nature thereof. The Kingdom is not *either* already *or* not yet, it is *both* already *and* not yet. Our responsibility is to seek to

---

[133] *The Gospel of the Kingdom* (Eerdmans, 1959) ISBN 0802812805; *A Theology of the New Testament*, 2nd ed., ed. Donald A. Hagner (Eerdmans, 1993) ISBN 0802806805, first published in 1974; *The Presence of the Future* (Eerdmans, 1996) ISBN 0802815316, previously *Jesus and the Kingdom* (Harper & Row, 1964).

[134] 1 Corinthians 12:11 KJV, RSV, LITV.

hear God's voice and to do what pleases Him in the moment-by-moment "passing on" of what we receive from the King, without demanding or prescribing when, what or how it should happen. The Kingdom, or authority, of God is discovered exactly in the humility and lack of control we confess when holding things in tension!

Living and serving as a Kingdom agent, therefore, will often call on us to hold seemingly contradictory things in tension. Most of the polarities of theology and ministry are answered with "both/and" rather than "either/or".[135] This is a metaphor that serves us well in considering the polarities of leadership: Are leaders born or made? Is it my gifting or my character? Is it fulfilled by grace or hard work? The answer is usually "both/and"!

To further expand on this model of dynamic tension to express the dynamics of the Kingdom of God, we may see it also as a series of overlapping circles, which converge to create a "new" reality in the overlap. When it comes to the spiritual gift of leadership, the Kingdom becomes manifest in the convergence of the concepts we have isolated. Words describing decisiveness and vision must converge with character and the loving humility of listening to people. The passion of the pioneer must converge with the grace of a shepherd. As Jesus was "full of grace and truth", so must be those He calls to lead on His behalf. We need to pursue convergence between all the words examined, all the definitions listed, if we are to see an expression of Christ's ministry of leadership through, under and over our own. As I will try to demonstrate later, such convergence also presupposes team function, as I do not believe any person has all of these qualities and functionalities in themselves. Thus, Thiselton says that the quality of and

---

[135]My friend, Rich Nathan, summarises these polarities and how we should approach them in an excellent work he wrote with Insoo Kim, called *Both-And: Living the Christ-Centered Life in an Either-Or World* (IVP, 2013).

requirement for diversity "challenges any self-styled leader who imagines that he or she alone is the church's 'answer' ... Christians need *all* the resources of God's gifts that are spread throughout the church, and encountered through different individuals and in different forms".[136]

Diagram 3: Convergence

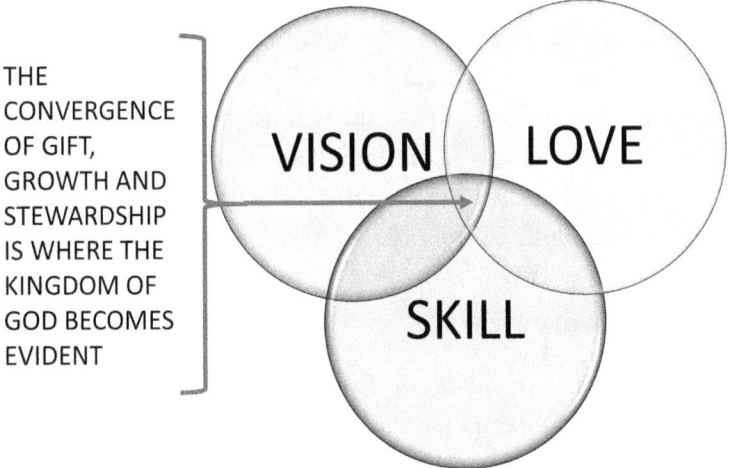

THE CONVERGENCE OF GIFT, GROWTH AND STEWARDSHIP IS WHERE THE KINGDOM OF GOD BECOMES EVIDENT

VISION   LOVE

SKILL

Specialisation of style and diversification, however, will never excuse a leader from not meeting the criteria that are commonly applicable to *all* leaders in God's Church, namely that we are to be motivated by love, to operate in compassionate community, and to seek the wellbeing of the whole, even at personal cost:

> *In its broadest definition, leadership is a relationship of influence. It is a relationship between two people in which one person seeks to influence the vision, values, attitudes, or behaviors of the other. This definition makes it clear that everyone exercises leadership. At one time or another, we all*

---

[136]Thiselton, *op. cit.*, p. 212.

seek to exert such influence and thus engage in leadership.[137]

In a statement quoted by Ascough and Cotton, Margaret Wheatley concurs: "What gives power its charge, positive or negative, is the quality of relationships. Those who relate through coercion, or from a disregard for the other person, create negative energy … Love in organizations, then, is the most potent source of power that we have available".[138] The authors later add, summing up Paul's mandate to leaders: "If Paul were a leadership coach in today's turbulent world, his bottom line, his non-negotiable benchmark for evaluating leaders, would be the degree of compassion they display in relationships … For Paul, without compassion, nothing else matters. Nothing!"[139] I think Paul would add: "… and without character, nothing else is sustainable. And without a servant heart, echoing Jesus, don't even *think* about leading God's people!"

Momentum maintenance

When Jesus had called the Twelve together, he gave them power and authority to drive out all demons and to cure diseases, and he sent them out to preach the kingdom of God and to heal the sick. (Luke 9:1–2)

In the New Testament, "power" is translated from the Greek word *dunamis*, which means (a) power, ability, physical or moral, as residing in a person or thing; (b) power in action, as, for example, when put forth in performing miracles. On the other hand, the word for "authority" is *exousia*, which is derived from the verb *ex-esti*, meaning "to be lawful". There are two ways in which *exousia* is used: The first has to do with mastery or ability into which a

---

[137]Wright, *op. cit.,* loc 320.
[138]Richard S. Ascough and Charles A. Cotton, *Passionate Visionary* (Hendrickson, 2006), p. 151.
[139]*Ibid.,* pp. 146-7.

person has grown through hard work, training and application; the second application refers to delegated authority, which a person earns by legal qualification or conferment by a higher authority. However, the important distinction to note is that, whereas *dunamis* means the actual force or strength to do and continue doing something, *exousia* means the permission or liberty to do that thing. It refers, in other words, to the legal right to exercise power. Authority is the right to give orders and see that they are followed. It is an issue of legality, not of strength. It is like the uniform worn by a policeman, or a badge of rank. Picture a traffic policeman on point duty, with a large truck approaching at 60 km per hour. The policeman does not have the power – i.e. the physical strength – to stop the truck. But, because of his uniform and his badge of rank, a simple gesture with upraised, white-gloved hand, causes the driver to apply the brakes and come to an obedient halt. That is authority. The policeman's badge trumps the truck's horsepower. To reverse the metaphor, power can be seen as the ability to press the accelerator so that the vehicle keeps moving. Authority is the right to turn the keys, start the vehicle and drive it through a particular gateway or down a particular route.

A careful reading of Scripture will show that, whereas anyone can receive a gift, and whereas God's grace is such that the gift remains with us, even if we take it for granted, there are ways in which we "put on" our uniform of authority, and qualify for greater and greater responsibility, by certain practices, disciplines and character growth. I have seen, in my life and in the leadership of others, that progress in ministry can be arrested, momentum can be stalled, even though the gift of leadership is still present. Ministry can move into a "holding pattern" instead of staying on a flight path. It can become a repeated journey around a traffic circle instead of taking the freeway to your destination. The ministry gift gives you the engine (power); God's call gives you the road map; but God's delegated authority gives you the keys (authority) to move and keep moving.

In this discussion, we are going to enter the long-standing conversation about grace and works, or the difference between God's part and our part in the growth and desired effectiveness of a leader. When Paul describes this dynamic in his life, he once again uses a "both/and" logic:

> *But by God's grace I am what I am, and his grace shown to me was not wasted. Instead, I worked harder than all the others – not I, of course, but God's grace that was with me.*
> (1 Corinthians 15:10)

What Paul is describing is the grace to do the work of ministry. When he speaks of "what I am", he means his identity and place as an apostle. It has been given to him by the grace of God, and that is the basis for whatever he does. This does not mean that he does not have to "work" – in fact, Paul says that he depends on grace, and works harder than any of the other (apostles). But looking back, he reminds himself, as much as his reader, that even the ability to work hard was given to him by the grace of God. Grace is essential, but working with, or "following" the grace, is what activates it to have its full effect.

Jesus' parting words to His remaining disciples, which are recorded in the four versions of the Great Commission, refer to the fact that, while certain things were "above their pay grade" to know or have authority over they, and the Church they would lead into God's mission, would operate on the basis of a power not their own. John had also referred, in more detail than the other Gospel writers, to the Person and work of the Holy Spirit in the life and ministry of believers. What is clear from all these exchanges is that, in order to complete the mission given to it, the Church was going to need a power beyond the ordinary. In Luke's version of the Great Commission "sermon", he emphasises the point, saying, in effect: "Don't go anywhere, or try to do this, without the Spirit's power!" The other thing that is clear is that the power will come in the form of a Person, the *parakletos*, or "helper", the One who is different-yet-the-same as Jesus Himself. Furthermore, this Person is "the promise of the Father", and is received as a "gift", not earned or bought, and not a right nor a merit badge.

As leaders in a humanistic environment, we need to be more mindful than ever of this fact. Our mandate and mission are to represent a Kingdom that, as Jesus said, is "not of this world" (John 18:36 NKJV). In order to truly represent Him and His Kingdom, we need to increase our dependence on and interaction with the source of that Kingdom's power. The Holy Spirit is that Source, and we will need to return repeatedly to Him for filling and refilling, and grow in relationship with Him, if we are to be His servants in every sense of that word. Paul, speaking of himself and the other apostles, puts it like this:

> *Such is the confidence that we have in God through the Messiah. By ourselves we are not qualified to claim that anything comes from us. Rather, our credentials come from God, who has also qualified us to be ministers of a new covenant, which is not written but spiritual, because the written text brings death, but the Spirit gives life.* (2 Corinthians 3:4–6)

In exchange for faith, then, we receive power. It is a gift. But authority comes in exchange for something more costly. Authority is spoken of as a legal mandate or credential. Scripture uses the concept of documented authority: being authorised to operate "in the name or on behalf of" or "having the (right to use) keys". Keys are used a few times in Scripture as a metaphor for authority, or the right to open or shut a door. In Western society, when a person reached adult "majority" at the age of 21, this was symbolised by giving them a key ("the key of the door"). When a person becomes some kind of hero to a city, they are given "the keys of the city", which symbolises their freedom to go anywhere and access any of the resources of that city.

Let us examine a few places where authority is taught about, and how it is obtained or gained, maintained or lost.

1. The first time authority was given to the apostles, it was because of obedience to a command to go:

> *The seventy-two returned with joy and said, "Lord, even the demons submit to us in your name." He replied, "I saw Satan fall like lightning from heaven. I have given you authority to trample on snakes and scorpions and to overcome all the power of the enemy; nothing will harm you. However, do not rejoice that the spirits submit to you, but rejoice that your names are written in heaven."* (Luke 10:17–20)

In explaining why they had authority, Jesus alludes to their legal status. Their names are written "in heaven". Most Christians make a mistake in the quoting and application of this text, by conflating this phrase with that found in the Revelation,[140] so that they misquote Jesus saying: "… rejoice that your names are written in the Lamb's book of life." While that may well be a good reason for rejoicing, that is not what Jesus is referring to. In Revelation, John hears about *arnion biblion zoe* as a register of those redeemed by the Lamb from before the world's founding. In Luke 10, Jesus is referring to the register of those whose names are written in the *ouranos*, a part of the word *epouranos*, which is translated "heavenly places" or "the heavenlies" in Ephesians 1:3, 20; 2:6; 3:10. This "place", in other words, is the "living room" of heavenly beings, including the devil and his demons. It is the wrestling

---

[140]Revelation 13:8; 21:27.

ring of prayer "against principalities, powers, and spiritual rulers of wickedness", and the locus of the throne from which Jesus reigns, and where we are seated "with Him"! In other words, it is a place that represents authority to rule. Jesus, in helping the disciples understand the basis of both their effectiveness and their safety, is making the point that their authority is not transient, but eternal and spiritual. It is not based on their immediate faith, but on their eternal status with God. Their names are recorded where His is stated, not just as a record of their being saved, but as part of heaven's "flow chart" of authority. When all else fails, and you are feeling at your weakest, this is your, and my, fall-back position. Your name is there, written in blood not your own, carved with the chisel of God's determined grace, alongside a Name that is above every other name.

2. A second place where authority is conferred is in exchange for servanthood. We will say much more about the concept of servanthood later, but let us hear Jesus on the subject at this point:

*Jesus called the disciples and said, "You know that the rulers of the Gentiles lord it over them and their superiors act like tyrants over them. **That's not the way it should be among you.** Instead, whoever wants to be great among you must be your servant, and whoever wants to be first among you must be your slave.* " (Matthew 20:25–27, emphasis mine)

There is a play on words here, between "lord it", "tyrant", "great" and "first", on one hand, and the other extreme of "servant" or "slave". The first set of words all refer to the having and exercising of authority. Jesus recognises that, in order to give leadership, a person will need authority. However, in His economy, the right kind of authority will not be demanded or exerted by manipulation or force, status or rank, but rather be given in exchange for servanthood. It is a powerful paradox, and an irreversible principle in a Kingdom that has been earned in the first place by serving, inasmuch as "the Son of man came not to be served, but to serve, and to give his life as a ransom for many" (Mark 10:45). It is because Jesus humbled Himself and took on Himself the place of servitude that God the Father has given Him the Name above all names (Philippians 2:6–9).

3. A third source of spiritual authority is an appropriate relationship with the Name of Jesus. Mark's version of the Great Commission reads as follows (16:15–18):

*Then he said to them, "As you go into all the world, proclaim the gospel to the whole creation. The one who believes and is baptized will be saved, but the one who doesn't believe will be condemned. These are the signs that will accompany those who believe: **In my name** they will drive out demons; they will speak in new tongues; they will pick up snakes in their hands; even if they drink any deadly poison it will not hurt them; and they will place their hands on the sick, and they will recover."* (Emphasis mine)

In my reading of this text, the phrase "in my Name" qualifies all that follows. Thus, we could read each clause as follows:

- In my Name, they will drive out demons.
- In my Name, they will speak in new tongues.
- In my Name, they will pick up snakes (and be saved from poison).
- In my Name, they will place their hands on the sick, and they will recover.

The Name of Jesus will be the basis on which all supernatural signs of His authenticity, of the claims of His gospel and the supremacy of His reign, will be given. In the following Scriptures, the major references to the phrase "in my [Jesus'] Name" show that ministry, prayer, leadership, and government in the church are all to be exercised in His Name. We need to understand what that means. Here they are:

- "… and whoever receives a little child like this in my name receives me." (Matthew 18:5)
- "For where two or three have come together in my name, I am there among them." (Matthew 18:20)
- "In fact, everyone who has left his homes, brothers, sisters, father, mother, children, or fields because of my name will receive a hundred times as much and will inherit eternal life." (Matthew 19:29)
- "These are the signs that will accompany those who believe: In my name they will drive out demons; they will speak in new tongues …" (Mark 16:17)
- "I will do whatever you ask in my name, so that the Father may be glorified in the Son." (John 14:13)
- "If you ask me for anything in my name, I will do it." (John 14:14)
- "But the Helper, the Holy Spirit, whom the Father will send in my name, will teach you all things and remind you of all that I have told you." (John 14:26)
- "On that day, you will not ask me for anything. Truly, truly I tell you, whatever you ask the Father for in my name, he will give it to you." (John 16:23)

The approach of many Christians to the use of the Name of Jesus is somewhat superstitious. We tag it onto the end of a prayer to validate the prayer's contents. We use it in sermons to give our statements weight. And we may sometimes be surprised if, having done the above, we do not seem to get the results that the texts promise. In my opinion, it is because we are taking to ourselves the authority of the Name, without first ourselves coming under the authority it represents. Jesus is calling us to something far deeper in meaning than what such practices involve. To do anything "in His Name" is, firstly, to recognise who He is. To give place to His sovereign status and, most importantly, to only do or say that for which He gives permission (authorisation). Secondly, it means to line our actions up with His character; to do things in a way that reflect who He is. To pray "in His Name" is another way of saying "because He told me to". To act "in His Name" means to be able to say "on His behalf" or "as though He were here Himself". It is only in this way that we qualify for His authority. This was, in fact, the basis of the effectiveness of Jesus' own ministry, as He explains when challenged by the religious leaders in John 5:19, 20, 22, 30:

> *Jesus told them, "Truly, I tell all of you with certainty, the Son can do nothing on his own accord, but only what he sees the Father doing, What the Father does, the Son does likewise. Just as the Father has life in himself, so also he has granted the Son to have life in himself, and he has given him authority to judge, because he is the Son of Man. I can do nothing on my own accord. I judge according to what I hear, and my judgment is just, because I do not seek my own will but the will of the one who sent me."*

Jesus is referring not only to His overall obedience to the Law of God, but to His moment-by-moment obedience to what He was seeing the Father willing and doing. He was seeing, and hearing, at two levels: what His human eyes saw on earth, and what His Father was doing or desiring to do about it in heaven. Jesus' effectiveness in ministry was derived from the fact that He was living on earth what God was willing in heaven. Consequently, He was a conduit of God's power, because He was under God's authority.

In the Vineyard movement we base our approach to ministry

on the Kingdom of God as the "breaking in" to this age of the power of the "age to come". This is so important, but no more important than the discovery of the Kingdom of God as coming under a different authority. It is the aspect of the Kingdom's advancement that will not only save, liberate and deliver people, but also transform each one into the full expression of God's image and nature we were designed to express. Baptism, instruction or training, obedience to all commands given, are all ways of responding to Jesus so as to qualify legally for the right to use His power.

To use the analogy of living in a nation: If you live in submission to its laws, you are free to partake of its benefits. Being a lawbreaker will lead to a loss of your liberty, your right to engage with its society, and less access to its benefits and blessings. Integrity (doing the right thing with our rights) gives us the legal standing to exercise our power, to go where we want, to drive a vehicle on the roads, etc. If you consistently break the laws, you may still have the vehicle, but your right to drive it will be suspended.

Integrity means being the same on the outside as we are on the inside. Following the regeneration we experience by grace through faith, we begin a process of growth and change, predicated on the constant repentance and mind renewal to which Jesus called His followers (Mark 1:13–15; Romans 12:1–3). This is vital if we are to see the Kingdom come in its fullness. Read again Matthew's version of the Great Commission, with my attempted elaboration in brackets:

> *Then Jesus came to them and said, "All authority in heaven and on earth has been given to me. Therefore, [as a result of my authority overflowing from within you, you are going to] go and make disciples of all nations [bringing them under my authority as well, as you] baptize them in the name of the Father and of the Son and of the Holy Spirit, and [as*

you] teach them to obey everything I have commanded you. And surely [then] I will be with you, [putting my stamp of approval on your words and actions] always [being proud of associating with you in word and deed, every inch of the way], to the very end of the age." (Matthew 28:18–20)

In Matthew 16:13–19, there is a precursor to the above Great Commission passage. In reply to the question: "Who do you say I am?" Peter makes the confession of Christ as the fulfilment of every messianic promise, as the incarnation of God's life, as the Lord of glory. In response, Jesus' promise to Peter – and through him, to the Church – was that He would entrust the keys of the Kingdom to human agency. This was His response to Peter's embracing of the revelation of who Jesus was, given to him by the Father. Jesus means He will give Peter the right of access to what is in heaven, while he is living on the earth. He will be allowed the use of the keys of the Kingdom to release heaven's waiting resources in God's service. The following references illustrate the principle of "opening and shutting", i.e. of authority increasing when we are lined up with God's ways, and decreasing when we are not:

1. Heaven is opened when we obey explicit commands, and shut when we disobey them:

   "Bring all the tithes into the storehouse so there will be enough food in My Temple. If you do," says the LORD of Heaven's Armies, "I will open the windows of heaven for you. I will pour out a blessing so great you won't have enough room to take it in! Try it! Put Me to the test!" (Malachi 3:10–12 NLT)

   When I speak here of heaven being "opened", I do *not* mean in the sense of access to God, or salvation. I believe that was accomplished irrevocably by Christ's once-for-all sacrifice. Rather, I am speaking here about heaven being opened from the "supply" side, in terms of what the prophet calls "blessings". And particularly, I am referring to the release of Kingdom authority. I am using an Old Testament "legal" text here purely to illustrate a principle, that when there is a clear law governing behaviour, to flout it is to invite the withdrawal of God's identification with us in the opening of the doorway of authority. A leader is to be an example to those he or she leads, and thus exercise the key of obedience.

2. Heaven is closed to us when we show a lack of respect, consideration or empathy:

Husbands, in the same way be considerate as you live with your wives, and treat them with respect as the weaker partner and as heirs with you of the gracious gift of life, so that nothing will hinder your prayers. (1 Peter 3:9)

In my opinion, this is another text which, though speaking narrowly (to marriage), affirms a broader principle. Peter implies here that an inconsiderate, disrespectful or abusive husband's prayers will be hindered (literally, "chopped out" or "shut off"). In the same epistle, as well as the epistle of James, there is a reference to God "resisting" or "opposing" self-centred or arrogant people.[141] The texts indicate that it is not so much the fact of praying, or the quantity of prayer, that makes us effective, but the motivation of the person praying and other attitudinal qualities that will either open or shut the windows of heaven to us. The centre of the Kingdom ethic is love, compassion, empathy, mercy and grace. Jesus highlights the presence of these characteristics, and the neglect of them, more than He does tithing, fasting, prayer and other spiritual disciplines.[142] If a leader is exemplary in these qualities, his or

[141]James 4:6–8, cf. 1 Peter 5:5–6.
[142]See Matthew 9:13; 12:7; 23:23.

her own prayer life will remain open and effective.

3. Prayer is the exercise of God's power through human agency under His authority. Having noted above the motivation or attitude in prayer, the fact remains that, once we have checked our motives, prayer itself is a vital key of the Kingdom. We could cite dozens of references on this point, but consider just one:

> *Truly, truly I tell you, whatever you ask the Father for in my name, he will give it to you. So far you haven't asked for anything in my name. Keep asking and you will receive, so that your joy may be complete.* (John 16:23–24)

Regular, specific, faith-filled prayer is essential if we are going to see God working in and through our leadership. Jesus teaches His leaders to ask for mountains to be moved, for workers to be sent, for faith to prevail over unbelief, for deliverance to come and for provision of every daily need. There are some prayers that we do not need special revelation to pray, because God has already told us in His Word to pray them. Beyond that, we are to listen in prayer, or as one of my old mentors used to say: "Pray that you may pray." A Christ-like leader will be a model of effective praying.

4. Make unity a priority:

> *Harmony is as refreshing as the dew from Mount Hermon that falls on the mountains of Zion. And there the LORD has pronounced His blessing, even life everlasting.* (Psalm 133:3 NLT)

Various translations render the Hebrew word *tsavah* (here just translated "pronounced") with different levels of strength. Some use "command" or "decree", which I think conveys the sense of sovereignty I believe the Psalmist intended. It is as if God becomes excited, intense and intentional about putting the signs of His favour on a community united under His authority. Where there is heart agreement and self-giving, sacrificial love, God is pleased to dwell and manifest His kind of authority. As I meditate on this Psalm, I hear an echo from heaven of what Paul writes in Philippians 2: "Fill me with joy by having the same attitude, sharing the same love, being united in spirit, and keeping one purpose in mind" (verse 2). What I mean is that, in its words, I hear a plea not only from the apostle, but also from the Lord Himself. A Christlike leader will be a model of peace and unity.

5. Worship positions us both to receive and to execute God's judgments against His enemies:

You are holy, enthroned on the praises of Israel. (Psalm 22:3)

The extravagant, Spirit-inspired worship of God literally makes the meeting place of the gathered faith community into a throne room, as if heaven descends on earth in the form of sovereign majesty and authority. There God "sets His throne":

Let the faithful exult in glory; let them sing for joy on their couches. Let the high praises of God be in their throats and two-edged swords in their hands, to wreak vengeance on the nations and chastisement on the peoples, to bind their kings with chains and their nobles with fetters of iron, to execute on them the judgment written! This is glory for all his faithful ones. Praise the LORD! (Psalm 149:5–9)

Notice that it is the high praises in (our) throats which are the two-edged sword in (our) hands. We do not worship *in order to* have this kind of authority; but, on the other hand, I have found that I am most receptive to revelation and spiritual gifts when I am in a place of worship. It is there that "the judgments written" in heaven are able to be read on earth. It is there, as we find ourselves in agreement with the Father and with one another, that we align ourselves for the amazing possibilities Jesus offers in Matthew 18:18–20:

I tell you with certainty, whatever you prohibit on earth will have been prohibited in heaven, and whatever you permit on earth will have been permitted in heaven. Furthermore, I tell you with certainty that if two of you agree on earth about anything you request, it will be done for you by my Father in heaven, because where two or three have come together in my name, I am there among them.

A leader, then, will be primarily a worshipper, representing the charge "love God and enjoy Him forever". He or she will thus model the role of the gathered congregation as a place for God to be enthroned in Kingly authority.

A leader is responsible not only to receive vision from God, and to envision a group with it. He or she is also responsible to maintain momentum on the journey toward it, by hearing and seeing, praying and obeying. In this way, the leader bears the group to a place where it may receive God's confirming authority. This is undoubtedly the Spirit's work, but leaders are the vehicle of that work, or at least hold the keys to the vehicle.

In Part One (chapters 1 to 3) we have discussed three characteristics of leadership that are common to all leaders, namely *influence*, *vision* and *hustle*. Although all leaders everywhere will have them in common, keep in mind that, while the *mechanics* are the same for spiritual leaders as much as secular leaders, the *dynamics* should always be different, in that the spiritual leader has to be dependent on God, led by the Spirit and imitative of Jesus.

PART TWO

KINGDOM LEADERSHIP

The section that follows (chapters 4, 5 and 6) will narrow the focus of what is essential, not to all leaders everywhere, but to those who would lead anyone or anything in faithfulness to the values of the Kingdom of God. By this I mean not just the Church and its work, but any group or organisation in which a Christian finds him or herself. Whether the workplace, the family, civic organisation or neighbourhood watch, NGO or Rotary club, or indeed a small group, ministry team or a congregation, once you have found yourself in leadership, you are accountable to a different set of standards. The chapters in this section will continue to populate the letters of my mnemonic, looking at those standards and how we may live them out in our leadership roles. They are:

1. Life quality, or the essential of *good character;*
2. Servanthood – becoming "great" in Kingdom terms by being the servant of all; and
3. Dividend – delivering actual beneficial change to every group we lead.

I often find myself a little surprised at how Christians, in their comments on social media and sometimes from pulpits, attempt to hold secular leaders accountable to standards like these. Whether presidents or parliamentarians, or even CEOs, civic leaders, etc., there will be criticism and cries of "Shame!" when these leaders lead from motives of self-aggrandisement, profit, status or power for its own sake.

The fact is – they can do no other, unless they are born from above! Until God places His nature and values within their hearts, opens their eyes to His Kingdom and turns them into followers of Christ, they will act according to their human instincts, with self firmly on the throne. Do not be surprised by this.

As for you who call Jesus Lord – read on, and follow!

CHAPTER 4

Life Quality: Grounded in Character

"In the last analysis, what we are communicates far more eloquently than anything we say or do." Stephen Covey

This is a statement that can be trusted: If anyone sets his heart on being a bishop, he desires something excellent. A bishop must have a good reputation. He must have only one wife, be sober, use good judgment, be respectable, be hospitable, and be able to teach. He must not drink excessively or be a violent person, but he must be gentle. He must not be quarrelsome or love money. He must manage his own family well. His children should respectfully obey him. [If a man does not know how to manage his own family, how can he take care of God's church?] He must not be a new Christian, or he might become arrogant like the devil and be condemned. People who are not Christians must speak well of him, or he might become the victim of disgraceful insults that the devil sets as traps for him. Deacons must also be of good character. They must not be two-faced or addicted to alcohol. They must not

use shameful ways to make money. They must have clear con-
sciences about possessing the mystery of the Christian faith.
First, a person must be evaluated. Then, if he has a good
reputation, he may become a deacon. Their wives [or, liter-
***ally, the women]** must also be of good character. They must*
not be gossips, but they must control their tempers and be
trustworthy in every way. A deacon must have only one wife.
Deacons must manage their children and their families well.
Those deacons who serve well gain an excellent reputation
and will have confidence as a result of their faith in Christ
Jesus. (1 Timothy 3:1–16 GW, my alternative translation
in brackets, emphasis mine)

It is interesting to note how little of Paul's admonitions to Timothy and Titus[143] with regard to the appointment of persons to the
offices of public church leadership, have to do with skills or ability. The only "skills" to which he refers are the ability to *manage*
their own households, and the ability to *teach*. The remainder of
both passages focuses on issues of character.

Character, as Bill Hybels defines it, is "who you are when no-
one's looking".[144] It is the inner, private you. Your leadership
gift, to have real meaning, significance or integrity in terms of
the Kingdom of God, needs to be the outward expression of an
inner character. All ministry is a matter of *being* as well as *doing*.
Being a leader is, first of all, the journey of becoming your true
self, and then allowing the essence of who God has made you, to
be expressed outwardly. This is what integrity means: being true
to yourself and to God's inner work in you. Another definition
of integrity is "living from the inside out". Understanding this
requires a working knowledge of the nature of identity.

---

[143]See Titus 1:6–9.
[144]Bill Hybels, *Who You Are When No One's Looking* (IVP, 1987), pp. 7–8.

Character and identity

I put these two words side by side to emphasise the fact that character, though expressed in what you *do*, is really the essence of who you *are*. Jesus' primary teaching on the subject of identity, or character, is found in the Sermon on the Mount (Matthew 5–7). Many commentators have written to expound and explain this sermon, which has been called the Manifesto of the Kingdom of God. As I read it in the context of a prophesied and later fulfilled *new covenant*, I believe Jesus is anticipating what grace was going to do in the hearts and minds of its recipients. Jeremiah's prophecy about this anticipates a covenant that is not only new in the sense of "current", but also in the sense of "a different *kind*", compared with the Sinaitic covenant:

> *"It won't be like the covenant I made with their ancestors on the day I took them by the hand to bring them out of the land of Egypt. They broke my covenant, although I was a husband to them," declares the LORD. "Rather, this is the covenant that I'll make with the house of Israel after those days," declares the LORD. "I'll put my Law within them and will write it on their hearts. I'll be their God and they will be my people."* (Jeremiah 31:32, emphasis mine)

Against the background of that prophecy, I read Jesus' words in this sermon as affirming and descriptive rather than as critical and prescriptive. His verbs should be read as more indicative than imperative in tone. He uses the term "you are", and then calls people to be, or to allow their inner reality to shine out. To paraphrase some of these: "You are the salt of the world – so be salty! You are the light of the world – so shine! You are the children of a holy God – so be a chip off the old block! ... You are a good tree – so sweeten the world's table!" (Matthew 5:13–16, 48).

One of the common errors in the church is a religious, externalist approach to virtue. This involves listing "dos and don'ts" of behaviour, requiring people to keep the rules before they are regarded as acceptable family members. It sees the expression of virtue more like a Christmas tree with its artificial, externally attached decorations, than like a fruit tree, where the fruit on the outside is a product and reflection of the sap flowing on the inside. The purpose of God is that we let His life shine out of us, that we "bear much fruit, and so prove to be [his] disciples" (John 15:8), that we relax into a sense of *being* in Christ. In fact, we could read the message of the New Testament, pertaining to Christian identity and behaviour, as a series of descriptive rather than imperative phrases. They describe, to use an expressive Americanism, what we "get to" do, rather than what we "have to" or "ought to" do!

Describing his function as a leader, Paul says: "But by God's grace I am what I am, and His grace shown to me wasn't wasted. Instead, I worked harder than all the others – not I, of course, but God's grace that was with me" (1 Corinthians 15:10). God's grace gave him identity, and with that identity, a leadership gift that he simply needed to allow to express itself. Yet, as he reflects on it, he is aware that even his "hard work" was enabled by that same initiating, empowering, enabling grace.

To change the metaphor, picture yourself as a toddler, dressed up in your mom or dad's clothes. The clothes look cute, but ridiculous on you, trailing behind you or tripping you up as you try to walk, but eliciting a broad grin from the parent who watches. God has done that: dressed you in His clothes; and then said: "You look great in my clothes! Now wear them, and grow into them!" There will be times when you feel your own clumsiness and unworthiness wearing His identity. But He is not ashamed of you. He has patience with you as you become more and more comfortable and adept at expressing His nature in how you live and behave. This is the journey of integrity, or character growth.

It is "living into the good" of who God has made you by grace, and expressing His grace in the form of gifts with which He has favoured you. You *are* what God's grace has made you. You *do* ministry as an expression of that grace in action. That is why, no matter how well or how badly you are doing your job as a leader, your identity, your value or worth to God is not affected, either for better or for worse. Be encouraged when you feel you are failing, in the knowledge that you can never ultimately fail in His eyes, and be duly humble when you see success, knowing that "apart from [him] you can do nothing".

As we have seen, part of the grace of God is expressed in spiritual gifts, like the gift of leadership. When leadership is an outward expression of what God's grace starts on the inside, it is effortless and carries the authority that comes with integrity. Without it, the result is one of two unconscious behaviour patterns: one destroys the leader him or herself, and the other destroys followers.

The first unconscious pattern is role/identity confusion, where the leader sees his role *as* his identity. He so strongly identifies with the function he fulfils, using language like "I *am* my ministry", that he becomes emotionally and spiritually absent from himself, his family and those he leads. He becomes obsessive-compulsive about his work, driving himself, not resting enough, experiencing a roller-coaster of emotion and self-esteem depending on the report card he gives himself for performance. Success or failure is judged by external criteria like compliments, converts, finances, church growth and various forms of recognition within his circle of significance. The end of this cycle can be anything from anger to disillusionment, burnout, substance abuse and marital/family destruction. The truth this person needs to remember is that, while character or identity is a basis for ministry, they are not the same thing. You are *not* your ministry!

The second pattern that arises, when there is a lack of integrity, and resultant authority "from the inside out", is where the "leader" resorts to external, worldly means of getting it. Things like titles, legalities, status symbols and strong-arm methods. The "leader" will dress in clothes and drive a car that express "power". He might have an impressively furnished office with deep-pile carpets, and a special, throne-like seat on the church platform. In his public preaching, he will seek to gain respect – when he feels it is needed – by increasing the volume of his voice, name-dropping, pretending a special status and "inside track" to God, or pulling rank. The follower, in such cases, may follow out of fear or favour, but is left feeling hollow or abused when the honeymoon ends. When the pressure to keep dancing to the leader's tune becomes unbearable, people will leave, bitter and burnt-out. They are the wreckage that litters the church landscape: the wounded, disillusioned ex-followers, who might still love Jesus, but hate or fear the church. Leadership without integrity will find you out, but unfortunately, often only after innocent followers have been seriously damaged.

At the risk of appearing to contradict myself, let me say I believe that, as leaders in God's Church, we do, in some way, represent Christ. Without going to the extreme of seeing ourselves as *vicarius Christi*,[145] we need to understand that when someone is sent "in the name of" another, he or she represents, speaks on behalf of, and is accountable to, the sender.[146] As Christian leaders, we are always to put our integrity of *being* before our skilfulness in *doing*. Joseph Allen, discussing ministry in the context of the "I

---

[145]"Vicar or representative/standing in place of Christ". A term used since the 6th century to describe the Bishop of Rome (the pope). Also referred to in Catholic catechism as a term for each bishop, as "vicar of Christ" to his diocese.

[146]So Paul, speaking for himself and other apostles, says: "Therefore, we are the Messiahs representatives, as though God were pleading through us. We plead on the Messiah's behalf: 'Be reconciled to God!'" (2 Corinthians 5:20)

am" sayings of Christ, says:

> *Each one describes who Christ says He is ... each tells us that*
> *he is doing more than comparing himself with these 'predi-*
> *cates'; he is what he is in these predicates; he is what takes*
> *place in these predicates ... his person and task are one. Thus,*
> *Christ and his ministry are one.*[147]

When this principle is extended to those who serve Christ as
ministers, it speaks both to the need to be examples to those we
lead,[148] and also to know that our example is in some way, in the
minds of those we lead, a model of Christ, for better or worse:

> *When the scriptural Referents to Prophet, King and Priest are*
> *made, they give to our understanding of ministry a personal*
> *rather than a functional character. Any one of these terms*
> *unites within itself the person and his task, the person and*
> *"his" office.*[149]

In the well-known text in which Matthew records the commis-
sioning (as opposed to the calling) of Simon Peter, Jesus refers
to this foundational substrate of leadership, when He says, in response to Peter's confession that He (Jesus) is "the Messiah, the
Son of the living God":

> *You are blessed, Simon son of John, because My Father in*
> *heaven has revealed this to you. You did not learn this from*
> *any human being. Now I say to you that you are Peter (which*
> *means "rock"), and upon this rock I will build My church ...*
> (Matthew 16:16–18)

From a man who would speak first and think later (Simon, from

---

[147]Allen, *op. cit.,* p. 26.
[148]Paul uses this as an exhortation to others to "follow me" (1 Corinthians
11:1; Philippians 3:17) as well as to his protégé Timothy (1 Timothy 4:12).
[149]*Ibid.,* p. 27.

Simeon, which means both "to hear" and to "make a noise"!), Jesus is anticipating Peter's transformation by grace into a rock (*petros*, "a piece of rock, a boulder").[150] Whether you think like a Catholic and believe *petra* refers to Peter himself, or like a Protestant and believe it refers to his confession of faith, what is clear is that Peter was going to be changed to a different person. Some blend of his faith and his character was going to be the basis for what Christ would do through him. We will return to Simon Peter when we discuss character change later in this chapter. Suffice it to say here that the essence of our gospel is the promise of radical change, a new birth,[151] a new creation.[152] Even with the worst background, pedigree, education or opportunities, you can become the person God intended you to be, in order to lead as He wants you to. As Samuel said by inspiration to the very dodgy King Saul (although it did not seem to do him permanent good):

> *The Spirit of the LORD will come upon you, and you'll prophesy with them and be changed into a different person.*
> (1 Samuel 10:6)

It has been well said that the only thing you will take to heaven is the person you have become by God's grace. I want to add that it is also the main thing we will give to the congregation, family or group we lead. To put it differently, if what we are contradicts what we say, people will "catch" or be infected with the former rather than the latter.

Returning to Paul in 1 Timothy 3:1–16 and Titus 1:6–9, a leader is first and foremost a model Christian man or woman.[153]

---

[150]A masculine derivation of the feminine *petra*, which means "a mass or stratum of rock" – used in the case of the second word translated "rock" in verse 18.

[151]John 3:3–5.

[152]2 Corinthians 5:14.

[153]The "women" referred to in 1 Timothy 3:11 are, in my opinion, women who were leaders, not merely the wives of male leaders. Thus: "… the exact

Anyone "desiring" a position of public leadership should show exemplary character as a first qualification. Reading these texts, note how little of the content of Paul's admonition to Timothy and Titus with regard to the appointment of public church leadership has to do with skills or ability. The only "skills" to which he refers are the ability to manage (again, the word is *proistemi*, "rule", or "lead") their own households, and the ability to teach. In other words, lead at home before you lead others. As Hugo Grotius wrote 500 years ago: "A man cannot govern a nation if he cannot govern a city; he cannot govern a city if he cannot govern a family; he cannot govern a family if he cannot govern himself; and he cannot govern himself unless his passions are subject to reason."[154] The passages in Timothy and Titus say nothing, or very little, about charisma, skill, charm or education, and focus rather on what cannot be faked or fudged, at least not long term. They focus on the issue of *character*. Walter Wright says:

> *I focused on the character of the leader that adds value to the organization and contributes significantly to the shaping of the organizational culture. Who you are matters. What you believe and how that shapes your character does in fact make*

---

replication of verse 8's sentence structure in verse 11 and the dependence of each verse on the initial *must* verb of the passage, verse 2, make a reference to women deacons equally possible. The question remains open; but it is well to keep in mind that in the absence of a technical term (deaconess), a reference to women in a code listing requirements for the office of deacon would have sufficed to direct attention to *those candidates who were in fact women* (compare Romans 16:1)", Philip H. Towner, *The Expository Commentary to the New Testament,* (IVP, 1994), italics mine. Here's how Eugene Peterson renders 1 Timothy 3:11: "No exceptions are to be made for women – same qualifications: serious, dependable, not sharp-tongued, not overfond of wine" (MSG).

[154]See also Proverbs 16:32b: "... anyone who has control of his spirit is better than someone who captures a city" (NLT).

a difference to the people you lead … [155]

Character, then, is the inner, private you, lived before God (an Audience of One) for the sake of others. Wright continues:

> *People of character become leaders whether or not they hold a position of leadership. They are people whose integrity and credibility earn trust. People listen and follow. In the context of Christian communities, we look for Christ-shaped character in our leaders, since leaders have a significant responsibility in shaping the character of our churches and organizations.* [156]

The character of Christ is seen in the gentle grace and humility of a person, rather than in their *charismata*. Character is an issue of who you *are*, not primarily what you *do*. Ministry, or leadership is firstly, the journey of becoming your true self by the grace of God. Walter Wright continues:

> *Leadership that produces fruit is rooted in the character of the leader. It is impossible to provide consistent leadership out of insecurity. Leadership emerges from secure people, from men and women who know who they are and live authentically in the security of that knowledge. The person who lives securely in the knowledge of the love of God will be a person whose influence is sought, whose leadership produces fruit.* [157]

The purpose of God is that we let His life shine out of us, that we bear much fruit, and so prove to be [his] disciples" (John 15:8). We are to relax into a sense of *being* in Christ, and then let His life "leak" out of us in what are called "the fruit[s] of the Spirit".

---

[155]Wright, *op. cit.,* loc 342.
[156]Wright, *op. cit.,* loc 1547.
[157]Wright, *op. cit.,* loc 342.

The chicken and the egg of character

Which came first, the chicken or the egg? Which came first, good character or leadership? I have said, based on the above texts, that good character is a trait required of a leader. But how much is enough? What is the pass mark? And what about the concept of being "wounded healers"? I have also seen people lead before they have proven character; and having their character refined while they led. My own experience is probably fairly common, and illustrates this. When planting my first church, I was a 23-year-old kid, really. Not much maturity, almost no experience, and I am not too sure if the basic character of godliness was visible at all! If I were God, I'm not sure I would have trusted that guy! And what about those who led the early church? Apart from the first apostles themselves, whose flaws are evident right up to the ascension of Christ and beyond, what about the next generation? Was Timothy a man of character before he became a leader, or did character emerge afterwards? There is a case for suggesting that some basic character issues needed to grow in young Tim; things like courage, for instance:

> ... *recalling your tears and longing to see you so that I can be filled with joy. I am reminded of your sincere faith, which lived first in your grandmother Lois and your mother Eunice, and I am convinced that this faith also lives in you. For this reason, I am reminding you to fan into flames the gift of God that is within you through the laying on of my hands. For God did not give us a spirit of timidity but one of power, love, and self-discipline. Therefore, never be ashamed of the testimony about our Lord or of me, his prisoner. Instead, by God's power, join me in suffering for the sake of the gospel.* (2 Timothy 1:4–8)

Is Paul suggesting that Timothy was timid, that he wept too easily, was reticent with his gift, was a bit embarrassed or perhaps fearful about persecution or imprisonment as a part of the price of ministry? Many commentators think so. However, there are also references to his "sincere faith", his desire to serve the church, his exemplary moral life – surely marks of underlying character.

The story of John Mark comes to mind.[158] Seemingly for a lack of courage, he abandons his first missions trip, which makes Paul so angry that he and Barnabas have a parting of the ways. Barnabas the encourager, however, pursues a young man in whose basic goodness he believes, and after mentoring him, Mark ends up being someone Paul calls "profitable to my ministry".[159] In John Mark, as in most of us, if essential goodness of character is present, what might destroy some will refine others, and good mentoring will draw it out.

Character, then, seems to be a foundational thing, which is proved and perfected in the crucible of experience, and especially suffering:

> *Not only that, but we also boast in our sufferings, knowing that suffering produces endurance, endurance produces character, and character produces hope ...* (Romans 5:3–4)

> *Son though he was, he learned obedience through his sufferings and, once made perfect, he became the source of eternal salvation for all who obey him ...* (Hebrews 5:8–9)

There is a clear link, in texts like these, between suffering and character. In the case of Jesus, He is even referred to as having been "made perfect" by obedience in suffering. But, in His case, we are confident that the raw material of good character was there to begin with. The pain He endured revealed it, matured it and

---

[158]Acts 12:25; 13:13; 15:37–39.

[159]2 Timothy 4:11. Paul uses of Mark the adjective *euchrestos* which means *easily used,* that is, *useful:* profitable, meet for use.

presented His life as a tried and tested platform for God to use.

It seems to me that character is the expression of a set of intangibles in a person's life. They include *being principle-driven, honourability, courtesy, otherliness,* a *"long-view" orientation, self-control,* and *the fear of God.* There may be others, but these will form the basis of our discussion here. They are principles which can be found in the Word of God, from the Torah, to the book of Proverbs, to the Sermon on the Mount. They are the foundations of the "Judeo-Christian ethic". Some people have had them instilled by parents and teachers, sometimes without consciously knowing the basis for them. Here is an example of a kind of "character check" from Psalm 15 (CEV, emphasis mine):

> *Who may stay in God's temple or live on the holy mountain of the LORD? Only those who* **obey God** *and* **do as they should.** *They* **speak the truth** *and* **don't spread gossip;** *they* **treat others fairly** *and* **don't say cruel things.** *They* **hate worthless** *people, but* **show respect** *for all who worship the LORD. And they* **keep their promises, no matter what the cost.** *They* **lend their money without charging interest,** *and they* **don't take bribes** *to hurt the innocent. Those who do these things will always stand firm.*

There seems to be a link between generations, in the sense that character is either inherited, imbibed with your mother's milk, or drummed into you by parents and early mentors. Timothy's "sincere faith" came to him through three generations. People like Nicodemus, Joseph of Arimathea, Cornelius, and Lydia, were called "righteous", "worshippers of God" or "God-fearers". They are commended for their care for the poor, their desire to help the righteous, or their interest in the gospel, before receiving grace by the gospel. I know that when my father "drummed" lessons about character into me as a boy (sometimes quite literally!), I was unaware that God was at work! Now I know differently. Grace comes to us before we know what it is, in many different guises and through many agencies, of which our parents can often be the most powerful.

The Proverbs show the link between good, firm parenting and character development:

> *A child's heart has a tendency to do wrong, but the rod of discipline removes it far away from him.* (Proverbs 22:15)

> *Don't withhold discipline from a child; if you punish him with a rod, he won't die. Punish him with a rod, and you will rescue his soul from Sheol.* (Proverbs 23:13–14)

> *The rod and rebuke bestow wisdom, but an undisciplined child brings shame to his mother.* (Proverbs 29:15)

Whatever you may believe about corporal punishment (symbolised here by the "rod" of discipline), and its continued relevance, the fact is that parents are instructed to use some means of placing moral boundaries – indeed, a moral *compass* – into a child's soul, through precept and example, as well as rebuke and reinforcement when he or she strays from them. Thus, there is a place to consider character, in some ways, as the product of a good upbringing, or as a friend of mine puts it, "breeding". A person with a good foundation in God's "precepts" will have an instinctive sense of the rightness of certain codes, ways of thinking, or behaviour patterns.

Paul says of his moral life before meeting Christ that he was "blameless". He was equally clear that his good breeding, upbringing and resultant character were not enough to perfect or justify him before God. Only Christ could do that. The nature of "the new birth" is that it fulfils God's pre-existing law inside us. It places in us the completed character of Christ. In an earlier part of the same letter, however, Paul exhorts the Philippians (2:12–13) to "continue to work out your salvation with fear and trembling.

For it is God who is producing in you both the desire and the ability to do what pleases him". What God inspires and motivates is only seen in our way of living, treating people, serving, etc. It reveals the character we actually have, or are allowing God's grace to form in us. I believe that the several passages that discuss Christian morality or character are guides for "taking our pulse", rather than a set of rules that we should work hard to make happen. They do not say: "Do these things and you will be 'saved', and become a righteous person." Instead they say: "If you have been born of God, you will want to do these things." You may have moments of failing, but your natural environment, the place you will want to make your home, will be the place of righteousness.[160]

I once heard a great illustration of this principle in a sermon by the great African evangelist and church leader, Nicholas Bhengu. He was illustrating the doctrine of perseverance, and spoke of a farmer who was crossing a muddy ditch by a narrow bridge, with a sheep under one arm and a pig under the other. He lost his balance and fell into the mud. After scrambling back to the high ground, he looked back to see the sheep bleating, kicking and struggling to get out of the ditch, and the pig rolling over, happily bathing in the mud! The point he made was that, while the sheep (Christian) may fall into the mud (sinful behaviour), it will hate the environment of sin and always seek to escape it. The pig, on the other hand, will enjoy sin as its natural environment. You can wash the pig, carry it and try to keep it away from the mud, but it will go back there eventually. External observance of moral rules without character change is what the Bible means by the word "hypocrisy".[161] It will eventually be exposed as play acting. Who we really are will be revealed – often through suffering.

---

[160]See, for example, 1 John 2:2–10.
[161]From the Greek words *hupo* ("under") and *kritos* ("to act"). It is derived from the theatrical stage, when actors would wear masks to depict different characters.

The English word "sincere" is derived from two Latin words *sine*, "without" and *cere*, "wax". It was originally applied to statues made of marble. When the sculptor made a mistake by taking too much marble off the sculpture, he would use marble dust mixed with wax to create a well-disguised "patch" for his work. A statue that was "sincere" (without wax) was, of course, more valuable. But how could the buyer be sure of its sincerity? By running a flame over it! (It gives a completely new meaning to the idea of a runny nose, doesn't it?) Just as a fake or wax-based nose will run off the face of the statue under the effect of heat, the fire of God's testing will reveal if our character is sincere!

Character change

Although the biblical texts giving qualifications for leadership indicate the non-negotiability of good character, I need to mention, once again, at the risk of self-contradiction, that the Bible also has many stories of real, fragile and flawed characters who were powerfully used by God. Many men and women seem to display the marks of poor character, of weakness in certain areas of their moral lives, and yet were both leaders and enjoyed the favour of God on their leadership. Some started well and finished badly (King Saul and other kings of Israel). Others were rogues from the start or middle, and were changed as they served (David). Yet others were weak, God used them, but they remained weak to the end (Miriam, Samson, King Saul). They are examples of how the grace of God proves the exception to every rule. This is especially true when you read the references to Old Testament leaders in the New Testament, where the "lens" of grace is held up over their stories. It's as though God only remembers their successes, and forgets their failures, in retrospect.

There is David, a serial adulterer, a murderer, a "man of blood", who is not allowed to build a temple for God because of this character flaw,[162] and yet is remembered in the New Testament as "a man after my heart, who will do all my will" (Acts 13:22). And Abraham, who we see in the Old Testament making some rather carnal arrangements to "help" God fulfil his promise (and what a mess that made!).[163] Yet, when his story is told in the New Testament, we read that:

> *He did not weaken in faith when he considered his own body, which was as good as dead (since he was about a hundred years old), or when he considered the barrenness of Sarah's womb. No unbelief made him waver concerning the promise of God, but he grew strong in his faith as he gave glory to God, fully convinced that God was able to do what he had promised.* (Romans 4:19–21)

The entire eleventh chapter of the letter to the Hebrews contains the "CVs" of Old Testament people whose elevation to sainthood is based on their faith rather than their good character. These are powerful reminders that God can make greatness with any material, and is testimony to the *grace* of the God we serve, whose heart is always to express His favour rather than judgment.

It is stories like these that give every one of us hope, that grace provides the "but God" element to every story, including mine; that apart from Him, I can do nothing; but by faith in Him anything, including personal redemption and change, is possible. I am trusting that the books in which my life's story are recorded in heaven have had the same lens of grace applied to that story, or heaven would be an embarrassing place! At the same time, I see in my own story the wonder of significant character change. As the old slogan has it: "I'm not what I want to be; I'm not what I ought to be; but thanks be to God – I'm not what I used to be, either!" I believe that the experience Jesus called being "born from above"

---

[162]1 Chronicles 22:8.
[163]Genesis 15–16.

is just that – a change of essence and nature by the power of the Holy Spirit, a regeneration that results in a brand-new species of being. I have witnessed it over 50 years in hundreds of people I have seen changed from hopeless addicts into servants of God's Church; from unfaithful husbands into pillars of integrity; from fearful introverts into the boldest of preachers. My confidence, however, is based not only on these examples, nor on my own wish to avoid potential embarrassment, but also on the biblical record of numerous weak people who, by co-operating with the grace and instruction they received, became examples of how character can be changed.

Character, as I said above, is shaped by our upbringing, which includes training in character, behaviour, relationships and skills for living. Most of our character development occurs in the first seven years of life, when children are exposed to models and taught precepts by the emotionally significant persons in their lives. If the child enjoys the company of those persons, he or she will internalise their values and beliefs and model their behaviours. Repeated beliefs become permissions we give or deny ourselves. Repeated behaviours become habits, and permissions, beliefs and habits together form our character. Correction or discipline and reinforcement or reward play major roles.[164]

As character has been shaped, so it can be reshaped by the same dynamics under the power of God's grace. Paul describes this process in texts like Philippians 2:12–13, where he encourages the Philippians to: "Work hard to show the results of your salvation, obeying God with deep reverence and fear. *For God is working in you, giving you the desire and the power* to do what pleases Him" (italics mine). He is saying, in effect, that our role in personal transformation is to repeatedly and consistently reflect outwardly

---

[164]The Proverbs make this point repeatedly, as in 12:1; 13:1, 24; 19:18; 22:15; 23:13, 14, 23; 29:15, 17, 19.

what God is activating and motivating inwardly, until we are "shining like bright lights in a world full of crooked and perverse people" (verse 15).

Transformation, then, involves a process with the following dynamics at play:

1. Repentance – changing our attitudes or mental habits to line up with God's;
2. Realisation that change is possible – see David's new self-awareness after repentance and appeal for "truth in the inward parts" (Psalm 51:6);
3. Radical encounter with God like that which changed Jacob into Israel (Genesis 32:24–28);
4. Replacement of old habits with new ones (Philippians 2:12–13; Colossians 3:5–15);
5. Reflecting Christ's character in mutually transparent, accountable community (2 Corinthians 3:18); and
6. Receiving and responding to the necessary disciplines of God (Hebrews 12:3–10, especially verse 10: "God does it for our good, so that we may share in his holiness.").[165]

Good character determines your basic orientation to life and people. Character, as Dallas Willard said, consists of "the permissions we give or deny ourselves".[166] It provides the "rules of engagement" by which you will think of and act toward people and things; whether you regard human beings as wonderful, valuable or woeful; it includes what you regard as good manners or courteous behaviour: whether you insult people, use bad language in polite company, respect people's dignity, privacy or reputations;

---

[165]1 Corinthians 15:33 states the negative power of bad company, so we may infer the opposite of "good company". In 2 Corinthians 3:18ff., Paul speaks of how we are changed by "reflecting" the character of Christ to one another in transparent, Spirit-empowered community.

[166]From notes taken at a retreat I attended with him in Cape Town, 2009.

whether you will use violent means to get your way, etc. These rules are, to some extent, culturally derived. Cultural norms have sometimes been confused with moral imperatives, which in turn causes great confusion when culture changes, and we can misjudge people if we do not allow for this fact. But the basics are still observable, and a person of character will ask questions of himself before acting. He will hold himself accountable to some value system. An internal "auditor", or what the New Testament calls "a good conscience"[167] is at work on the inside of a person of character. In contrast to this, the New Testament uses the term "lawless"[168] to describe a certain category of sinful people. Here's an example, using Eugene Peterson's rendering:

> *It's true that moral guidance and counsel need to be given, but the way you say it and to whom you say it are as important as what you say. It's obvious, isn't it, that the law code isn't primarily for people who live responsibly, but for the irresponsible, who defy all authority, riding roughshod over God, life, sex, truth, whatever!* (1 Timothy 1:9 MSG)

So, whether your internal "rules" or values are the same as someone else's is less important than the main point: Do you have any? And are you living them? People of character instinctively ask themselves the "May I?" questions, the biggest of which are answered by God's clear statements of "good and evil" in the Law, and the character of Christ, expressed in His life story. A Christian will want to follow Christ in character as well as charisma (e.g. Galatians 5:22–23). I believe that the Law has been fulfilled in Christ, and its curse (expounded in Deuteronomy 28:15–68) has been negated by the Cross. That does not mean, however, that the moral imperatives it upholds are redundant. If anything, the Sermon on the Mount makes it clear that, in the new covenant,

---

[167] 1 Timothy 1:5, 19.
[168] 1 Timothy 1:8–10.

their applications are internalised and intensified![169] But biblical statements do not answer every question. The "grey areas" increase as human society crosses more and more boundaries through science and interaction in the global village. In the absence of a clear "Yes" or "No" from God's Word, we need to return to the "May I?" question as a basis for good judgment. Paul asks the question, and answers it in three ways:

All things are lawful to me, but not all things profit. All things are lawful to me, but I will not be ruled by any. (1 Corinthians 6:12)

All things are lawful to me, but not all things profit. All things are lawful to me, but not all things build up. (1 Corinthians 10:23)

The answer he gives twice, "not all things profit", is an essentially personal character consideration. If there is no personal character growth to be derived from something, Paul says he will not consider that thing an option. Essentially, he is saying: "Before I can lead anyone else, I need to lead myself to a better place." The second answer has to do with personal power or autonomy. He will not allow himself to be "ruled", enslaved or manipulated by anything. The final answer places personal ethics in the context of the faith community. Not all things "build up" or serve the spiritual growth of others. Paul will not allow himself a behaviour that interferes with, or in fact does not promote, the positive growth of the life of Christ in the church.

In my opinion, the very fact that a person asks questions like these is a mark of good character. When someone is asking essentially self-centred questions, looking for the loopholes, the minimum pass mark, or the lowest criteria of goodness, it betrays some suspect aspects of character. Alexander the Great

---

[169]Matthew 5:17–28, etc.

once sought to recruit a new driver for his personal chariot. He had each candidate steer the chariot around a cliff edge, and each tried to go closer to the edge than the last, thinking their skill would impress the emperor. He chose the one who had stayed furthest away from the edge, saying: "I trust most the charioteer who would steer me furthest away from danger, not the one who would flirt with it." We should not be asking: "What's the least I can get away with?" but "How can I really grow into Christ?" and "How may I serve the growth of others?" It is not about what *feels* good; it is about what *is* good (and yes, there are still ways of telling!). Good and evil, right and wrong are not relative terms, no matter how much humanistic, post-modern society wishes they were. There are rules of engagement. But, a person of character sees them not merely as external laws, but as an internal compass. Let us unpack a few I listed earlier:

1. *Being principle-driven*: A person of character has lines drawn in the sand, his points of no retreat, no compromise, where he will say: "Here I stand, I can do no other, so help me God." As a modern saying puts it: "If you don't stand for something, you'll fall for anything!"

2. *Honourability* simply means keeping your word. Eugene Peterson translates Psalm 15:4: "They keep their promises, no matter what the cost." It was translated in old English by the phrase "swears to his own hurt". It means letting your "yes" mean "yes". It links the sense of worth your name carries to your word and behaviour. A person who constantly prevaricates, who "runs with the hares and hunts with the hounds", is going to let everyone down at some stage.

3. *Courtesy:* Do people feel safe in this person's company? Does he or she treat others in a way that values both their comfort and their participation? Courtesy believes that it is not only possible,

but also important for your own sake, to say and do things toward others "nicely". Courtesy provides for the psychological safety of others in your company. Max de Pree calls it "civility".[170] A person of character is both effective and gracious.

4. *Otherliness,* or being other-directed.[171] It means to live toward and for the wellbeing of others. It is an attitude of consideration, that seeks to provide for the benefit of the other. A person of character is not self-centred, but shows that love for his neighbour which Paul says sums up the Law of God.[172] That is, to do for and to others what you would love someone to do for you. Not as a response, but as a proactive habit. Not toward those who deserve it, or who will repay you, but toward the least and poorest among you. To be otherly is difficult in a cynical, abusive and self-driven world. However, a person of character will still believe it to be worthwhile, and live by its rule.

5. A *long-view orientation* refers to a person's ability to defer compensation, to wait for a future day of reckoning for reward or vindication. A person of genuine character will not always have to appear right, or to be applauded. There is a Day coming in which all that we have done will be revealed, evaluated, applauded or rewarded, and the person of character is willing to wait for that Day. She has the capacity to do what is right, without need of instant gratification. This, too, flies in the face of a society of "instant" everything!

6. *Self-control:* We will look at the idea of "self-management" at the end of this chapter. But self-control is at the core of character. It has to do with what I refer to elsewhere as "an internal locus of control". The person of character will not be controlled

---

[170]De Pree, *op. cit.,* p. 21.
[171]See https://www.collinsdictionary.com/dictionary/english/other-directed.
[172]Romans 13:8–10.

by circumstance, impulse, fears, pragmatism or other people, but will derive her motivation from within herself. He will seek to live by objective standards, and bring his spirit into obedience to the values chosen before the tests begin. Paul speaks about beating his body to make it his slave (1 Corinthians 9:27). David makes his soul obey what he decides, rather than simply following its whims (Psalm 42:5, 11). These are marks of the self-control that is essential to good character.

7. *The fear of God:* This phrase, often misunderstood and abused to misrepresent God as an angry ogre, rather has to do with reverential love, or willing, worshipful submission to God and His Word. It is an attitude that does not first seek to excuse or vindicate itself, but delights in God Himself and in doing His will. It is a longing to please Him, and a heart longing never to disappoint Him, no matter who else sees or knows about it. In other words, it is living before an Audience of One, this One, who has become, for a Christian, the centre, the circumference and everything in between, of their life (see Proverbs 1:7; 14:26; 19:23; 22:4).

Character before charisma

In the 1 Timothy 3 passage we have been considering, Paul emphasises the character issue even more strongly when he says "[having] a good reputation" (RSV), a phrase otherwise translated as "blameless". This is an interesting term, meaning "not liable to arrest", or "not having anything to lay hold of". That is, there should be no legitimate arrest warrants issued against him. This phrase has to do with the legal right (authority) that Satan, God's enemy and ours, has to "bind" us to our sin in such a way as to paralyse our ministries. He can only do this to the extent that we give him permission by entertaining wilful sin. It is not the occasional behavioural lapse that gives "the accuser of the brothers"[173] a hand-hold in our lives, but character flaws, or hidden habits of sin.

Of course, to some extent "blamelessness", like beauty, is in the eye of the beholder. Jesus was blamed by the religious leaders of His day, yet He was confident of His blamelessness before God (John 8:46). He knew that the devil had no "hold" on Him (John 14:30). That is, there were no *legitimate* (or legally valid) grounds for moral or spiritual warrants of seizure against Him. Paul, in the same way, refused the judgments of people against him, saying: "I don't even examine myself. For my conscience is clear, but that doesn't vindicate me. It is the Lord who examines me."[174] In another place, Paul says of himself, even before his conversion, that he was "blameless" (in relation to the requirements of the Law). What does this mean, and how does the concept of "blameless-ness" apply to leaders?

First, let us be clear that differences of opinion on morality *that is not specifically regulated by Scripture,* or even of ministry practice, cannot be the basis for blame. The concept is not subjectively derived. Nor should an occasional lapse or action disqualify a leader. If character is who you are when no one is looking, then a blameworthy character is one who *regularly* misbehaves in secret, who does not deal with his or her failings "in the light" (1 John 1:7). The thing about a secret life is that it does eventually "find you out"![175] When dealing with moral lapses in a leader and deciding about their possible restoration, John Wimber used the criterion of whether the person immediately confessed his sin, or lied about it and/or only "confessed" after he was found out. In the latter case, it was not just the "sin" that was at issue, but a

---

[173]Revelation 12:10.

[174]1 Corinthians 4:3b–4.

[175]See Numbers 32:23, which is preceded by the exact topic under discussion – the interplay between "blamelessness" and hidden sin, which Moses assures the people will eventually manifest itself, or be discovered.

character flaw, i.e. deceitfulness. In Psalm 51:6, David says that God's requirement is "truth in the inward being" (ESV). Eugene Peterson translates the verse as follows: "What you're after is truth from the inside out. Enter me, then; conceive a new, *true* life."[176]

For John Wimber, refusal to face one's own sin betrays a lack of truth about oneself, and failed the character test. As a result it was a matter of disqualification from leadership rather than merely a "stumble" requiring a process of restoration. Paul's approach to this matter is expressed in Galatians 6:1, where he speaks about a person who is overtaken (that is, surprised or run down) in a fault (a "side-slip" or "lapse", as opposed to a wilful act or habit of sin).[177] In such cases, he or she is to be restored gently. Compare the much more severe treatment of the elder who keeps sinning (having a habit of sin or a character flaw) in 1 Timothy 5:20, where Paul instructs Timothy to publicly rebuke a leader who displays that kind of flawed character.

Paul tells the Ephesians, in the context of correcting or refusing habitual sin, not to give the devil a "place" or "foothold" in their lives (Ephesians 4:27 NLT). The word used here is *topos* which, among other meanings, can apply to a scabbard or sheath, i.e. a place to store a sword or a dagger. The word picture suggests that unresolved sinful patterns – in this context, bitterness or unforgiveness – leave a place for the enemy to store a weapon in our lives, which he may use against us in the future. A blameless leader is not someone who has never had such a "scabbard" in his or her

---

[176] *The Message* translation of the Bible by Eugene Peterson, italics mine.

[177] John's use in his first epistle of different Greek words for "sin", confusingly translated by just the one English word in older translations, is helpful here. He says of all of us (1:7–9) that we "sin" (*hamartia* = acts of sin) and that if we say we do not, we are kidding ourselves; but then (3:6, etc.) says that if we "sin", we have never known God or been born of Him! Here he uses the word *hamartano*. (also used in present continuous tense form in I Timothy 5:20), which describes a lifestyle or habit of sinfulness. It implies unregenerate character rather than behavioural lapses.

soul, but someone who has worked through them, closed them off and discovered truth or integrity "from the inside out".

I will return to this concept of integrity later, but for now, keep in mind that the life of integrity is lived when our deepest values and beliefs are expressed in our behaviour; when our identity and our profession of faith are integrated; when there is harmony between yourself, your stated values and your relationship with God, private as well as public. God's desire for us is that what is seen on the outside is an authentic expression of what he has done on the inside. God's desire is that leaders wear no masks, that they are men and women of transparency and integrity. "WYSIWYG", i.e. "What You See Is What You Get", is a well-known mnemonic that describes the character of a person who may be trusted, in private as well as in public, to be honest and open, vulnerable and real, for the delivery, in lived-out form, of their promises.

John Wimber used the analogy of infectious disease when describing ministry and ministers. Some people in leadership are like a man who has chicken pox, but tells others he has measles. He might describe his measles, elaborate on its cause, its symptoms and sensations, etc. But, people who touch him will catch not what he *says* he has, but what he *really* has. They will catch chicken pox. This is another way of saying "the truth will out", or "your sin will find you out" (Numbers 32:23). As a leader, you are infectious in unconscious ways. You are the seed you plant. People you touch are going to catch what you *are* (have), not what you *say* you are, for better or for worse.

Of course, all this has particular significance in the context of the Church and Kingdom of God, because we are in the business of passing on a life quality, not just vision, advice and decisions. In secular society, presidents, monarchs, prime ministers, executives and other leaders have had a greater or lesser degree of accountability for their character. However, in many modern contexts, character does not seem to count for very much. Charisma, charm, or a healthy profit share can cover a multitude of sins. Adultery is forgivable if federal taxes are reduced by the same adulterous leader, or if she or he "wins the war" or "fought in the struggle".[178] Often a kind of "balance scale" principle is used to assess people. If they have done good things, these are packed on one side of the balance scale. Any bad things they then do are placed on the opposite side. So, a leader who served in the struggle for justice in South Africa, may be forgiven immorality, corruption, even murder, forever afterward. It is a humanistic and, in my view, irresponsible way of evaluating leaders, because usually, what is currently at issue may have nothing to do with the past. Nor does my clean track record vis-à-vis other crimes earn me a free pass to avoid having to pay a speeding fine!

This kind of thinking disregards the value of character, and would have us believe that "the end justifies the means". Of course, those who make such judgments are often doing so through a warped and non-biblical lens. We should not be surprised when unregenerate people think in unregenerate ways.

Unfortunately, some of these standards for evaluating have been adopted in the church. The fact that a church is growing, that the leader is "anointed", that sick people are healed, or that "souls are being saved" through them, is an excuse for character flaws and even habitual sin to be overlooked in a pastoral leader. In one case, a leader's "right to happiness" was cited as a reason to deal lightly with a clearly unresolved "scabbard" in his life. It all reminds me of a line from a song in the 80s which said: "How can it be wrong when it feels so right?" This was the mantra of the hippie counter-culture: "If it feels good – do it!" What a self-serving way to decide on the rightness of decisions or behaviour!

---

[178]This is a phrase used uniquely in South Africa, referring to the resistance movement against apartheid.

Unfortunately, however, it is not that rare. It seems as if God's people, who are supposed to be governed by principle, are easily lured into the same false system of measurement as is used in the secular environment.

Accountability in leaders

The fact is that we are required to measure, and to be measured by, one another as Christians. The church, through its members and its leadership, is responsible to call to account, to require integrity of leaders, and even to exercise righteous judgment of behaviour by one another (see 1 Corinthians 5:12–6:4). Leaders are called to higher standards, stronger scrutiny, and public accountability. The more public the role, the more public is our accountability for how we play it. In the Kingdom we are inheriting, we are accountable, not only for ultimate outcomes, but also for current behaviour in at least three "court rooms".

We are accountable, firstly, *to our fellow leaders*. Every leader needs people to whom we can entrust our souls. Two or three colleagues who we cannot deceive; who know us well enough to detect when we are lying; who know what our secret struggles and sins are; who pray with us and for us. We need to keep short accounts with these people. I have a long-standing friend with whom I talked, over many years, through the following questions every month:

1. What have you been reading?
2. How are you doing with your spiritual disciplines?
3. Have you been getting physical exercise?
4. What has God been saying to you?
5. How are things between you and your wife?
6. How are you doing on the issue of (*that* area of vulnerability)?
7. Have you seen any sexually explicit material since we last

talked?

8. In the past 10 minutes, have you lied to me?

The questions are designed to provoke talk about ourselves at a character level. We want to be accountable for our growth as persons, for our marriages, for our morality and sanctification. Of course, such vulnerability presupposes trust between two people. The person with whom you share this confidence can be a mentor/leader, or a friend/colleague. We all need a trusted and trustworthy colleague-confessor. I remember an old joke in which three pastors go fishing together. During the day, in a boat in the middle of a lake, one suggests that they each share their besetting sin with the others. The first one says: "I am a secret drinker. I get drunk by myself every night. Neither my wife, my church council nor my flock know about it." The second says: "I have a problem with stealing. I take $500 out of the offering every week before it is counted. I can't help myself. No one in my life knows about it either." The third says: "My sin is gossip, and I just can't wait to get back to town!"

Secondly, we are accountable *to our followers*. By taking a leadership role, we have agreed to uphold certain values and standards of conduct, faith and ministry, in terms of our lives as well as how we will treat those we lead. They have the right to call us to account for walking our talk. The idea that a minister stands "six feet above contradiction" is false and dangerous. A popular modern trend in some churches involves the (ab)use of a phrase from the Old Testament text found in 1 Samuel 24:6, 10 and 26:9, 11, which says, in summary, that it is a sin against God to raise your hand against His "anointed". It is applied in these churches to teach that the pastor ("the anointed") should not be criticised. To do so is a sin against God. It suggests a kind of papal infallibility for pastors or elders: "If you disagree, don't speak – just pray for them and leave them to God" is a phrase used in these abusive systems.[179] It is important, however, as in the study of any biblical text, to understand the Samuel text in its context. It is a story in which David is in a specific case refusing the right to exact vengeance. If you read the full story, you will see that he criticised Saul, to his face. He appealed to the king on the grounds of God's Word and standard, but he would not take revenge. He believed that the final action required in bringing a leader to book, is to be God's. It did not mean that David should surrender his sense of righteousness, or allow Saul to abuse him again. It simply meant that, in this case, David was prepared to defer judgment to God. Additionally, and perhaps even more significantly, those who hold this view might need to examine the New Testament and discover that "the Lord's anointed" is in fact the entire Church!

You have an anointing from the Holy One and know all things. (1 John 2:20)

The anointing you received from him abides in you, and you do not need anyone to teach you. (1 John 2:27)

Do verses like these suggest that Christians do not need leaders, that in addition to "the priesthood of every believer", we also have "the leadership of every believer"? No, I am not suggesting that all have the same role to play in giving leadership to the church, nor that the Church is a democracy. However, we need clear biblical perspective regarding the way leaders relate to those they lead. Leaders need to know that every "follower" has equal standing *before God*, the same access to His truth, the same internal ability to assess it, the same divine Teacher or Counsellor, as does the leader. Followers are to weigh the leader's words, to hold

---

[179]This dangerous teaching and practice is what I believe Jesus was describing in Revelation 2:6, 15, where he refers to both the practice and the doctrine of the "Nicolaitans". The word is derived from two words *nikos* and *laos* (to conquer the people), i.e. the doctrine and practice of the abuse of power to subdue ordinary people.

them accountable to the truth, as the Bereans did (Acts 17:11). The leader who puts himself above them, quoting the text from 1 Samuel, while abusing or manipulating them is, ironically, himself guilty of "raising his hand against the Lord's anointed"!

Leaders are responsible to respect those they lead, to listen to them often, and to have the integrity to keep the promises, spoken and unspoken, that were used to call them into followership. This also means that leaders should not only remain open to, but should in fact *invite*, examination of both their lives and teaching. Paul seems to indicate such transparency in his leaders in places like 1 Timothy 4:12, 15 and 16:

> *Do not let anyone look down on you because you are young, but be an example for other believers in your speech, behavior, love, faithfulness, and purity ... Think on these things. Devote your life to them so that everyone can see your progress. Pay close attention to your life and your teaching. Persevere in these things, for if you do this, you will save both yourself and those who listen to you.*

Thirdly, we are accountable now, and will give ultimate account, *to the Lord of the Church*. The apostles who wrote the New Testament, and notably Paul, were acutely aware that we live under God's scrutiny, and lived their lives daily in the light of the last Day. Listen to Paul's searingly honest way of saying this:

> *So whether we are at home or away from home, our goal is to be pleasing to him. For all of us must appear before the judgment seat of Christ, so that each of us may receive what he deserves for what he has done in his body, whether good or worthless. Therefore, since we know the fear of the Lord, we try to persuade people. We ourselves are perfectly known to God. I hope we are also really known to your consciences.* (2 Corinthians 5:9–11)

This text is not about the fear of hell, but about the desire to present a life back to God that is commendable and pleasing to Him. We will give an account to Him on that Day, not for our souls, but for how we have lived and served and how we have treated others. Let us therefore show as leaders that "*that* Day" is part of the motivation for *this* one. We are all like the stewards of whom Jesus spoke in Luke 12:35–48, who were to live daily in the watchful expectation of the day of accounting. The truth is that every one of us is only a heartbeat away from the Judgment seat. In that context, says Peter, our constant question should be: "How should we be conducting ourselves today?" (2 Peter 3:11–14).

Christian leaders, says Paul, are subject to a higher standard of scrutiny than others in the church. How much more scrupulous, then, should we be than leaders in the worldly context? We have been entrusted with huge privilege. Therefore, says Jesus, we have huge responsibility. Eugene Peterson translates Luke 12:48: "Great gifts mean great responsibilities; greater gifts, greater responsibilities!"

But, all the scrutiny will not be left to the last day. It happens along the way, in the form of tests and trials. Just as a new invention or a piece of equipment has to be tested, so is the character of any who would lead God's people. Tests come in the form of *pain, frustration,* or *suffering* of some kind. They come in the form of *opposition,* of *failed dreams* (see what happened to Joseph), and of *human inadequacy* in ourselves and others. Directly or indirectly, the devil will be a part of the process, because, before face-to-face confrontation with him occurs, he will be used to call into question the very things you have heard from God. Thus, Jesus had to face the tests of the opposition before He qualified to embark on His mission (Luke 4:1–14). It is interesting to note that he went, or "was led" into the wilderness "full of the Holy Spirit" (verse 1), and returned after the temptation "in the power [or full flow] of the Spirit" (verse 14). Could it be that, just as exercising increases blood and oxygen flow to the muscles and brain, so the "full flow" of spiritual power is an outcome of passing the tests we encounter? As it was for Job, so it is for us. Although the devil is the agent of the test, God is its Author. His intention is that you will pass it, grow by it and come out the better for it.[180]

> *In this you rejoice, though now for a little while you may have to suffer various trials, so that the genuineness of your faith, more precious than gold which though perishable is tested by fire, may result in praise and glory and honor when Jesus Christ is revealed.* (1 Peter 1:6–7)

> *But if when you do right and suffer for it you take it patiently, you have God's approval.* (1 Peter 2:19)

Testing also sometimes takes the form of *success*. Simon Peter is confronted with his own fallibility, and the primacy of Christ's claims on his life, when he brings in the biggest catch of his life (Luke 5:1–9). Will his success make him proud and self-reliant? Will it distract him from his calling? Sometimes the true measure of a person is how success affects their attitudes to self and others. Peter learns, as must we all, that the gifts by which we make a living, conduct a life, teach the Truth or preach a sermon, come from God. He knows us and our work better than the most qualified expert does. We all, like Simon, are "sinful people", and we need daily to come to our knees before the Giver of our gifts, for formation, shaping and cleansing the vessels that may carry such grace! The test of success is whether we will become self-satisfied, or remain hungry for more of the God who gave it, and go deeper with Him. Thus, the same Peter writes, years later:

> *For this very reason make every effort to supplement your faith with virtue, and virtue with knowledge, and knowledge*

---

[180]Job 1:6–12; 2:1–6.

> *with self-control, and self-control with steadfastness, and*
> *steadfastness with godliness, and godliness with brotherly af-*
> *fection, and brotherly affection with love. For if these things*
> *are yours and abound, they keep you from being ineffective*
> *or unfruitful in the knowledge of our Lord Jesus Christ.*
> (2 Peter 1:5–8)

The question is not *if,* but *when* and *how,* we will be tested. In the test, remain focused on, and accountable to, the God who has called you. He has been there, and knows how to strengthen you. Passing the test will earn you greater trust from Him, greater capacity to take the load of leadership He wants to place on you. There is no other way.

Under new management

Returning to the text with which we began in this chapter (1 Timothy 3:1–16), let us take a closer look at the character qualities of a leader, and specifically, his or her blamelessness. He or she is to be blameless, or above reproach, with regard to:

1. Family management (verses 2, 4)

A leader is to be a faithful person, monogamous in heart and deed if married, who stewards their family relationships in ways that are worthy of imitation. A person qualifies for ministry by the quality of their marriage and family life. A call to the ministry should not be an excuse for neglecting responsibilities to spouse and children. This passage of Scripture flies in the face of those who say their ministry comes before their spouse and children. That view is another symptom of the confusion between role and identity of which I spoke earlier. One friend of mine was asked, "How do you balance your family and your ministry?" He replied, "My family *is* my ministry!" He was so right. Before and after appointing someone to leadership, we could benefit by asking their spouses and children: "Would you follow their leadership, or go to the church they lead, if you didn't have to?"

2. Self-management (verses 2b, 3)

There should be no aspects of the leader's life that are out of control, or under the control of any substance, spiritual force, emotional or behavioural habit or material thing. Compulsive or addictive patterns are disqualifications for a leader. Proverbs 16:32 says: "He that rules his own spirit is stronger [better] than he who takes a city." While this originally referred to controlling one's temper, I believe the principle can be applied to other aspects of what makes up my spirit or "soul". Paul mentions six areas of self-management:

- *Mental:* They should be *circumspect*, ordered or vigilant; he should be focused and not easily distracted, and operate by what is called "an internal locus of control"; thinking about themselves constantly, in the sense of guarding, or managing, their thought life. Is this person stable in thought and theology? Do they change their mind often? Are they easily distracted? Are they true to their word?
- *Emotional:* The leader is to be a *self-controlled* person, keeping their passions under control; appropriate and moderated in emotional responses. This means that they are governed by *principle* rather than *preference*. Watch how a prospective leader reacts in a crisis. Are they easily panicked? Do they regularly "lose it" when things go wrong, or remain calm? Are they subject to regular mood swings, or are they reasonably stable? The area of *substance abuse* (verse 3a) is included in this. "Not a drunkard" is the way the phrase is best translated. In New Testament Mediterranean life, where alcohol was served with meals, this would have been easy to observe. The issue was clearly not one of abstinence, but of control or

moderation, the ability to enjoy food and wine without allowing these to rule them.

- *Behavioural:* The leader is to be a *decorous*, or decent person; a person of seemly conduct, who will not get into a brawl(!). In other words, someone who is not violent, whether with words or fists. To state it positively, Paul says leaders should be "gentle men" (verse 3b), thus making this a character quality, not merely one reflecting a behavioural score or track record. Is his or her general disposition gentle? In evaluating leaders, one of the traits I observe is how a person relates to children. A gentle spirit is one that invites, embraces and includes the kindred gentle spirit found in children. Are children at ease with them? Are they attracted to their company? Does the leader notice them, like them and celebrate them? Watch not only how a leader relates to the child, but also how the child relates to the leader. These little ones are usually excellent judges of character!

- *Social:* "A lover of guests", or a *hospitable* person; managing a home that is open to others; a person of warmth and openness, who generally enjoys people. Is the prospective leader a hermit or a host? Is their home usually filled with people, or a lonely, forbidding place? This does not mean that all leaders should have the same level of extroversion, which means *seeking* human company and contact, but they should at least show social grace and be open to *discover* human company. This word also describes the spirit of welcome that was expected to be given to importunate strangers and travellers in Middle Eastern cultures, which is also a major part of African social custom. When friends or strangers "pop in", or need a bed, a meal, or company, how should a leader respond? With a warm, welcoming and helpful spirit. Furthermore, says Paul, leaders are required to have proved themselves in the outside world. I think this includes the workplace and the wider community. What is their *reputation* like? Are they conscientious, reliable workers? Do they deliver on their promises? Do they steal time, or watch the clock inordinately? Too many ministers are refugees from the real world of work, and stand on the platforms of the Church without having proved themselves on the platforms of secular responsibility.

- *Financial:* The leader is a person who keeps his or her *material* desires under management. They will have a good credit rating, and not be living under a debt load. Ministers need to live balanced lives in the material sense, neither in poverty nor in ostentation, but at a respectable level, which is not driven by greed for gain, or "covetousness". In Hebrews 13:5, the same word is used, and punctuated with "be content with what you have". A leader is someone who lives simply in himself and generously toward others, not the other way around. They will know "how much is enough".

- *Spiritual:* The leader is not to be a "novice" or *recent convert*, not because a new believer's spirituality is inferior, but because it is untested. As such, he or she is vulnerable to pride (when they are doing well) or depression (when they are doing badly). They have not come to terms with their own fallibility yet, and are self-focused in the sense of performance-orientation. A true leader, on the other hand, is known not only by his achievements, but also by his limp! (See Genesis 32:24–31.) He or she knows that frailty is to be faced, and managed, and that the true mark of spirituality is that God has conquered him in the context of his weak self, and redeemed that very self as a vehicle of service. This translates into a "reverence before the mystery of the faith" (verse 9) in a good conscience.

3.   Ministry growth

There are several references in 1 Timothy 3:1–16 to a process of "proving" or "being proven". The leader is to be like a bridge that can take a load; a person whose ability to serve without resentment or ambition has been demonstrated; someone who does not merely "talk a good game", but who has borne the fruit of faithful service. What do the people among whom they have served, say about them? They need to have borne fruit at home before they are sent abroad; to keep their own backyard clean before they tackle the neighbourhood. Nehemiah, whose leadership model we will study in depth chapter 8, set each leader in the city to repair the wall "opposite his house" (see Nehemiah 3:10, 23, 28, 29). It seems logical that, if every person managed his own sphere of responsibility, a whole city, or a nation, could be restored. In the same way, a leader should have proved his or her mettle in faithful serving in the unseen arena of home and small group, before being entrusted with greater responsibility. This is a simple but often neglected principle. Would you send someone to plant a church if they had never gathered unchurched people and won them to Christ? Would you hire someone as a pastor who showed a disregard for, and avoidance of, people?

The Wheel of Life

With regard to life management, a measuring instrument for self-evaluation and focus, on which I have written elsewhere and which others have found helpful, is the "Wheel of Life".[181] I use it here in an adapted form (Diagram 4 below).

---

[181] Costa Mitchell, *Learn to Love Yourself* (Vineyard International Publishing, 1991).

Diagram 4: The Wheel of Life

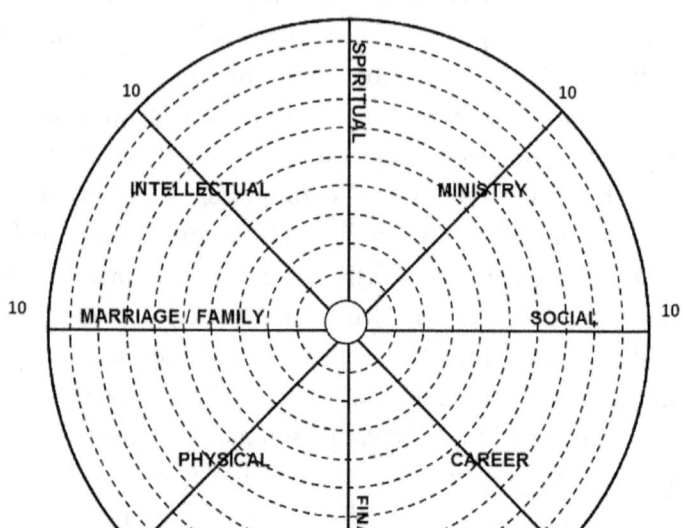

The diagram shows a wheel with eight spokes, each representing an area of life, labelled and graded from 0 (at the centre) to 10 (at the circumference). If you were to answer the question: "How am I doing at managing this area of my life?" or "Do I have, and am I living intentionally to accomplish, my God-given goals in this area of my life?" Where would you put your mark on that spoke? Make a mark on each line. After you have marked all eight spokes, "join the dots", drawing a line that goes from mark to mark, until you have the equivalent of a circle. What does your "wheel" look like? Is it round and balanced, or wobbly and disproportionate? Are you managing each area of life appropriately? And if not, what should you be doing about the areas in which you are not managing? How can you better "take charge" here? Good character is not the same as perfection; rather, it speaks of maturity, or responsibility. The wheel might indicate areas for attention. The questions are: "Whose job is it to change this? Are you doing better at self-management this year than last? Who is in charge of *you*?"

> But the Holy Spirit produces this kind of fruit in our lives: love, joy, peace, patience, kindness, goodness, faithfulness, gentleness, and self-control. There is no law against these things! Those who belong to Christ Jesus have nailed the passions and desires of their sinful nature to His cross and crucified them there. Since we are living by the Spirit, let us follow the Spirit's leading in every part of our lives. (Galatians 5:22–25 NLT)

> In view of all this, make every effort to respond to God's promises. Supplement your faith with a generous provision of moral excellence, and moral excellence with knowledge, and knowledge with self-control, and self-control with patient endurance, and patient endurance with godliness, and godliness with brotherly affection, and brotherly affection with love for everyone. The more you grow like this, the more productive and useful you will be in your knowledge of our Lord Jesus Christ. (2 Peter 1:5–8 NLT)

Success in any field, including church leadership, is not a matter of the *size*, but of the *manner* of its achievement. You can win or inherit a fortune, and not be a successful person. You can be earning and managing a tiny income well, and show yourself to be a giant in God's eyes. Thus, it does not matter if the goals you are achieving are "small". The question is: Are they God-given, in balance, and are you the one managing your progress toward them? A leader is someone who is in charge of him or herself, under

God, who lives in secret with a clear conscience, who lives a joyful life before an Audience of One, whose character is *blameless*.

Good character might occur before you met Christ or develop afterwards; your growth process may be smooth or fraught with difficulties; you might have grown up with poor models and been deprived. Whichever of these apply to you, before you step to the front in order to lead a group, basic, good character development needs to have been accomplished in your life. Otherwise, you risk infecting those you lead with the unhealed viruses of your own "stuff", rather than blessing them with the fragrance of Christ.[182]

---

[182] 2 Corinthians 2:15–16.

CHAPTER 5

Servanthood: The Heart of Leadership

"Everybody can be great, because everybody can serve. You don't have to have a college degree to serve. You don't have to make your subject and your verb agree to serve ... You only need a heart full of grace, a soul generated by love."
Martin Luther King Jr

Then the mother of Zebedee's sons came to Jesus with her sons. She bowed down in front of him to ask him for a favour. He asked her, "What do you want?" She said to him, "Promise that these two sons of mine will sit, one at your right and one at your left, in your kingdom." Jesus replied, "You don't realize what you're asking. Can you drink from the cup that I'm going to drink from?" They told him, "We can." He said to them, "You will indeed drink from my cup. But it's not up to me to grant you a seat at my right hand or at my left. These positions have already been prepared for others by my Father." When the ten heard this, they became furious with the two brothers. But Jesus called the disciples and said, "You know that the rulers of the gentiles lord it over them and their superiors act like tyrants over them. That's not the way it should be among you. Instead, whoever wants to be great among you must be your servant, and whoever wants to be first among you must be your slave. That's the way it is with the Son of Man. He did not come to be served, but to serve and to give his life as a ransom for many people." (Matthew 20:20–28)

The heart and soul of leadership

I have referenced the above text several times, because I believe it forms the core and the subtext of any authentic expression of the spiritual gift of leadership, and demands of spiritual leaders an attitude and conduct that distinguishes godly leadership from other forms. It is the text which emphatically expresses the non-negotiable quality of a Christian leader of whatever "type" he or she may be, namely the quality of servanthood. With regard to leading God's people, spiritual leaders should not entertain any ideas of domination and rigorous rule, control or subjugation, let alone abuse of any kind (Matthew 20:25–28). Commenting on the above text, Joe S. Ellis writes: "Jesus sets forth a relationship between leader and people in which servant-leadership is to prevail. The leader in this case is not *over* but *among* people. The role is not one of authority but of service ... the group responds best to a leader who is perceived as 'one of us'."[183] The idea of pretentiousness or entitlement, regarding oneself as superior or seeking to be first, is even more antithetical to godly, spiritual leadership (Matthew 23:1–11). Jones and Armstrong write: "But we long for leaders who are focused, not on themselves, but on helping institutions to embody a faithful witness to God."[184] Walter Wright

[183]Joe S. Ellis, *The Church on Purpose* (Standard, 1982), p. 130–131.
[184]L. Gregory Jones and Kevin R. Armstrong, *Resurrecting Excellence: Shaping*

concurs: "Servant leadership points people away from the leader to the mission of the community and empowers their individual contributions toward that mission."[185]

Jesus speaks in the strongest terms about His requirements for a Kingdom leader. He describes the essence of a secular leader as one who exercises unquestioned authority or power; who rules over or "against" his people; who seeks his own benefit; that is, "greatness" or "privilege", by ruling. Having thus described this kind of leader, Jesus here uses the "absolute negative" in an emphatic way – "*Not so* among you!" He is saying: "Don't even think about it! *No! Oxi! Nada! Hayi khona! Nooit! Never! We don't go there!*" It is important to say here that Jesus is not necessarily addressing *style*, but *essence*. He is not saying: "Don't step forward to lead" or "Don't take initiative"; He is saying the way you do that is "from the bottom up". It is important to remember that certain elements of style will also have to be surrendered before Jesus' "*Not so!*" word, because style is not always value-free. It may express values about the people we lead, the purpose for which we lead them, the church itself and the Kingdom of God.[186] Jesus is suggesting in this all-important text that Kingdom leadership is not about adjustment, but replacement. The dictatorial, pretentious, self-aggrandising models of this world cannot be accommodated in the church. They must be disavowed and repented of, so that they may be replaced.

Jesus uses two Greek words to describe the servant leader. The

---

Faithful Christian Ministry in the *Pulpit & Pew* series (Eerdmans, 2006), Kindle edition, loc 1710.

[185]Wright, *op. cit.,* loc 357.

[186]I think, for instance, that a style of sermon delivery, which is at maximum volume, with angry tone and near-hysteria in body language, expresses a view that hearers are naughty children, and that the voice of authority needs to be loud and in their face. These are values in action, not mere stylistic considerations.

first is *diakones*. There are two possible derivations for the word, both of which are very descriptive. The common one is *diako*, which means "to run", by implication "on errands". Hence, the leader is one who takes his orders from his master, and runs to deliver them. He or she is not above being a "gofer" for the Lord. This term is not referring to the American ground squirrel ("gopher"). It is American slang for someone who is paid just to stand around near to the boss, where he or she could be told: "Go for a cup of coffee"; "Go for a doughnut"; "Go for this"; "Go for ..." (Go...fer = gofer!). Therefore a *gofer* is someone who is ready for anything, eager to serve, to do what is necessary for the wellbeing of others and the accomplishment of their goals, without acclaim or reward. A servant is someone who will run quickly, without waiting, to do his master's bidding.[187]

The other possible inference is that it comes from *dia* (through) and *konis* (dust). This implies that the servant is a person who "raises dust" in his haste to do his master's will. He is also not above getting "down and dirty" in his work. He is not concerned about appearances, or status. Jesus contrasts this with the desire to be great (*megas*). "Do you want to be big? Then be small (get in the dust)!"

Andrew Clarke quotes Eduard Schweizer, who writes in *Church Order in the New Testament*: "... as a general term for what we call 'office', namely the service of individuals, there is, with few exceptions, only one word: *diakonia*. The most common usage of the word had to do with 'waiting at table'."[188] Schweizer goes on to say: "Thus the New Testament throughout and uniformly chooses a word that is entirely unbiblical and non-religious and

---

[187]Read an interesting story about a young gofer in 2 Samuel 18:19–32. It is especially readable in *The Message*!
[188]Dr Eduard Schweizer, *Church Order in the New Testament* (Wipf & Stock, 2006), pp. 173–174.

never includes association with a particular dignity of position,"[189] but "came to describe service marked by a peculiarly Christian value of love and self-giving".[190] It is a word that, in later usage, conveyed the dignity of being a trusted "go-between", namely "spokesman, emissary and mediator" or "mandated authority".[191] But, that is not where it started its etymological journey. It nicely illustrates the point that the way up is downward. If you want to be a trusted emissary, get down and serve!

The second word Jesus uses is *doulos*. It is an even stronger word, describing a slave, or bondservant. That is a person who has *no option but* to do her master's bidding, because she is not her own. She belongs to her master, as property. She is subject to her master's every whim, and he even has the power of life or death over her. The word is contrasted with *protos* ("first"), and so Jesus says: "You want to be first? Then go to the bottom of the food chain!" He is not saying: "Don't desire greatness, or leadership," but if you do desire it, you start at the bottom. The way to leadership is voluntary subservience for the sake of the One who has called you. It is also the way to fulfilment. Albert Schweitzer said it well: "I don't know what your destiny will be – but one thing I know: the only ones among you who will really be happy are those who have sought and found how to serve."[192] I conclude, with Wright, that: "Leadership is the use of power to serve the people. We have been

---

[189]Clarke, *op. cit.*, p. 233.

[190]Clarke, *op. cit.*, p. 235. He goes on to quote Wilhelm Brandt, *Dienst und Dienen Im Neuen Testament:* "... diakonia [denotes] ... a caring kind of service exemplified in its most sublime form in the actions of Jesus at the supper, where he described himself 'as one who serves', and in the self-giving which led to his death." So, quoting John Collins: "... apostle, presbyter, and believer, we are to take it, found common cause with him who came to serve" (p. 236).

[191]Clarke, *op. cit.*, p. 239.

[192]Albert Schweitzer, "Happiness" on www.cybernation.com, quotation centre.

given an awesome responsibility: to feed the sheep of God, to care for the people of God. We are accountable to God for the use of the power he has given us. The prophets are watching. How will we use our power?"[193] This last is a poignant and prophetic challenge, worth a few hours of reflection and soul-response before we lift a finger to lead anything that belongs to God!

Servanthood – the essence of leadership

Servanthood is not to be seen as an "optional" module to be added to the leader's qualifications, nor a tactical manoeuvre. The risk, in talking about *servant leadership*, is that it can be interpreted as a consumerist tactic, so that a person serves in order to gain a "market share" among those they serve. As Miroslav Volf puts it:

> *One of the things a gift's skeleton has to have to come alive is the willingness of givers to impart more to recipients than they expect to receive. If, to the contrary, we want to receive more than we impart, we are not giving. The recipient or some other observer, who could, like God, peek into our hearts and discern our intentions, would quickly dismiss our giving. We are slyly and gently extracting, not giving.*[194]

In the words of my former colleague, Gary Best,[195] we are not to be "leaders who serve" (i.e. leaders first, serving to increase credibility), but rather "servants who lead" (i.e. servants without an agenda, serving with an Audience of One, imitators of Jesus, who gave Himself away and left the "results" to Him who judges justly).[196] The motivation, no matter what style is employed, is

---

[193]Wright, *op. cit.,* locs 2485-2505.
[194]Volf, *Free of Charge, op. cit.,* loc 1564.
[195]*The Vineyard as an International Movement,* document written for the Vineyard International Consortium, 1999, parentheses mine.
[196]1 Peter 2:23.

to model exemplary life, selflessness of motive and goal-directed momentum toward the good of the whole Body, and never pretentiousness, pride, abuse or self-focus.

Therefore, more than seeking this kind of personal "downward mobility", servant leadership also seeks to create "a community of followers within the organisation" and thus cultivate, as a corporate culture, an environment "marked by kindness, love, and altruism".[197]

> *A consumerist culture urges us to measure the costs of our involvement: What will I get out of this? Is this a good investment of my time? A cross-shaped community, however, trades in a different kind of economy. We do not make room for the stranger to have our needs met. We engage in these relationships because our needs already have been met in the friendship of God made known to us in the life, death, and resurrection of Jesus Christ.*[198]

Walter Wright makes the point that one of the ways servanthood works in a community is by the recognition that we only truly discern accurately when we do so with others. True community, he says:

---

[197]Winston and Ryan, *op. cit.*, continue: "Patterson's model of servant leadership begins with 'agapao' love as presented in Winston's (2002) work to love in a social or moral sense, embracing the judgment and the deliberate assent of the will as a matter of principle, duty, and propriety (p. 5). The unique term *hesed* is difficult to translate in English but is often rendered as steadfast love and kindness by translators. The Mediterranean concept of *hesed* and its Greek equivalent *agapao* carry the meaning of an active involvement in the world marked by kindness, love, and altruism (Knight, 1999). It is important to note here that one concept alone, in this case Ubuntu, is not reason enough to accept servant leadership as global but rather to see that there are various concepts around the world that speak to a humane consideration of others."

[198]Jones and Armstrong, *op. cit.,* loc 936.

> *... requires visionary leaders who can see what God wants to accomplish with their organization and what their church or organization can look like with Christ present in its midst. It requires relational leaders who make themselves vulnerable by making an accountable commitment to a stated set of values. It requires servant leaders who have learned to depend upon God and who expect to see God at work in their organizations in the years ahead. Vision, values, and vulnerability – maybe that is what relational servant leadership is all about ... This is the point where the relational character of servant leadership is most visible. In the interdependent relationship of leader and follower we hear the heartbeat of servant leadership most clearly.*[199]

This is a risky business. "The world's way of leadership may seem safer ... But ... we must expose ourselves to misunderstanding and doubt until the integrity of our lives and the supernatural work of God in the hearts of His people brings response to Him."[200] Servanthood, then, is to be our essence, our orientation, our "poise"; our cost-free investment in living a life of love, imitating the attitude and lifestyle of Jesus. In the context of the Church and the Kingdom of God, servanthood is not a choice of one between many styles of leadership. It is the only way we should be.

A parallel biblical setting for understanding the relationship of servanthood to leadership is found in 1 Corinthians 12:31, where Paul concludes his discussion about spiritual gifts by saying: "But earnestly desire the higher gifts. And I will show you a still more excellent way." He is not contrasting spiritual gifts with love on an "either-or" basis; instead, he is introducing love, which he is just about to highlight as the ruling principle of all spiritual ministry; as the dynamic that should guide the use of spiritual gifts. In the

---

[199]Wright, *op. cit.,* locs 1928, 2106.
[200]Richards and Hoeldtke, *op. cit.,* p. 121.

same way, servanthood is the guiding principle that makes leadership godly, and whose absence disqualifies it from godliness. It is not a better alternative to leadership – it is its qualifier.

Kenosis – example, mandate and empowering to serve

If then there is any encouragement in Christ, any consolation from love, any sharing in the Spirit, any compassion and sympathy, make my joy complete: be of the same mind, having the same love, being in full accord and of one mind. Do nothing from selfish ambition or conceit, but in humility regard others as better than yourselves. Let each of you look not to your own interests, but to the interests of others. Let the same mind be in you that was in Christ Jesus, who, though he was in the form of God, did not regard equality with God as something to be exploited, but emptied himself, taking the form of a slave, being born in human likeness. And being found in human form, he humbled himself and became obedient to the point of death – even death on a cross. Therefore God also highly exalted him and gave him the name that is above every name, so that at the name of Jesus every knee should bend, in heaven and on earth and under the earth, and every tongue should confess that Jesus Christ is Lord, to the glory of God the Father. Therefore, my beloved, just as you have always obeyed me, not only in my presence, but much more now in my absence, work out your own salvation with fear and trembling; for it is God who is at work in you, enabling you both to will and to work for his good pleasure.
(Philippians 2:1–13)

The opening verses of Philippians 2 set out, according to Paul, the "ethical implications of union with Christ".[201] The context of the

---

[201] J. Todd Billings, *Union with Christ: Reframing Theology and Ministry for*

chapter is Paul's general admonition to the Philippian church "to adopt that common *phronesis,* or practical reasoning, that he has argued for in 2:1–4. We might do well to follow Wayne Meeks' paraphrase: "Base your practical reasoning on what you see in Christ Jesus.' ... practical reasoning is a pattern of thinking, feeling, and acting."[202] Paul makes the connection between chapter 1, where he describes his suffering and "life and death struggle" to pursue God's mission, and his admonition introducing chapter 2, using the words "if ... then". He calls them to display real unity of mind and heart, and to manifest it in selfless serving, caring and love in action. To enable such followership in action, says Paul, will require a set of attitudes: "... a high demand is made here upon the inward disposition of believers."[203] Christ is presented here as both an example and an empowering, alternative life-force. The text begins with Paul relating why our obedience is possible. It is based on the reality of courage, love, compassion, sympathy and interactive power (the Spirit) shared in a vital union with the Christ who is there, alive, near at hand. J. Todd Billings, commenting on this passage as a template for ministry, makes the excellent point that it is not, as many suggest, a call for "incarnational ministry", but rather a call to an *attitude* which was exemplified in Christ. Where authors like Alan Hirsch,[204] emphasise the former, Billings concludes that "... there is no necessary connection between these and the notion of imitating God's act of becoming incarnate ... they are [attitudinal] imperatives of

---

the Church (Baker, 2011), p. 137.

[202]Stephen E. Fowl, *Philippians* in the *Two Horizons New Testament Commentary* series (Eerdmans, 2005), p. 90.

[203]Jac J. Müller, *The Epistles of Paul to the Philippians and to Philemon* in *The New International Commentary on the New Testament,* ed. F. F. Bruce (Eerdmans, 1980), p. 77.

[204]Alan Hirsch, *The Forgotten Ways: Reactivating the Missional Church* (Brazos, 2006), p. 133.

the New Testament for Christian witness that … can be properly rooted in the Christian's union with Christ the servant".[205]

I believe that the primary call of Paul, here as well as in 2 Corinthians, is for the imitation of the attitudes that are exemplified by Jesus Christ. In Jesus, they were intrinsic because of the unique blend of divine and human natures (although He still had to choose their expression in both the incarnation and the cross). In us, they are only possible to imitate by accessing the Christ-nature, which is in us by virtue of regeneration (Galatians 2:19–20). Billings builds his entire thesis around this text, stating that the idea of union with Christ is reflected in John 20:21: "… the Johannine theme of sending actually relates to union with Christ and to the way that those who belong to Christ bear witness to Him."[206] Taken together, then, Paul and John are both saying, in my view, that the indwelling Christ is capable, and willing, to replace our nature with His, to literally live His life and love His loves through us. I believe that neither transformation of personal character nor authentic Christian ministry are possible without this dynamic, indwelling, ruling presence. Miroslav Volf quotes Archbishop Rowan Williams, saying: "The inconceivable self-emptying of God in the events of Good Friday and Holy Saturday is no arbitrary expression of the nature of God: this is what the life of the Trinity is, translated into the world … the life of God is a life of self-giving and other-receiving love."[207]

What Paul emphasises in terms of Christ's example is self-emptying (verse 7), which "is a single choice taken on by the Son in the incarnation".[208] It thereby "displays something crucial about the character of God. In refusing to use his participation in the

---

[205]Billings, *op. cit.,* p. 129, parenthesis mine.

[206]Billings, *op. cit.*

[207]Volf, *Exclusion and Embrace* (Abingdon, 1996), Kindle edition, locs 2555-1563.

[208]Fowl, *op. cit.,* p. 95.

glory of the God of Israel for his own advantage and adopting, instead, the disposition of self-emptying ... Christ is actually displaying the form of God, making the glory of God manifest to humans."[209]

What was involved in Christ's *kenosis* or self-emptying? He emptied Himself not of His deity, but of "his independent exercise of [divine] authority",[210] "... so that He could exchange the appearance of God for the appearance of man. This exchange denotes more than just 'the form of man'; it depicts servitude and subjection, unattractiveness and lack of distinction ..."[211] In essence, what Christ exemplified was a series of decisions, based on an attitude of surrender to the will of the Trinity, to descend through six "layers" of existence. Jesus Christ descended, as Paul illustrates, from a place of:

> Supremacy as **God**,
>> to **human form**,
>>> to **poverty** and **rejection**,
>>>> to a life lived as though it was not His to control
>>>> (a **Servant**),
>>>>> to judgment as a **criminal** and
>>>>>> to an agonising, lonely **death**.

"He came," continues Müller, "as an ordinary man, in all things made like unto us (sin excepted), in the form of a servant in which the divine glory did not reveal itself."[212] The element of Christ "emptying himself", laying aside His rights as God (verse 7: "gave up His divine privileges" – NLT, MSG) – is important to our

---

[209] *Ibid.,* p. 96.

[210] William Hendriksen, *A Commentary on the Epistle to the Philippians* (Banner of Truth, 1963), p. 108.

[211] Müller, *op. cit.,* p. 82.

[212] *Ibid.,* p. 83.

discussion of servanthood, because it demonstrates that serving is a choice. Christ *chose* to become human; Christ *chose* to be humbled; Christ *chose* the cross; Christ *chose* the way of servanthood. "From the manger to the cross He trod a path of humiliation",[213] and it was a moment-by-moment choice, because at any time in His earthly sojourn, He could have reasserted the divinity that lay close at hand, and served His own purposes and needs. Instead, He chose to serve ours.

Having been empowered by the indwelling Christ, the example, too, is Christ. But, if this call to imitate Christ were simply "a new law", it would discourage rather than encourage any who read it. I believe, however, that this passage is set in the context of grace, offering an invitation to embrace the "mind ... *that you have* in Christ Jesus", instead of an admonition for us to imitate the "mind ... *that was* in Christ Jesus".[214] "Paul's readers are already 'in Christ', the living Christ to whom the Spirit is conforming them. Christ is alive; thus we are incorporated into Him."[215] Billings goes on to quote Gordon Fee on this vital point of interpretation. Fee wrote: "The Philippians – and we ourselves – are not called upon to simply 'imitate God' by what we do, but to have this very mind, the mind of Christ, developed in us."[216] John Calvin, quoted by Billings, held the same view: "In union with Christ, Christ lives in the Christian – the same Jesus Christ who shows us what it means to be humble, obedient servants before God."[217] Therefore, like Paul, we will always have the tension between two answers to the question: "Who is adequate for such

---

[213] *Ibid.*, p. 86.

[214] Billings, *op. cit.*, p. 138.

[215] *Ibid.*, p. 141.

[216] *Ibid.*, p. 142, quoting Gordon D. Fee, "Paul's Letter to the Philippians", in the *New International Commentary on the New Testament* (Eerdmans, 1995), p. 228.

[217] Billings, *op. cit.*, p. 151.

things?"[218] The two answers are: "*Not that we are sufficient* in our-selves to claim anything as coming from us, but *our sufficiency is from God, who has made us sufficient* to be ministers of a new covenant."[219] We are not so much called to imitate Christ as to ap-propriate Him! In Christ, and through Christ in us, we can serve in self-emptying grace.

Paul expounds on this grace in his great essay on ministry in 2 Corinthians 3 to 5. Overall, two things constitute Paul's com-pelling motivation as a leader: a desire, as a response to grace, to please Christ above all; and the love of Christ as expressed in His serving of others. The reason we serve, preach, have boldness and hope, do not lose heart, are up to the task, is because life itself, and ministry in particular, extract something like a fragrance, or life-force, out of us. When we are humiliated or persecuted, mis-understood or even killed, and do so with our eyes on the One who died for us, called us and whose glory lives in us, the result is life for the people to whom He sends us, literally, "life from our death".

What Paul is saying, and this is an essential point, is that in order for ministry to release this life, this Kingdom quality, to the people, it *must* cost us our lives, our reputations, our comforts, our "firstness". Although in 2 Corinthians 2:14 Paul speaks of his ministry travels as "triumphal procession", in 1 Corinthians 4:9 he expands the metaphor to say: "It seems to me that God has put us apostles on display at the end of the procession, like men condemned to die in the arena. We have been made a spectacle to the whole universe ..." He is drawing from a familiar scene in Roman life, where generals would ride into Rome after a military conquest, with slaves in shackles tied behind their chariots. Those condemned to die in the arena would become gladiators, owned

---

[218] 2 Corinthians 2:16.
[219] 2 Corinthians 3:5, italics mine.

by that general, to live or die at his pleasure. Thus, Paul's use of language here is an ironic paradox. Christian leaders – apostles, in this case – are not the general in the chariot, but the slaves running in shackles behind him! In the "triumphal procession" of being a leader, it is *Christ's* triumph over us that is displayed, never our mastery over our task or the people we lead. As a result of this, says Andrew Clarke: "... the content of Paul's lifestyle ... did not consist in a strategy of empire building, but in a quality of selflessness ... The substance of this imitation is ... that they are not to seek their own good, but the good of many."[220]

It is, then, this "lastness", this raising of dust in servanthood, this self-emptying attitude, that releases the fragrance of Christ (2 Corinthians 2:14) from a leader; that enables us to write Christ's words on people's hearts (3:3); that qualifies us as ministers of the new covenant of life (3:6). When we, like Moses, die to ourselves in face-to-face encounter with the Lord, we reflect His transform-ing glory to others (3:18). When "we preach not ourselves, but Jesus Christ as Lord, and ourselves as your servants for Jesus' sake" (4:5), the result is that people see "the light of knowledge of the glory of God in the face of Christ" (4:6). Here Paul pauses to emphasise that ministry involves "death at work in us, but life at work in you" (4:12). The leader who sees his "death" resulting in "life" (i.e. God's real life) for others will not lose heart, will not become fatigued or resentful, will not dry out or burn out, but be inwardly renewed day by day (4:16).

It is at this point that Paul reminds those who would be leaders, that it is not a job for wimps! First he lists the "troubles" he had faced because of his calling to leadership (4:8–9). Then, he sums it all up in the phrase "our light and momentary troubles" (4:17)! Is he kidding? Is he being ironic? Is he being a bit of a triumphal-ist? No. He is simply "paying his bills in advance", contrasting the

---

[220]Clarke, *op. cit.*, pp. 235-236.

payment of the servant's "bill of serving" in this life, with what he or she receives in the age to come. He is calling us all to a different perspective on our lives and ministries. And in summary of his own life, he is saying: "The exchange is worth it!" The servant serves with his or her eyes on the unseen, eternal results of the life-exchange he or she is making (4:18); this life is merely a blip on the screen compared to the immensity of the age to come. The reality of heaven more than balances the hardships of earth, not only for us, but also for those we lead. We are not just bringing change, growth and joy for this life, but we will take with us to heaven those who receive our ministry of reconciliation. Christ's love compels us, and causes us to serve out of this singular motive: "We make it our goal to please Him." The books will be closed, and account will need to be given. Not to your church, your leaders, your denomination, or your colleagues, but to the Christ who will judge every man's servanthood, "of what sort it is".[221]

Jesus' servanthood model

In John 13, we are given a visual aid of what servanthood means. Jesus is facing His final night on earth as a man. He shares it with His closest friends, and wants to leave them His final, most earnest and powerful statements about their identity, their security, their calling and their destiny. One of the ways He does this is by fulfilling a practical need while illustrating a spiritual principle:

> [1]*Now before the feast of the Passover, when Jesus knew that his hour had come to depart out of this world to the Father, having loved his own who were in the world, he loved them to the end.* [2]*And during supper, when the devil had already put it into the heart of Judas Iscariot, Simon's son, to betray him,* [3]*Jesus, knowing that the Father had given all things into*

---

[221] 1 Corinthians 3:13 KJV.

his hands, and that he had come from God and was going to God, ⁴rose from supper, laid aside his garments, and girded himself with a towel. ⁵Then he poured water into a basin, and began to wash the disciples' feet, and to wipe them with the towel with which he was girded. ⁶He came to Simon Peter; and Peter said to him, "Lord, do you wash my feet?" ⁷Jesus answered him, "What I am doing you do not know now, but afterward you will understand." ⁸Peter said to him, "You shall never wash my feet." Jesus answered him, "If I do not wash you, you have no part in me." ⁹Simon Peter said to him, "Lord, not my feet only but also my hands and my head!" ¹⁰Jesus said to him, "He who has bathed does not need to wash, except for his feet, but he is clean all over; and you are clean, but not every one of you." ¹¹For he knew who was to betray him; that was why he said, "You are not all clean." ¹²When he had washed their feet, and taken his garments, and resumed his place, he said to them, "Do you know what I have done to you? ¹³You call me Teacher and Lord; and you are right, for so I am. ¹⁴If I then, your Lord and Teacher, have washed your feet, you also ought to wash one another's feet. ¹⁵For I have given you an example, that you also should do as I have done to you. ¹⁶Truly, truly, I say to you, a servant is not greater than his master; nor is he who is sent greater than he who sent him. ¹⁷If you know these things, blessed are you if you do them." (John 13:1–17)

What do we learn about servanthood from this story? I believe it illustrates four essential attitudinal dimensions of servanthood.

Firstly, Jesus operated as a servant out of *a secure sense of identity and self-worth*. He knew where He had come from, what His purpose was before God, and where He was going (verses 1–3). He knew these things in the face of the world's verdict regarding His value, which had just been paid by Judas (the equivalent of about six months' wages for a labourer). As Jesus begins His final actions of loving servanthood, He consciously reminds Himself, and measures His worth, by the Word of His Father rather than the going rate, or the standard of the least convinced.

Secondly, Jesus was *not concerned with His image* (verse 4). Anyone observing this scene, taking into view how He was clothed, the seating positions of the guests, and the work being done, would have assumed that Jesus had the lowest status in the room. The role He was fulfilling was usually done by the lowest slave in the household. Evidently He not only did not mind, but, in fact, also insisted on that role.

Thirdly, He did not merely symbolise serving; He actually *sought to benefit those He served* with compassion (verse 5). Their feet were hot and dirty, caked with dust and who knows what else. He may or may not have been praying for them, or speaking encouraging words to them as well. But He actually improved their lot, and made them feel better, because of what He did, without expectation of reward or thanks.

Fourthly, He teaches Peter, and through him, all of His disciples, that serving someone is *the key to genuine fellowship with them* (verses 6–8). Servanthood is not only the key to leadership, it is the essential ingredient in creating relationship between leader and follower. John Wimber, echoing what Jesus says here, often said: "You can't lead anyone you haven't served." Leadership, like all ministry, goes hand in hand with relationship, shared life, shared vulnerability and intimacy. To receive something from another is an admission of need. In the case of Jesus to Peter, this connection was crucial, because not admitting that he needed the "washing" of Jesus would mean Peter could not enter the relationship with God Jesus was offering him. In the case of a leader at our human level, even with spiritual interests at their core, there is a secondary application of this. If a "follower" will not show the humility of admitting need, and recognising that the leader can meet it, there will only be frustration in the relationship. Of course, there are degrees of relationship between any leader and his followers, as there were degrees of closeness between Jesus and the 12, the intimate three, and the beloved disciple, John. Nevertheless, each level of connection requires a relative degree of willingness to give and receive servant ministry.

As Jesus chose the serving role, so He calls His leaders in the new covenant to do likewise. It is the place where we will meet Him in ministry, find fellowship with Him, draw on His power, and exude His Life.

The servant of the Lord in Isaiah

In the sections of his prophecy that have been called "the servant songs" (roughly, chapters 41–53), Isaiah describes the qualities that were to be exemplified by the Servant of the LORD. The servant in the songs probably refers to three things, either simultaneously or, as the context reveals, individually: Israel and her destiny, the remnant within Israel who would fulfil what the nation in general had failed to fulfil, and an individual who would suffer redemptively on behalf of the nation.

I think that Jesus was aware of being sent as the fulfilment of the Isaiah prophecies, and saw his mission as that of the Servant of Yahweh. That self-awareness informs the mandate Jesus gave His disciples, both here and in John 20:21: "As the Father has sent me, so I send you." While the context of the particular "Servant Song" will clarify whether Israel or Messiah is the subject, we may draw on each of them to illustrate the nature of the Servant's serving.[222]

---

[222]Certainly, Jesus did not shrink from claiming the identity of the Servant, in using Isaiah 61:1–2 (admittedly, not directly a Servant Song, but having the same dual subject of Zion herself and, in Jesus' usage, the Messiah) as His ministry mandate, concluding with "today this Scripture has been ful-

I want to expand on some of these characteristics of the Lord's Servant, which may serve as a set of "orientation beacons" for His leaders, in any time, in any context:

- **Chosenness and calling** (41:8, 9; 42:1; 44:1–2, 21; 45:4; 48:15). He is chosen specifically, and called by name. His servanthood is neither his idea, nor the result of popular acclaim. The leader is not there to pursue "his" calling, so much as to fulfil *God's* purpose (Hebrews 10:7, cf. Psalm 40:6–8). Calling carries the idea of love, ownership and sovereignty, the promise of protection and providence, and the seed of fulfilled purpose. Only the chosen, called leader will persevere throughout his life and ministry, because perseverance depends on the God "who called [us, who] is faithful" (Hebrews 10:23), and will hold us up despite even our own fickleness. Our faithfulness is a reflection of the faithfulness of God who called us, not of our strength or self-effort. The servant leader is *called by God*.[223]

---

filled in your hearing" (Luke 4:21). In *The College Press NIV Commentary*, the authors state: "The New Testament identifies Jesus with the servant in numerous passages. Jesus' healing ministry is cast as the fulfillment of the first servant song (Matt 12:15–21). Jesus exhorts his disciples to recognize that the greatest among them must be their servant (Matt 20:26), even as he has come to them not to be served but to serve, and to give his life as a ransom for many (Matt 20:28) It is in this role as ransom that Jesus is most closely linked to the final servant song. He is the Lamb of God, who takes away the sin of the world (John 1:29). The Ethiopian eunuch is reading about the suffering servant when God sends Philip to him to explain that the prophet is speaking about Jesus, leading to the eunuch's conversion (Acts 8:26ff.). Peter calls Christians who suffer for their faith to look to the example of Jesus who, though sinless, silently accepted mistreatment and in the process 'bore our sins in his body on the tree' (1 Pet 2:21–25)."

[223]F. Duane Lindsey, "The Call of the Servant in Isaiah 42:1–9" in *BIBLIO-THECA SACRA* 139 (553) (Jan. 1982): 12-31 (Dallas Theological Seminary, 1982) writes: "... vss 1–4 constitute Yahweh's designatory call of and promised accomplishments by His servant."

- **Character formation** (49:2; 50:5–7). If the servant is called, her circumstances and suffering are part of that calling. She will be refined by suffering, equipped and completed by the One who called her. Suffering is not a tragedy; even rejection says nothing about her worth; rather it is the means of finding out, and perfecting, the character of the servant in the image of the God for whom she speaks. This is as much the purpose of God in calling us, as is our effect on others. If Jesus had to be perfected by His obedience through suffering (Hebrews 5:8–9), how much more is this true of the fallen, broken people God wants to make into ministers of His grace? The servant leader is *trained in character.*

- **Empowerment for the job** (42:1; 49:8–13). The Lord puts His Spirit on His chosen servant, to strengthen him, uphold him and redeem others through him. The power to do God's work comes from God, and is therefore, supernatural or extraordinary. God will confirm the servant's word (44:26) by releasing prisoners, healing the oppressed and restoring justice. The way Jesus used His God-given power displayed the selflessness for which servants ought to be known. He would not "put on a show" for the curious, or allow the recipients of healing to make a noise about who He was. He was not in the ministry for success or status, title or turf, but because He loved the lost, the poor and the broken. He had compassion, and the lesson of His life is that God empowers compassion. The servant leader is an agent of *empowered compassion.*

- **Confidence in God's final vindication** (41:11–12; 43:1–6; 45:14; 49:6–7; 50:7–8; 52:13). The servant has times of near despair, but is reassured repeatedly by the knowledge that God will preserve and vindicate him. More than this,

God will vindicate His own Name through the accomplishments of His servant. What seems like failure is not failure, if the servant maintains the long view. The sense of destiny, or long-term hope, is a vital ingredient for true servanthood. The servant leader is *quietly confident in the final outcome* of his or her life.

- **Blind and deaf to all agendas but God's** (42:19–20). Although it probably refers to the former meaning of who the Servant is, namely Israel, and her disobedient deafness,[224] I want to use some "prophetic licence" (with its New Testament fulfilment in mind) and apply this enigmatic passage more positively to the Servant himself. It is suggestive of a single-minded obedience, in which the servant shuts his ears to anything but "the law of the Lord". In 50:4–5 he speaks of this single-mindedness as the basis for his ministry. He hears with humility; therefore he can teach with authority. Jesus put His ability to perform miracles down to this one principle: "The Son can do nothing on his own accord, but only what he sees the Father doing" (John 5:19). He listened, He watched, He obeyed the Father. Therefore, He bore the Father's fruit. The servant leader is *understated and single-minded.*

- **A spirit of quiet grace** (42:2–4; 50:4; 53:7). His words are grace to the weary; he does not trumpet his status, his rights, his authority or even his message. When unjustly accused, he is silent. His gentle spirit is what commends him to the "bruised reed" and the "smouldering wick". He is able to strengthen and heal the bruised to make them useful again, and to blow the diminishing spirit gently

---

[224]Most commentaries consulted give this interpretation, e.g. John Oswalt, *The Book of Isaiah 40–66* in *New International Commentary on the Old Testament* (Wm. B. Eerdmans, 1998), p. 131.

into full flame. This spirit of grace is probably the standout characteristic of Jesus in the Gospel accounts, as He gives God's generous, redemptive acceptance to the broken, the discouraged, the marginalised and rejected. The abuse of spiritual authority that is evident in the snuffing out of hope and freedom to believe in the lives of weak followers, or the breaking of the little strength left in those bruised in the climb, is an indictment on modern leadership. The servant leader *adds the value of grace* to those he leads.[225]

Robert T. France's article in *The Zondervan Pictorial Encyclopedia of the Bible* sums up the Servant Songs in this way:

> *The Servant was chosen by the Lord (42:1; 49:1) and endued with the Spirit (42:1); He was taught by the Lord (50:4), and found His strength in Him (49:2, 5). It was the Lord's will that He should suffer (53:10); He was weak, unimpressive, and scorned by men (52:14; 53:1–3, 7–9), meek (42:2), gentle (42:3), and uncomplaining (50:6; 53:7). Despite His innocence (53:9), He was subjected to constant suffering (50:6; 53:3, 8–10); He obeyed Him (50:4–5), and persevered (50:7) until He was victorious (42:4; 50:8,9).*[226]

Richards and Hoeldtke add a poetic touch in affirming this view: "The Servant portrayed here is a source of special delight for the Lord. He is gifted with the Spirit, adopts a gentle and quiet lifestyle, and works for the birth of justice. Although He meets with resistance, He is neither discouraged nor fails but succeeds in carrying out the purpose to which He is called."[227] Jesus asks those He appoints to leadership, to emulate Him in the way they lead (Mark 10:45). Leadership is a call to follow in His steps (1 Peter 2:21).

---

[225]Lindsey, *op. cit.*

[226]Ed. Merrill C. Tenney (Zondervan, 1975) vol. 5, p. 361.

[227]Richards and Hoeldtke, *op. cit.*, p. 104.

Anyone who would rise to a position of leadership in God's Church would do well to pause and reflect on what it will cost us to do so.

The servant's mission

> *We do not put an obstacle in anyone's way. Otherwise, fault may be found with our ministry. Instead, in every way we demonstrate that we are God's servants by tremendous endurance in the midst of difficulties, hardships, and calamities; in beatings, imprisonments, and riots; in hard work, sleepless nights, and hunger; with purity, knowledge, patience, and kindness; with the Holy Spirit, genuine love, truthful speech, and divine power; through the weapons of righteousness in the right and left hands; through honour and dishonour; through ill repute and good repute; perceived as deceivers and yet true, as unknown and yet well-known, as dying and yet – as you see – very much alive, as punished and yet not killed, as sorrowful and yet always rejoicing, as poor and yet enriching many, as having nothing and yet possessing everything.* (2 Corinthians 6:3–10)

Paul's retrospective mission statement gives a poignant focus, fulfilment and spiritual ECG of leadership. A true leader is a man or woman who exemplifies servanthood in contrast to self-seeking, and answers every temptation to power, prestige, pleasure or the line of least resistance, with the single ambition of being "unworthy servants".[228]

If servanthood is the essence of leadership, it is important to know how to apply it to our leadership functions. Toward whom does the Christian leader direct his humility? An early mentor in my life would often use the expression: "Don't serve the people for the Lord's sake; serve the Lord for the people's sake." That is

---

[228]Luke 17:10 NLT.

to say, give ministry as though Christ is its beneficiary. Preach as if He is your sermon's only hearer; "treat people as if they were Jesus". This last has become a well-known quote by Mother Teresa of Calcutta, who was asked how she could keep up her work of selfless caring for street people without tiring. She replied: "Each one of them is Jesus in disguise. I treat each one as if he were Jesus. There is always the danger that we may just do the work for the sake of the work. This is where the respect and the love and the devotion come in – that we do it to God, to Christ ..."[229]

> *Untethered from God, self-giving love cannot stand on its own for long. If it excludes God, it will destroy us, for we will then deliver ourselves to the mercy of the finite, and therefore inherently unreliable, objects of our love. The only way to ensure that we will not lose our very selves if we give ourselves to others is if our love for the other passes first through God, if we, as Augustine put it succinctly and profoundly, love and enjoy others in God.*[230]

In 1988, I learned and have since applied this principle to my life and ministry. I was pastoring two congregations at the time, while also being bi-vocational, managing the sales department of a large company from 8 till 5, Monday to Friday, and one or two nights a week as well. You could say I was running on fumes, enjoying my work but a little fatigued, to say the least! At that time, at the end of each Sunday night, I would come home from church, eat supper and destress by watching sport or *M*A*S*H* on television, before falling into bed exhausted. And virtually every Monday

---

[229]http://www.iloveindia.com/indian-heroes/mother-teresa/quote.html. This, then, is a reverse of the message of the WWJD (What Would Jesus Do?) bracelet, which requires that the "doer" be Jesus. Mother Teresa instead suggests that Jesus be seen as the recipient rather than the doer of the deed.

[230]Volf, *Free of Charge, op. cit.,* loc 1589.

morning, I would awake with a tension headache.

I was reading and reflecting on the parable Jesus tells in Luke 17:7–10. It is the story of a servant who, having worked all day in the fields, does not rest when he comes home, but first sees to his master's needs. He feeds, serves, and celebrates his master before seeing to his own needs. Suddenly I saw the point of the parable, which is, to use a popular phrase: "It's not about me!" From that time on, each Sunday night, both on the way home and after getting home, I would immerse myself in worshipping and enjoying God for Himself and His faithfulness, before watching TV or anything else. As my focus changed and I established a habit of ministering to the Lord Himself after every service, I found myself sleeping well, being stronger and waking refreshed, pain and stress-free every Monday morning.

An episode from the Gospel of Luke is also pertinent here.[231] We have probably all heard dozens of sermons on the story of Mary and Martha (sisters of Lazarus, from Bethany). Many of the sermons I have heard say the same thing, namely that Martha should have stopped her "many things" in favour of Mary's "one thing" (enjoying time with Jesus). I am sure that is an accurate spiritual lesson from the story itself. However, on an everyday basis, most of us are involved with "things" – to do, achieve, perform, care for, see to … I will address the issue of "restful work" elsewhere, but want to suggest that Jesus is opening Martha's, and subsequent generations of readers' minds, to the possibility of daily doing the "many things" of service while our hearts remain fixed on the "one thing" of worshipful and obedient connection with Jesus. Doing what we do, in other words, "as to the Lord".

Paul develops this thought in addressing actual slaves, in Ephesians 6:5–8 and Colossians 3:22–24. He says that the Christian slave is not serving his earthly master, but the Lord Christ.

---

[231] Luke 10:38–42.

Therefore, he exhorts them to serve "as working for the Lord, not men". This brings an element of worship to everything the servant does. It allows her to receive life back from Him for life expended, irrespective of how her earthly "master" treats her. It brings the renewal, the secret joy, of knowing that, even if no human being notices, rewards or thanks her, He who sees all things done in secret always does. Jesus taught that pretentiousness, popularity and prosperity are their own reward (Matthew 6:1–24). If you look for people's recognition or gratitude for your prayer life, fasting or tithing (or, indeed, any other discipline), you will get precisely that, and only that, out of it: human recognition of how "spiritual" you are![232] The point he makes is that these "rewards" are superficial, temporal and destructible, but that the Kingdom nature within us longs for something deep, eternal and incorruptible. The servant is the ultimate expression of a willingness to defer compensation, to work for no immediate gain, but to realise that, apart from the immediate satisfaction of the secret joy mentioned above, our rewards are "out of this world". Stanley S. Grenz places the entire endeavour of being the Church and working for the sake of the Kingdom of God in this context when he writes:

> *Only as we obey Christ can we indeed be the eschatological covenant community God intends us to be. Our goal is to embody and advance the program of God until our Lord returns. Hence, the church exists for the sake of eternity.*[233]

So do its leaders!

---

[232]I enjoy the NLT rendition of the ironic phrase Jesus uses about reward in this text: "that is all the reward they will ever get" (verses 2, 5, 16).

[233]Stanley S. Grenz, *Theology for the Community of God* (Eerdmans, 2000), p. 570.

CHAPTER 6

Securing a Dividend

"True leadership must be for the benefit of the followers, not the enrichment of the leaders." **Robert Townsend**

> *For we do not preach ourselves, but rather Jesus the Messiah as Lord, and ourselves as merely your servants for Jesus' sake … We are always carrying around the death of Jesus in our bodies, so that the life of Jesus may be clearly shown in our bodies. While we are alive, we are constantly being handed over to death for Jesus' sake, so that the life of Jesus may be clearly shown in our mortal bodies. And so death is at work in us, but life is at work in you.* (2 Corinthians 4:5, 10–12)

The concept of leadership being qualified by whether it brings about benefit for those being led, is closely aligned with the subject of the previous chapter. From the inception of the Hebrew people of God through the calling of Abram, there was a promise of resultant benefit, or blessing, coming to the world, as Yahweh promises Abram that "through you *all the people of the earth will be blessed*" (Genesis 12:3, italics mine). The Hebrew word *barak* used here, as it applies between humans, carries the idea of causing happiness or joy in the recipient. This is echoed by the Greek word *makarios* (literally, "happy") used in the Greek rendition of Jesus' Sermon on the Mount in Matthew 5. In some ways, it goes without saying: serving people brings a benefit to them. Benefit means that those who receive the input, or the service, of the leader, experience a resultant improvement of their condition, either in material, emotional or spiritual ways. For example, Peter's reply to Jesus' poignant question: "Are you also going to leave?" in John 6:67–68, is that they would not leave Jesus because He "[had] the words that give eternal life" (NLT). They had "tasted and seen" through Him that the Lord was good. We are to serve people, not for symbolic reasons (or, as I emphasised in the preceding chapter, in order to win authority with them), but so that their situation, personal or corporate, is improved. Leaders (e.g. political ones) who line their pockets, build palaces and otherwise "fleece" their people for personal gain, are not leaders in the biblical sense, but exploiters of their people and abusers of power.

I use the word "Dividend" here to fit with my LEADERSHIP mnemonic. It helps to convey the idea that leadership is a gift you get to *give*, and keep on giving. It is giving in the progressive continuous tense. Jesus spoke about blessing one another in Matthew 10:42: "And whoever gives one of these little ones even a cup of cold water because he is a disciple, truly, I say to you, he will by no means lose his reward." Even refreshing one another on the journey of discipleship is a fulfilment of the Abrahamic prerogative. The size of the benefit is not as important as the fact and its motivation. Once, while reading John 7:37–39, I was struck by two things. Jesus was, at the time, probably standing ankle deep in the water of purification that had been poured through the temple courts at the climax of the feast of purification:

On the last and most important day of the festival, Jesus stood up and shouted, "If anyone is thirsty, let him come to me and drink! The one who believes in me, as the Scripture has said, will have rivers of living water flowing from his heart." Now he said this about the Spirit, whom those who were believing in him were to receive, because the Spirit was not yet present and Jesus had not yet been glorified.

The two things that impacted me as I read the text, were:

1. Why did Jesus change the subject?
2. Where is the Scripture to which He is referring?

The answer to my second question actually provides the answer to the first. There is no Old Testament text that uses these exact words, but the closest I found is Isaiah 32:1–2:

*Look, a king will reign in righteousness, and rulers will rule with justice. Each one will be … like **streams of water in the desert**, in the shadow of a great rock in an exhausted land.*
(Emphasis mine)

Isaiah changes the subject quickly, from announcing the king to describing His "viceregents". The effect of the King is rulers who rule on His behalf, and each one of them becomes a resource of shelter, refreshing and shade. They receive the King's righteousness, only to give it away as justice and mercy. They are blessed to be a blessing. Thus, as Jesus in John 7 invites His followers who are thirsty to "come to me and drink", He quickly announces, in effect, that they would be so abundant in resource, that in giving, they will receive, in blessing, they will be blessed. "Are you thirsty?" he asks. "Then come to me and drink, and you will have water so abundant that it will fill you while it waters the world."

When Jesus did the work of the lowest servant in the household, by washing the feet of the disciples, He was making a statement about leadership, and establishing a precedent and example for His future leaders to follow in principle and in practice. But,

He was also serving a basic need, and bringing a basic benefit to some tired, hot and dirty feet! I have over the years heard people say that the reason they "signed up" with a particular leader was that he gave them a sense of safety; another that "He believed in us!" The benefit may be anything from the security of belonging, to the satisfaction of accomplishing; to comfort or fame; enjoyment to development. But personal and group benefit is part of the fulfilment of a long-held promise, made to Abraham, fulfilled through Jesus and "rolled over" into the hands of those He calls.

Here are some examples:

- If a leader is a teacher-leader, the group they lead will be better informed and equipped.
- If he is an administrator-leader, they will be secure and organised.
- If he is a pioneer, or catalytic leader, they will have advanced toward a mutually acceptable goal in new "territory".
- If he is a pastoral leader, they will feel loved, embraced and empowered.

In each case followers, or beneficiaries, will feel a gratitude and loyalty toward the leader, and give them greater authority or permission to lead them further. They will find in the leader a safe place, a source of help, warmth, dignity and growth. This, again, is what will stimulate continued following. Relationships begin, and are sustained, when people spend time with one another and add value to one another's lives. A leader adds value to a follower in a unique way. This value-addition will usually take the form of either *achievement, information, security* or *inspiration*. A group exists to make a difference, to touch the world, to achieve a vision. It needs internal coherence, or a substantiated belief system, which is provided by sound teaching. It also needs the security of solid relationships, a sense of belonging and care. Then, it needs to be enjoyable or entertaining. Its gathering should, as Bill Hybels says, be "made memorable".[234]

Just as in a jointly held company, shareholders can expect dividends or returns on their investment, so members of any group sign up with the group because there is a benefit they anticipate. These are the elements of group cohesion. Their presence at appropriate times in the group's life determines the reason why individuals become, and stay, involved. They are the fine print, the coloured-in details of the big picture or vision announced at the group's inception. They are the benefits for which people "sign up".

The various schools of psychology were developed around particular answers to the basic question: "What motivates people?" In other words, what is the "Why?" for the "What?" and "How?" of any behaviour? For the sake of simplicity and brevity, we could say that Sigmund Freud believed people's basic motivating drive to be "Pleasure"; Erik Erikson suggested it was a sense of "Ego Identity"; Carl Rogers proposed "Potentiality" as the basic drive; and Viktor Frankl said it was "the will to meaning". Dr Abraham Maslow developed an idea which, in summary, included "all of the above". He believed that every person grows through a hierarchy of needs, beginning at the most basic and culminating with the most altruistic. Each level needs to be satisfied before the next can be addressed.[235]

When you seek to draw any group of people toward a vision, you would do well to remember that they will range throughout Maslow's hierarchy and, accordingly, respond very differently to your message or leadership. There is possibly an echo of this diversity of need in Peter's answer to Jesus' offer of foot washing. Maybe he was uncomfortable that Jesus was offering him such a

---

[234]From his talk at an early edition of the Global Leadership Summit, Cape Town, October 2007, http://www.willowcreekglobalsummit.com/downloads/gls_2007_report.pdf.

[235]A. Maslow, *Motivation and Personality* (New York: Harper, 1954).

mundane service, wanting rather to be considered as having higher interests in mind. He might have explained: "Lord, I am way more spiritual than this. My connection with you is about much more than clean feet! Why are you reducing our relationship to *this?*" Jesus' reply to him illustrates an enduring principle of leadership, which was well articulated by John Wimber with the adage I mentioned earlier: "You can't lead anyone you haven't served."

When you step up to the plate[236] of leadership in any capacity, you will find a range of motives mixing, not only among the group members, but also in your own heart. Depending on factors as wide-ranging as your age and experience, spiritual state and maturity, you will be motivated by a mixture of joy and terror. Joy that your gift can be used, and terror that God knows your heart and true motives. You will feel reluctance and enthusiasm in tension. You will be too afraid to act, and too afraid not to act, these two fears working against each other within you. Your body, your mind, your reputation will scream against it and, simultaneously, you will know that you must. You will have within you an echo of Paul's exclamation in 1 Corinthians 9:16–17:

> *For if I preach the gospel, I have nothing to boast about, for this obligation has been laid on me. How terrible it would be for me if I didn't preach the gospel! For if I do this voluntarily, I get a reward, but if I am unwilling to do it, I am still entrusted with an obligation.*

Paul had been able to reach this point of honesty and compulsion because he had taken his motives past the cross, and lived in the light of the last Day. He had concluded that motivations will always be unclear, to both the person serving and those he or she serves, until that Day makes them clear:

---

[236]A term derived from the game of baseball, used when a player has come to his or her turn to bat (hit the ball).

*It is a very small thing to me that I should be examined by you or by any human court. In fact, I don't even evaluate myself. For my conscience is clear, but that does not vindicate me. It is the Lord who examines me. Therefore, stop judging prematurely, before the Lord comes, for he will bring to light what is now hidden in darkness and reveal **the motives of our hearts.** Then each person will receive his praise from God.* (1 Corinthians 4:3–5, emphasis mine)

The place of self-abandonment in a leader is secured by what Paul expresses in the final phrase: his confidence that each of us will receive "*praise* from God". God knows our hearts best and, once we have aligned ourselves with Him and our need of His grace, that settles the basic question of motivation. It provides an inner compulsion that drives the leader to the goal toward which the grace of God has equipped us to lead. We, like Paul, will always minister to others with a measure of self-suspicion. We will know that we are inadequate, unworthy and untrustworthy, while we simultaneously "make it our aim to please Him".[237] We should respond to our self-doubt with a willingness of heart tempered by a complete reliance on the grace of God.

What I look for in a leader is a healthy tension between reluctance and compulsion. Reluctance to push him or herself forward, and a compulsion that comes from God's gracious energy within. When you lead, you will know that the end you serve is worth your own loss, whatever that means. Affirm over your life that your gift matters; that your offering is sanctified by the cross, and is acceptable to God because of Christ. Affirm the fact that your desires have been sanctified by the same atoning sacrifice that cleansed your sins, and that you may expect to do what you do for the sake of God's eternal purpose with you and the people you serve.

---

[237] 2 Corinthians 5:9 ESV.

I said in chapter 2 that a key ingredient of leadership is the casting, communication and achievement of vision, in the form of goals. In the interests of staying in touch with reality in this regard, it is a good idea for a leader to take a periodic inventory of the effects of your gift, and the goals it is accomplishing. What have people thanked you for doing? Have they been encouraged, built up and comforted? Do they love Jesus more? Are they more aware of and motivated about the Kingdom of God and its values? Are they lifted out of the mundane and temporal concerns of their lives, to focus on the eternal and spiritual ones? Does your presence and ministry leave a sense of life on them? Then you have probably operated in a spiritual gift of leadership. Paul encouraged the Corinthians to "strive to excel in building up the church."[238] I believe this is something we may measure by the setting and achieving of God-given goals.

Leaders are noticed, then, because they lead. Something happens to the group because of their function. The group is led into cohesion, growth, momentum and achievement. The leader is not more valuable, or gifted, or holy, than those he or she leads. However, unless their gift is exercised, the group exists without purpose, and without experiencing the benefit for which it was designed. As Paul faces his end, he reveals this tension in his letter to the Philippians, in its ultimate form:

> [21]*For to me, living means living for Christ, and dying is even better. *[22]*But if I live, I can do more fruitful work for Christ. So I really don't know which is better. *[23]*I'm torn between two desires: I long to go and be with Christ, which would be far better for me. *[24]*But for your sakes, it is better that I continue to live. *[25]*Knowing this, I am convinced that I will remain alive so I can continue to help all of you grow and experience the joy of your faith.* (Philippians 1:21–25 NLT)

---

[238] 1 Corinthians 14:12 ESV.

Jim Collins, in his book, *Good to Great*, traces the growth of a leader through five levels. Level 1 is the "Highly Capable Individual", who makes productive contributions through talents, knowledge, skills and good work habits. Level 2 is the "Contributing Team Member", who contributes his or her capabilities to enable the achievement of the group's objectives. Level 3 is the "Competent Manager", who organises people and resources toward the effective and efficient pursuit of predetermined objectives. Level 4 is the "Effective Leader", who catalyses commitment to and vigorous pursuit of a clear and compelling vision, stimulating higher performance standards. The Level 5 leader, which Collins calls the "Executive", "builds enduring greatness [into the organisation and its people] through a paradoxical blend of personal humility and professional will". This kind of leader is both self-effacing and fiercely ambitious. Ambitious not for self-aggrandisement or gain, but for the company/group he or she leads to become great. In the Matthew 20:25–28 text we looked at, Jesus is not preaching against the idea of greatness. Instead, He is preaching about the way to true greatness, which is that he is greatest who seeks the greatest good for others:

> *You know that the rulers of the Gentiles lord it over them and their superiors act like tyrants over them. That's not the way it should be among you. Instead, whoever wants to be great among you must be your servant, and whoever wants to be first among you must be your slave. That's the way it is with the Son of Man. He did not come to be served, but to serve and to give his life as a ransom for many people.*

Thus, says Collins, and I think Jesus would concur, a great leader is "a study in duality: modest and wilful, humble and fearless". In His teaching about leadership in the above text, Jesus evidently does not mind someone wishing to be "great [or first] among you". However, He says that in order to become truly great, you will need to deliberately take the lowest role, to desire to see others, or the group, become great. The "great" leader is someone who is energetically, intentionally and passionately focused on the wellbeing of the group he or she leads, to his or her own personal cost. True leaders are only happy when the group they lead succeeds, or looks great.

Collins uses the analogy of the "window and the mirror" to illustrate this. Picture an executive in an office overlooking his company's factory. He can see his employees at work through a large window. On the other wall of his office is a mirror. When things are going badly, the bad leader looks out of the window for something or someone outside him or herself to blame. When things are going well, they look in the mirror and credit themselves for it. Conversely, when things go badly, a Level 5 leader looks in the mirror and asks: "What could I be doing better?" When things are going well, they look out of the window and say: "What great people I have to lead. They made all this possible!"

In chapter 1 I mentioned Daniel Goleman's concept of "Emotional Intelligence"[239] or "EQ", which can be summed up under the heading of *empathy* and, I would add, *altruism*. The person with a high EQ will constantly be thinking about others in the room, feeling with them and putting their needs above and before his own. The phrase that sums up the Sermon on the Mount ("Whatever you want people to do for you, do the same for them" – Matthew 7:12) covers all interactions at every level of relationship for a follower of Jesus, and applies to the leader's calling of seeking the wellbeing of the group they lead.

When it comes to the objectives that group achieves, the leader with high EQ is also not interested in receiving the credit for its achievements. To paraphrase the words of Ronald Reagan: "There is no limit to the amount of good you can do if you don't care who

---

[239]Goleman, *op.cit.*.

gets the credit."[240]

Other images from the Sermon on the Mount are equally pertinent here. In that sermon, Jesus reserves some of His strongest
words for people who want recognition for their acts of charity or
spirituality. I referred to these in the last chapter, but repeat the
reference here. Jesus' repeated assessment of the actions of those
who practise their religious duty because "they want everyone to
praise them", is to say: "That's all the reward they will get" (Matthew 6:2 ERV).

In Luke 14:28–33, Jesus seems to say both that His disciples
should, and should not "count [estimate, calculate] the cost" of
discipleship (and, we might say, ministry) before embarking on
that journey. He begins by asking "which of you would" start a
construction project without doing so? However, His final comment is seemingly contradictory, when He says: "And so whoever is not ready to give up all he has may not be my disciple"
(verse 33). What is He telling us? I believe Jesus is contrasting two
economies and their practices. He is contrasting the profit-driven,
consumerist economy that depends on a cost-to-benefit calcula-
tion, on one hand, with a Kingdom economy on the other. He is
contrasting "which of you" with "whoever wants to follow me".
And the concluding equation is that, in tower building, or in wag-
ing war, you need to calculate and ensure you have what it takes
to finish (and that the effort is worth the benefits). But in discipleship and leadership, realise ahead of time that: (a) you probably don't have what it takes; (b) it's going to cost you everything;
(c) the benefits are internal and will probably need to be deferred;
but (d) do it anyway! Pay your bills in advance. Remove from
yourself the option of quitting, or of disillusionment because the
cost exceeds the benefits. On the one hand, the benefits to you
will never be enough. They may also only be awarded to you in

---

[240]Quoted on the website http://www.goodreads.com/quotes/29359.

private, or not at all. And actually, they were never yours to begin with!

On the other hand, benefits (dividends) are supposed to accrue to those you lead. A leader who has been tamed by the Spirit of God will seek the growth, the security and the godly destiny of those she leads. Here are a few examples of biblical characters showing the characteristics of a Level 5 leader:

> [31]*So Moses returned to the LORD and said, "Oh, what a terrible sin these people have committed. They have made gods of gold for themselves.* [32]*But now, if You will only forgive their sin – but if not, erase my name from the record You have written!"* (Exodus 32:31–32)

> [13]*I assigned supervisors for the storerooms … These men had an excellent reputation, and it was their job to make honest distributions to their fellow Levites.* [14]*Remember this good deed, O my God, and do not forget all that I have faithfully done for the Temple of my God and its services.* (Nehemiah 13:13–14)

> [14]*"If you keep quiet now, help and freedom for the Jews will come from another place. But you and your father's family will all die. And who knows, maybe you have been chosen to be the queen for such a time as this."* [15]*Then Esther sent this answer to Mordecai: "Mordecai, go and get all the Jews in Susa together, and fast for me. Don't eat or drink for three days and nights. I and my women servants will fast too. After we fast, I will go to the king. I know it is against the law to go to the king if he didn't call me, but I will do it anyway. If I die, I die."* (Esther 4:14–15)

> [17]*… Jesus said to him, "Take care of my sheep.* [18]*The truth is, when you were young, you tied your own belt and went where you wanted. But when you are old, you will put out*

your hands, and someone else will tie your belt. They will lead you where you don't want to go." [19](Jesus said this to show how Peter would die to give glory to God.) Then he said to Peter, "Follow me!" [20]Peter turned and saw the follower Jesus loved very much walking behind them ... [21]When Peter saw him behind them, he asked Jesus, "Lord, what about him?" [22]Jesus answered, "Maybe I want him to live until I come. That should not matter to you. You follow me!" (John 21:17–22)

[16]*Even when I was in Thessalonica you sent help more than once. [17]I don't say this because I want a gift from you. Rather, I want you to receive a reward for your kindness. [18]At the moment I have all I need – and more! I am generously supplied with the gifts you sent me with Epaphroditus. They are a sweet-smelling sacrifice that is acceptable and pleasing to God. [19]And this same God who takes care of me will supply all your needs from His glorious riches, which have been given to us in Christ Jesus.* (Philippians 4:16–19)

These are examples of leaders who did not count their own lives as precious, but laid them down to see others, and the cause of God's Kingdom, thrive. Some of them lost their lives for it. Others lost families, reputations or careers. Yet they did not hold anything back, though in some cases they were told ahead of time what it would cost them. They, like the people described in the book of Hebrews:

"[13]... died still believing what God had promised them. They did not receive what was promised, but they saw it all from a distance and welcomed it. They agreed that they were foreigners and nomads here on earth. [15]If they had longed for the country they came from, they could have gone back. [16]But they were looking for a better place, a heavenly homeland.

> *That is why God is not ashamed to be called their God, for he has prepared a city for them.*" (Hebrews 11:13, 15–16 NLT).

The principle translates into every level of activity, and every configuration of people being served. If you are serving, or destined to serve, in vocational ministry, you will soon discover that it includes many opportunities to quit. As I said in chapter 2, a calling to serve Christ is not for the faint-hearted.

It is also not for the self-centred!

PART THREE

UNIQUE LEADERSHIP STYLES AND PROCESS LEADERSHIP

In Part One we explored factors, character traits and practices that are common to all leaders, whether in the Church or in the secular environment. In Part Two we examined those unique characteristics and practices that are non-negotiables for "Kingdom" or Christian leaders. The final part will look at what makes each Kingdom leader unique, notably their style, gift-mix or way of applying what *all* leaders need to do, to what *this* leader needs to do.

Stylistic differences are noticed primarily in the public functions of a leader. In church leaders, they usually appear when he or she is in the pulpit, and in the effects the leader's decisions and actions have on the "feel" or ethos of the leadership group. For example, the style a visionary leader will display in public will be inspirational and motivational, whereas an analytical leader's style will come across as more instructional and foundational. The former will usually be more extemporaneous, the latter more structured and "chapter and verse" based. The visionary leader will be more future-focused, whereas the teacher will want to anchor the group in the past and present. Other styles we will discuss include the more adventurous, outward-focused leader and the community-building, inward-focused one.

The following section of the book will examine how these styles are designed to complement one another, to form a cohesive and comprehensive resource for the maturing and visionary success of any and every church or Kingdom endeavour.

The letters of the LEADERSHIP mnemonic as set out in my Preface, which I will discuss in the last section, are Empowering; Relationality; Implementation and Potentiality. Each of these will not have its own chapter, but they will be seen together in a dynamic relationship in the chapters that follow.

CHAPTER 7

The Functions of Leadership

"You can do what I cannot do. I can do what you cannot do. Together we can do great things." **Mother Teresa**

I therefore, the prisoner in the Lord, beg you to lead a life worthy of the calling to which you have been called, with all humility and gentleness, with patience, bearing with one another in love, making every effort to maintain the unity of the Spirit in the bond of peace. There is one body and one Spirit, just as you were called to the one hope of your calling, one Lord, one faith, one baptism, one God and Father of all, who is above all and through all and in all. But each of us was given grace according to the measure of Christ's gift. Therefore it is said, "When he ascended on high he made captivity itself a captive; he gave gifts to his people." (When it says, "He ascended," what does it mean but that he had also descended into the lower parts of the earth? He who descended is the same one who ascended far above all the heavens, so that he might fill all things.) The gifts he gave were that some would be apostles, some prophets, some evangelists, some pastors and teachers, to equip the saints for the work of ministry, for building up the body of Christ, until all of us come to the unity of the faith and of the knowledge of the Son of God, to maturity, to the measure of the full stature of Christ. We must no longer be children, tossed to and fro and blown about by every wind of doctrine, by people's trickery, by their craftiness in deceitful scheming. But speaking the truth in love, we must grow up in every way into him who is the head, into Christ, from whom the whole body, joined and knit together by every ligament with which it is equipped, as each part is working properly, promotes the body's growth in building itself up in love. (Ephesians 4:1–15 NRSV)

I believe that, in any local church context, everyone is gifted and needs to play a role, and the role of a gifted senior leader in that church will need to be the prayerful and sensitive facilitation of "every member ministry". Leadership is the gift that distinguishes some people, and the "wattage" or capacity of that gift will determine the scope and impact of their leadership. However, what is the content of each person's leadership? What style, what effect, characterises each leader's serving? In my view, there are all kinds of leaders in the church, and if they lead by the grace God gives them, the overall result will be a group of people taken to a specific goal. If a leader is given an apostolic grace, the goal reached will be the gospel preached in new environs, and a church built and established; if a prophetic grace, a group will be inspired and encouraged; if a teaching grace, new understanding of truth; if a pastoral grace, people will be secure in love and care for their souls. The effect of leaders will be determined by the focus and the capacity of the grace God has bestowed on them for the sake of the church. In Ephesians 4, Paul introduces what he is going to say about gifts, with the same phrasing he uses in Romans 12.

Grace (*charis*) has been given to him as an apostle as well as to "each of us", as the basis and nature of the ministries he will discuss (verse 7). Thus, in what follows, Paul is going to address the grace in him, as well as the grace that is in every member of the Body of Christ, and to explain the arrangement and interdependent function of each.

What is immediately striking is the fact that Paul introduces the gifts as the "apportioning … of the ascended Christ",[241] as distinct from the Holy Spirit, whom he names as the dispenser of the *charismata* of 1 Corinthians 12. The old (unattributed) explanatory statement about the Trinity says that "where any person of the divine Trinity is present, the others are not absent". However, Scripture often distinguishes the member of the Godhead who initiates in certain actions or ministry functions. The *charismata* are always spoken of as manifestations of the Holy Spirit. He "gives what he wants to each person".[242] On the other hand, when it comes to the gift ministries in this text, the role of the ascended Son is emphasised. Christ as the Builder of His Church features in the distinctive way in which He ensures that His nature and personhood are represented in the gift ministries He dispenses. As I will emphasise later, Paul also uses a different word for "gifts" in the text *(domata* rather than *charismata).*

The introductory verses of Ephesians 4:8–11 are from Psalm 68:18, with its theme of conquest and the receiving and distributing of the spoils of war by a conquering monarch. The Psalm was probably set in the context of David's conquest and capture of Zion from the Jebusites,[243] but also spoke prophetically

---

[241] F. F. Bruce, *The Epistles to the Colossians, to Philemon, and to the Ephesians* (Wm. B. Eerdmans, 1984), p. 91.

[242] 1 Corinthians 12:11.

[243] E. K. Simpson and F. F. Bruce, *The Epistles to the Ephesians and the Colossians* in *The New International Commentary on the New Testament* (Eerdmans, 1968), p. 92.

of "David's greater Son".[244] The Hebrew wording of the Psalm translates as "received gifts *among* (or *from*, or *for*) men" in most translations but, in the opinion of Bruce, who refers to the Targum's rendering, Paul changes the direction of the verb so that it becomes "gave gifts *to* men".[245] Bruce continues: "Paul and other NT writers occasionally give evidence of using targumic renderings ... especially where such renderings are better suited to the argument to which they are applied than the Hebrew or Septuagint wording would be."[246] I. Howard Marshall sees in the language "a descent subsequent to the ascent, that is, Christ descending in and through the Sprit's bestowal of gifts on the church".[247] Other commentators make less of an issue of Paul's change of direction, saying that Paul "does not intend to quote literally but rather ... to elucidate a passage by showing how that which in the Psalter was said concerning *God,* attained its fulfilment in *Christ*" and that "*the apostle had every right to make this application, for the Victor receives the spoils with a view to giving them away. The giving is implied in the receiving* ... Now Christ *received* in order to *give*".[248]

A subtle, but important, change has occurred in Paul's description of how leadership is to work in the Church. He uses, for the first time, the word *domata* to describe the gifts bestowed on the Church by the ascended Christ. The word means, not a transient "manifestation", nor a ministry perfected by practice, but rather a permanent bequest. It is derived from a verb describing the action

---

[244]*Ibid.*

[245]Bruce, *op. cit.:* An early targumic rendering is found in the Peshitta: *"Thou hast ascended on high; thou hast led captivity captive; thou hast given gifts to men".* A later amplification appears in the traditional Targum on the Psalter: *"... thou hast taught the words of the law; thou hast given gifts to men."*

[246]Bruce, p. 342, see his footnote.

[247]I. Howard Marshall, *Ephesians* in *Eerdmans Commentary on the Bible,* ed. James D. G. Dunn (Eerdmans, 2003) p. 1390.

[248]William Hendriksen, *Ephesians* in *New Testament Commentary* series (Banner of Truth, 1976), pp. 190–191.

of bestowing *(didomi)*, and thus is always noticed by the fact that it is not deserved or developed, but received as a gracious endowment. Therefore, Vine explains, *domata* "lends greater stress to the concrete character of the gift, than to its beneficent nature".[249]

The strength of meaning can be gleaned from Paul's construct in Ephesians 4:11: "He gave some *'as'* [or *'to be'*] apostles ..." In order words, *He gave the gifts, and the gifts were* people. Hendriksen writes: "The person is the gift, and the gift is the person; the person *becomes* what God wants to express of Himself, and do in a particular context. The emphasis in this passage does not lie on the apostles, prophets, etc. as officers, but as gifts of Christ to his church."[250] Calvin puts it: "That we have ministers of the Gospel is His gift; that they excel in necessary gifts is His gift; that they execute the trust committed to them, is likewise His gift."[251] Simpson and Bruce add, rather poetically, that "[a]postles and prophets do not spring up at random; they are largesses from His royal exchequer of grace, shafts of His polishing, arrows hid in His mighty quiver".[252] Bruce, in his other commentary, suggests a distinction between the "varieties of gifts" in Corinthians and what Paul is dealing with here:

> *Whereas in 1 Corinthians 12:4–11 the 'varieties of gifts' are the diverse ministries allocated by the Spirit to individual members of the church, ... here the 'gifts' are the persons who exercise those ministries and who are said to be 'given' by the ascended Christ to his people to enable them to function and*

---

[249] *Vine's Expository Dictionary of New Testament Words* (Macdonald, undated), p. 487.

[250] Hendriksen, *op. cit.,* p. 195.

[251] John Calvin, *Calvin's Commentaries on the Epistles of Paul the Apostle to the Galatians, Ephesians, Philippians and Colossians,* trans. T. H. L. Parker (Eerdmans, 1979), p.178.

[252] Simpson and Bruce, *op. cit.,* p. 94.

develop as they should.[253]

Good and godly leaders at this level, then, are not only gifted; they *are* in themselves a gift, made up of a mixture of the gifts and talents built into them by the Creator; the gift of parents and mentors, who have grown their character and skills; and then the "graces" which come with the Gift of the Holy Spirit. They have become, to quote John Wimber, God's "pocket change", which He can spend as He wishes.

In enumerating the gift ministries (verse 11), "It is not Paul's intention to furnish us with a complete list of office-bearers"[254] but, as most commentators agree, he is creating a representative rather than an exhaustive list of "styles". However, we may make a case for the fact that some are essential (and called "foundational") to the Church's existence and nature.[255] Their work is to take God's missional people into God's presence in worship, to discern the missional direction in which God's presence is leading them, and to advance God's missional purpose with and through those people, taking them to their God-appointed destiny.

This latter point raises the idea that there are four basic types of leader, with styles or expressions of personality that appear in the context of the leader's work of leading so that, when all four are, or have been, in play, the outcome is wholeness, maturity or balance among those being led. The overall goal of godly leaders of the four basic kinds which Paul lists (apostle/evangelist,[256]

---

[253]Bruce, *op. cit.,* p. 345. (See his footnote, where he says "in the Corinthians passages about gifts the Greek words are *diaireseis ... carismaton*" and adds "neither word is used in Ephesians".)

[254]Hendriksen, *op. cit.,* p. 195.

[255]F. F. Bruce, commenting on this passage compared with Ephesians 2:20 and 1 Corinthians 12:28, emphasises apostles, prophets and teachers as the "offices of most import" (*op. cit.,* p. 346).

[256]I place these two side by side because of their pioneering, gospel-advancing nature and effect, although where the evangelist evangelises (proclaims

prophet, pastor and teacher), is two-fold:

1. to equip the members of the church to do their jobs (verse 12a); and
2. to lead the church to maturity of faith and efficiency of function (verses 12b–16).

The idea of "equipping" has to do with faith as well as function, with the repair of the person and making them battle-ready.[257] The three phrases in the text were fatally separated by commas in the older English translations:

> *For the perfecting of the saints, for the work of the ministry, for the edifying of the body of Christ.* (KJV)

"There should be no comma between the first and second phrases"[258] and, in fact, some commentators suggest, "no comma at all in the verse".[259] "The resultant idea is that Christ gave some men as apostles ... etc. for the purpose of 'perfecting' ... or *providing the necessary equipment* for all the saints for the work of ministering to each other so as to build up the Body of Christ."[260] Paul concludes the section with what I see as the missional goal of every church, which is that: "*as each part is working properly*, promotes the body's growth in building itself up in love" (verse 16, emphasis mine).

---

the gospel to unbelievers and invites their commitment), the apostle does that and more, by laying the foundations of good doctrine, community formation and leadership so that the result is, not just new believers, but a new church.

[257]The word is *katartismos,* meaning to *complete thoroughly,* that is, *repair* (literally or figuratively) or *adjust:* – fit, frame, mend, (make) perfect (-ly join together), prepare, restore. It was used of the mending of nets (Matthew 4:21) and, in common usage, the setting of a broken limb.

[258]Hendriksen, *op. cit.,* p. 198.

[259]*Ibid.*

[260]*Ibid.*

*From a Pauline perspective, we will argue against any vision of ministry that sees ordained leadership as the constitutive mark of the churches' life. Ministry lives for the service of the church as the church lives for the service of the gospel in the world. We start with the body and derive from that the functions of its members, not with official functionaries as if somehow the body derived its meaning from them. We will call into question the claim that those who are ordained as priests or ministers should take to themselves the whole diversity of gifts that Paul thought belonged to the body of Christ. Why should any one person be expected or required to be equally adept at administration, preaching, pastoral care, spiritual healing, spiritual direction? More often the gift of leadership today lies in discerning and encouraging in each congregation the recognition and development of those gifts the spirit distributes among us. However, Paul recalls to us the centrality of proclamation in the mission and up-building of the church. When he puts apostleship first among the gifts, it is not the apostle as overseer or orderer he stresses, but the apostle as **diakonos**, intermediary between God and humankind, proclaimer of the word.*[261]

In other words, the church is the primary vehicle through which every believer should discover, be trained in and released to use their gifts and thus grow by giving those gifts to the whole Body. Therefore, I note, with others, that the goal is not the fame and prominence of the leader/s, but their eventual redundancy! "The New Testament affords no hint of a priestly caste … but at the universal priesthood of believers … In the theocracy of grace there is in fact no laity."[262] The gift ministries have a role in relation to the "saints", namely equipping, resourcing, making ready,

---

[261]Bartlett, *op. cit.,* p. 55.
[262]Simpson and Bruce, *op. cit.,* p. 95.

building aptitude in them for the task of ministry.

This is the church being missional, in that every believer is seen, valued, trained and released to follow Christ in His Mission, inside and outside the church's walls. Before they "disappear", leaders will need to have given themselves away, to have taught, modelled, trained, encouraged, nurtured and then released every member of the church into full functionality.

The Levites and the Ark

In the Old Testament, when God chose to live among His covenant people Israel, He instructed Moses, their leader, about the structure within which He would be accommodated, and His Nature revealed. The Ark of the Covenant, and specifically the mercy seat between the cherubim, was the place where God would reside, and the *Shekinah*,[263] or manifest presence of God, was signified by a pillar of cloud by day and a pillar of fire by night, which rested on the mercy seat. Whenever the cloud lifted and moved, it was a signal to Israel that they needed to break camp and follow.[264] The Ark was made at God's instruction, and there were specific guidelines for its storage, its erection and its transportation. In this latter regard, responsibility to care for and carry the Ark was given to a very specific order of Israelites, the Kohathites, one of the

---

[263]"... the radiance, glory, or presence of God, 'dwelling' in the midst of His people, is used by Targumist and Rabbi to signify God Himself ... The Shekinah, the nearest Jewish equivalent to the Holy Spirit, became, with other Old Testament ideas or derivatives, Word, Wisdom, Spirit, etc., a bridge between man's corporeality and God's transcendence. If the term is late, the concept saturates both Testaments. It underlies the notion of God dwelling in His sanctuary (Exodus 25:8, etc.) or among His people (Exodus 29:45f. etc.). These and other cognate passages use the root verb *shakan,* 'to dwell', from which Shekinah, the abiding presence, is derived", ed. J. D. Douglas, *The New Bible Dictionary* (Inter-varsity Fellowship, 1967), p. 1174.
[264]Exodus 40:34–38, etc.

Levite clans (Numbers 3:28–31; 4:4, 5, 15; cf. 10:33–36). They led Israel over the Jordan into their heritage (Joshua 3). They led Israel into battle on numerous occasions (e.g. Joshua 6:6–7), carrying the Ark on their shoulders. When the Ark was captured by the Philistines, and later recaptured by David, the first attempt to return it to Jerusalem was flawed (it was carried on an ox wagon), resulting in God's displeasure and judgment (2 Samuel 6:1–11). When the correct discipline was restored, and the Ark was carried on the shoulders of appointed and anointed leaders, the result was revival (2 Samuel 6:12ff).

From this account, I want to apply some lessons about leadership:

- God's manifest presence is promised to His people, symbolised by the Ark and the accompanying cloud;
- God's glorious presence (*Shekinah*) is the focus of worship (and, in fact, where He "meets" a worshipping people. See Psalm 22:3 in the ASV, BBE, KJV, RV, renditions);
- God's accompanying presence is the guarantor of guidance and victory for a missional people; and
- God appoints a tribe to serve Him (Levites), a clan from within that tribe to be priests to Him (Aaronites), and a sub-clan among that clan to serve and carry His Presence (Kohathites).

Leaders in the modern Church can take (and often have taken) these lessons too seriously or too lightly; too seriously in that they become the literal, only mediators of God's presence *(vicarius Christi)*, and thus create an unbridgeable gap between clergy and laity; or too lightly in that they forget that they *are* to facilitate the coming together of God's Church as a Temple, where every stone has a purpose, every gathering is about God's presence dwelling among us, and the worship of God is its motivation for community and mission. Leaders are no substitute for the present

God being manifestly among His people, nor can they manipulate God's presence by what they do. However, they do need to take, with the right amount of seriousness, the fact that God uses human means to facilitate His presence and ministry, and that this is their primary work, rendered by faith and prayer and sensitively responding to the promptings of God the Holy Spirit.

The throne and the creatures

Two descriptions of creatures carrying the presence of the Creator are found in Ezekiel 1:4–11a and Revelation 4:6–8, where we encounter four creatures who surround God's throne and also seem to carry it.[265] It is interesting that the Jewish Talmud taught that the four quadrants of Israel's encampment in the wilderness were "fronted" by the four primary tribes of Judah, Dan, Ephraim and Reuben, and that their banners held the images of Lion, Eagle, Ox and Man respectively.[266] And that a long time before they first appeared to Ezekiel. Ezekiel's vision records the creatures as having four faces each, namely the faces of a human, an ox, a lion and an eagle. John's vision in Revelation describes each of the four having a single face: one a human, one an ox, one a lion and one an eagle. The Church Fathers, as well as numerous modern commentaries and traditions, refer to the creatures as symbolic of the four Gospels. Thus, for example, they suggest that Luke writes a very "human" story of Jesus; Mark's Gospel symbolised by the ox; John in his Gospel, expresses glory and awe, soaring

---

[265]Jesus Asurmendi Ruiz, *Ezekiel* in *The International Bible Commentary*, ed. William Farmer (The Liturgical Press, 1998), pp. 1057-8, writes: "… what we see here is a way of speaking of the personal presence of God … The interest of this passage [lies] in the affirmation of God's presence in the midst of the people, wherever they are."

[266]Carl Friedrich Keil and Franz Delitzsch, *Commentary on the Old Testament* (Hendrickson, 2002), 1:659-660, quoting Flavius Josephus, *The Complete Works of Josephus* (Kregel, 1981), s.v. Ant. XVIII, v3.

beyond all other views and, like the eagle, looking at Jesus on earth from a heavenly vantage point. Other authors have arranged their parallels differently from the one I suggest above. Examples from church history show how authors attributed a "type" to each Gospel, as illustrated by the following table from the Catholic Resources website:[267]

EARLY CHRISTIAN AUTHOR	HUMAN	LION	OX	EAGLE
St Irenaeus of Lyons	Matthew	John	Luke	Mark
Augustine of Hippo	Mark	Matthew	Luke	John
Pseudo-Athanasius	Matthew	Luke	Mark	John
St Jerome	Matthew	Mark	Luke	John

Richard Burridge, in his book, *Four Gospels: One Jesus?* concurs with St Jerome's arrangement, describing the four Gospel writers seeing Christ as human (Matthew), lion (Mark), ox (Luke) and eagle (John).[268] In addition to the connection between each symbol and the Gospel writers, consider that Matthew's genealogy of Jesus starts from Abraham (Judaic), Mark's from Isaiah's Messenger (Pioneer/Missional), Luke's from Adam (Human) and John's from God (Eternity, Glory).[269] What is common to all the above

---

[267] www.catholicresources.org/Art/Evangelists_symbols.htm.

[268] Richard A. Burridge, *Four Gospels, One Jesus?* (Eerdmans, 1994), pp. 24-27.

[269] Judson Cornwall opts for a similar arrangement in his book, *Profiles of a*

views is that there is rich diversity in expressing the dimensions of the character of Christ, which have prevailed from early in the history of the Church.

I want to take the liberty here to present my own associative categorisation of the four creatures in relation to the four Gospels, as: Matthew/ox (representing workmanlike attention to detail); Mark/lion (action, power and territorial advancement); Luke/ human (compassion and inclusivity); and John/eagle (revelation and mysticism).

But how do the Gospel writers and these traditions address the subject of leadership? In their book, *Resurrecting Excellence*, L. Gregory Jones and Kevin R. Armstrong state that one of the measurements of excellence for missional churches and their leaders is "how congregations and pastors are bearing witness to the presence and power of God".[270] They continue: "What if excellence were articulated as a response to the question, 'Where is the presence and power of God being manifested in this congregation's life, in this person's life, in this person's pastoral leadership?'"[271] While, as mentioned earlier, the extreme application of this position has led in the past to the elevation of clergy as *vicarius Christi*,[272] the point is made well enough to establish an important and, I think, biblically supported criterion of success for leadership.

Keeping in mind these symbolic expressions of God's presence, whether on a throne (John) or a chariot (Ezekiel), being "carried"

Leader (Logos International, 1980).

[270]Jones and Armstrong, *op. cit.,* loc 151.

[271]Jones and Armstrong, *op. cit.,* loc 141.

[272]Jones and Armstrong put it this way: "... in one view, a high church sensibility, the pastor is sent from God to serve as the mediator of God's word in the pulpit and the sacramental presider in Christ's stead at the table; in the other view, a low church sensibility, the pastor is called out from the community to serve particular functions that the community needs to have fulfilled", *op. cit.,* loc 1055.

by the four creatures, I propose that an acceptable metaphor of worshippers (with the missional purpose of escorting, promoting or carrying God's manifest presence) and, therefore, of four types of leader, calls our attention to:

- The leader as *pastoral person* – the face of a *human* (Luke)
- The leader as *prophetic visionary* – the face of an *eagle* (John)
- The leader as *teacher/informant* – the face of an *ox* (Matthew)
- The leader as *apostolic pioneer/builder* – the face of a *lion* (Mark)

These are not watertight categories, and there is much overlap between them. Nor can one be dogmatic about them regarding each symbol and its meaning – these are merely mine. Additionally, I want to make the disclaimer that I do not propose, nor support, the easy allocation of titles such as "Prophet" and "Apostle" to spiritual leaders (in fact, I question whether leaders should have "titles" at all). I rather propose that we learn something more about our work from these metaphors, without indulging in the pretentiousness of title-seeking. The metaphors provide a framework to describe the specialised role distinctions of a category of New Testament Church leadership which Paul calls *domata*.[273]

---

[273]In the NT, the words "lead", "leadership" or "leader" are derived variously from seven Greek words; two of these are used pejoratively, but illustrate very important elements of the kind of leadership God approves:

i. *Katakurieuo* is the verb used by Jesus in contrasting the way the rulers of the Gentiles lead or rule (Matthew 20:25, etc.) which is to lord it over, to control or subjugate. It implies harsh measures of control, and the abuse of people by positional power. It is used in 2 Corinthians 1:24, where Paul disavows the use of this kind of power by himself and his team. He says, in effect, that genuine Kingdom leaders would never do that, and that, while its effect on people is subjugation and demoralisation, the apostolic goal is rather joy for those they lead.

ii. *Archo*, similarly, refers to the act of being first, to rule by outranking. Jesus uses it as a parallel, explanatory phrase in Mark's rendering (10:42) of what we discussed above; thus, those Gentile rulers who put themselves first exercise harsh control over them. He contrasts these leadership attitudes (firstness and harshness) with the kind that would characterise Kingdom leaders, namely put yourself last, be a servant/slave, and God will give you His kind of authority. The Kingdom is an upside-down Kingdom. It lives by dying, it rises by descending, it leads by serving.

iii. *Hegeoumai* is used 27 times as a verb in the middle voice, which means to command or to lead by both example and rank. Some of its most striking usages are in Hebrews 13, where the writer calls the church to remember (7), obey (17) and salute (24) those who lead them, and who have acquired that position by their example and by their care/concern for the people.

iv. *Kratos* is used in adverbial or in noun form, 12 times in the NT. It means vigour(ous) or might(y), and is applied to mean dominion or strength, thus Revelation 1:6.

v. *Poimen/Poimaino* – The noun (*Poimen*) is used as the very evocative title ("Pastor" or "Shepherd") of one of the gift ministries of Ephesians 4:11, albeit in a grammatical format where it is adjectively linked to "teacher", thus making the fourth gift ministry the "pastoring teacher" or, as some have translated it, the "teaching pastor". It conveys the caring, nurturing function of a leader as a shepherd, leading his flock by walking ahead of them, providing sweet grazing and refreshment, protecting them from predators and guiding them to safety and destiny (Psalm 23). It is introduced in Matthew's rendition of Micah 5:2 (Matthew 2:6) and, interestingly, to describe the Messiah's rule with a rod of iron in Revelation 12:5, 19:15.

vi. *Hodegēo*, from *Hodēgos*, means to conduct, guide, or show the way, thus also conveying the idea of walking ahead to lead followers to a destination. It is applied to the Messiah's saving action (Revelation 7:17) and to the illuminating guidance of the Holy Spirit (John 16:13).

vii. *Proistemi,* and its derivation *Proistomenos,* is the word used in the primary New Testament text I have been exploring, i.e. Romans 12:8. It is a very evocative verb, which literally means to stand to the front and, by implication, to step to the front with intent to take a group to its goal. It is used, in its variants, to describe the rule of elders (1 Timothy 3:5; 5:17). Thus, it carries the idea, not only of leadership, but of stewardship or management.

Secular business models

The list of different types of leaders offered by Paul in Ephesians 4:11 runs in interesting parallel with modern proponents in the secular field of leadership development. Dr Christo Nel has designed a measurement instrument to define whether a leader's style and its effect on the group takes the form of improved Vision, Interdependence, Structure or Action. His management model therefore uses the acronym VISA.[274] Other organisations offer different headings, such as Wilson Learning's Social Styles of Driver, Amiable, Expressive, and Analytical;[275] or the Myers-Briggs categories, which identify temperaments of the persons in an organisation, including leaders, as SJ or Realistic Achiever; SP or Sensual Entertainer; NT or Thinking Organiser; NF or Sensitive Shepherd.[276] Dr Itschak Adizes presents a similar model, in which he identifies the four leadership types as Producer, Administrator, Entrepreneur and Integrator.[277] The basic distinctions are between issues of how a leader treats followers (with greater or lesser levels of assertiveness); and which socio-emotional "tone" or personality is prevalent as the leader does his or her work. Most of the models I have studied, work in a quadrant, as illustrated by Diagram 5 below, so that four basic styles, or types, of leadership are observable. What we will discover is that some people fit into one quadrant more clearly than others, while some are on a

---

[274]Dr Christo Nel, *VISA to the HILT* Workshop, in the *PEAK Leadership Seminar* (© The Village Leadership Consulting, 2012).

[275]Wilson Learning Corporation, *Managing Interpersonal Relationships* (Wilson Learning, 1978), p. 4.

[276]Roy M. Oswald and Otto Kroeger, *Personality Type and Religious Leadership* (Alban Institute, 1988), Kindle edition, loc. 540, cf. also David Keirsey and Marilyn Bates, *Please Understand Me II* (Prometheus Nemesis Books, 1998), chapter 9.

[277]Ichak Adizes, *Management/Mismanagement Styles: How to Identify a Style and What to Do about It* (Adizes Institute Publishing, 2004).

boundary between two or more of the quadrants, resulting in a mixture of gifting or styles. Thus, for example, using the categories of the Wilson Learning organisation, a leader may be an "Expressive Driver", an "Analytical Driver", an "Amiable Expressive" or an "Amiable Analyst".[278]

Paul's list, in my opinion, has much in common with the categories just described and illustrated below, especially if we think of them by outcome or effect. All the gift ministries of Ephesians 4:11 have a leadership component, but their *way* of leading (style) will be unique to their specific gift-mix, and will be noticed by their effect on a group.

> *Ephesians 4:11–13 indicates that certain ministries in the form of individuals (apostles, prophets, evangelists, pastor-teachers) are given to the church by Christ, in order that the church fulfill her present task (verse 12), and, at the end, reach the goal set for her (verse 13). These ministries of leadership are given to enable the church to carry out its fundamentally missiological purpose in the world: to announce and demonstrate the new creation in Jesus Christ. This purpose necessarily involves leaders in* **equipping and guiding the body in those ecclesial practices that form the community** *in a oneness that is a living demonstration of the ethics of God's reign.*[279]

Stanley Grenz explains the functions of the four-fold gift ministries (gifts to the wider church) as follows:

> *Apostles played a significant foundational role in the early church as the guardians and pioneer propagators of the gospel. Prophets served as mouthpieces for special divine communication. Evangelists carried on itinerant missionary work, using*

---

[278]Wilson Learning Corporation, *op. cit.,* p. 9.
[279]Guder, *op. cit.,* loc 3295 (emphasis mine).

churches established by the apostles as a basis (for example, Apollos in Acts 18:27–28). The example of Timothy's sojourn in Ephesus suggests that pastors and teachers worked more directly within a specific locale for an extended period of time in order to edify the congregation through this focussed ministry. The pastor exercises leadership within a local congregation, but with ramifications beyond the local setting. Fundamentally, the pastoral office is to facilitate the well-functioning of the community. To this end, the pastor keeps before the members the vision of the community ideal ...[280]

Thus, the *apostolic/evangelistic* gift will seek new frontiers and lead the group toward advancement or *achievement*; the *prophetic* gift will lead the group through instilling a sense of *excitement* or *encouragement*; the *teaching* gift will instil a sense of *stability* in the group through imparting timely biblical information; and the *pastoral* gift will develop the group's *security* by modelling and instilling a strong sense of love and community. The leadership component has to do with *moving the group toward its goal*. The stylistic component has to do with how the group are going to change and feel along the way while this particular person leads them, and also determines some of the specific sub-goals that will be achieved.

---

[280]Grenz, *op. cit.*, pp. 562-3.

Diagram 5: The Leadership Window

OX	NT ORGANISER ANALYST THINKER ADMINISTRATOR DIRECTOR STABILISER STRUCTURE TEACHER	SJ AUTOCRAT DRIVER CATALYST ENTREPRENEUR ACHIEVER PIONEER ACTION APOSTLE	**LION**
HUMAN	NF DEMOCRAT AMIABLE MAINTAINER INTEGRATOR COUNSELLOR ENABLER INTERDEPENDENCE PASTOR	SP VISIONARY EXPRESSIVE ENTERTAINER PRODUCER EXHORTER INSPIRER VISION PROPHET	**EAGLE**

In addition to these, several authors use, as a model of ministry, the three offices of leadership mentioned and modelled in the Old Testament and which, in many traditions and commentaries, are ascribed to the Messiah, namely Priest, Prophet and King.[281] Daniel Migliore is one author among several who uses this triad to create a model for leadership in the missional church:

> *The missionary activity of the church should be understood as a participation in the mission of Jesus Christ (in) his three-fold office as priest, prophet, and king. The doctrine of the threefold office of Christ also brings clarity and direction to the understanding of the church and its mission. The church is called to participate in his work and to be guided by it. Hence the church's mission will always include the priestly*

---

[281]Osmer, *op. cit.,* pp. 28-29, and Dr Coenie Burger, *op. cit.*

activity of proclaiming forgiveness and reconciliation in the
name of Christ; it will always include the prophetic activity
of teaching God's will made known in Christ and denounc-
ing injustice and oppression as opposing God's will; and it
will always include the royal activity of being a protector and
advocate of the weak and lowly and using what resources and
influence it has not for its own sake but for the sake of God's
coming reign of justice and peace that has dawned in power
in the royal life, death, and resurrection of Christ.[282]

These three "anointed" offices, later all displayed in Jesus the Anointed One, were expressed through leaders appointed by God, at God's discretion, so that those who play a role in God's missional story fall into one of the three categories, whether Aaron and succeeding high priests, Saul and David the first kings, or the prophets from Samuel to Malachi. For the sake of consistency and completeness, I want to propose the addition of a fourth, the Teacher/Sage. This is not just so that the four-fold quadrant idea is neatly completed by these offices, but also because this function of leadership is alluded to in the Old Testament, especially in the post-exilic period (Ezra 7:6, 11, 12 and Nehemiah 8:1, 4, 9, 13), and specifically mentioned in prophetic literature in the context of the restored covenant (Isaiah 30:20–21). The concept of the "Rabbi" was introduced and later entrenched in the intertestamental period, where "teachers of the law"[283] were linked with every synagogue, and those who could comment or teach on any biblical issue were accorded the title. Jesus is called "Rabbi" on many occasions, as referenced in Matthew, Mark and John.

The continuity between Matthew's church and the synagogue

---

[282]Daniel Migliore, *Faith Seeking Understanding: An Introduction to Christian Theology*, 2nd ed (Eerdmans, 2004), Kindle edition, locs 5335-5343, cf. Barrett, et al., Osmer.
[283]Luke 5:17, etc.

provides one possible model for contemporary ministry – that of the Rabbi ... The model of religious leader as interpreter of Torah is one that deserves careful consideration ... this is to say that the religious leader not only preaches the gospel but interprets the range of the canon for faithful people ... the religious leader is given those keys that "bind and loose", i.e. the Christian scribe helps the community of faith determine which regulations are binding and which are not. Shifted to our time, this suggests that the Christian minister might consider the obligation to take more seriously her or his role as moral guide for the community of faith, a role often denigrated in our worry about "moralism".[284]

It also runs parallel to the idea of the "Sage" as a purveyor of wisdom, who was consulted by the people of God for better understanding and application of truth.[285] Thus, "Rabbis" led the people through truth, giving them necessary, godly information and securing them in obedience to God's Word, and giving discernment or judgment in ethical and other practical matters. It is thereafter assumed as a necessary role of leaders throughout the New Testament, and notably by Paul (Romans 12:8; 1 Corinthians 12:29; Ephesians 4:11, etc.).[286] In the church of Acts, the

---

[284]Bartlett, *op. cit.*, p. 87.

[285]The Judges, whose story is told in the biblical book of that title, fulfilled this role in the period between Joshua and the appointing of the first king. The word "judge" refers to governance or leadership, but includes dispensing wisdom (see, especially, Deborah in Judges 4:4).

[286]*Ibid.*, p. 50: "Teachers are mentioned only in this paragraph (1 Corinthians 12:28–29) in Paul, so we really have no context by which to decide how he understood their function. (There may be a parallel in Romans 12:7 where 'the teacher' is to use that charism 'in teaching'.) A sheer guess would be that unlike the Apostles and Prophets, Teachers were local leaders and it may be that while the Prophets spoke oracles, the teachers interpreted tradition. We simply do not know. Apostleship is the first gift listed, and the implication here as elsewhere is that special authority accrues to the

functional necessity of teachers, alongside those of apostles and prophets, is assumed by Luke (Acts 13:1ff.), and Paul also makes it the primary skill required in leaders who are to be remunerated for their ministry (I Timothy 5:17–18).

Richard Osmer, although initially only referencing "the three-fold office of Christ" (i.e. prophet, priest and king),[287] nevertheless also goes on to discuss ministry as completing *four* tasks, viz. Priestly Listening (Priest); Prophetic Discernment (Prophet); Servant Leadership (King) and Sagely Wisdom (Teacher).[288] I will use those four categories for the reasons stated above, and invite you to think about your style and its application using my model as one of its discerning lenses. In this model, the apostolic function parallels that of the "king" of the Old Testament *charisms*, in that the king is the builder who establishes and shapes the "kingdom", lays its foundations and expands its influence. "Nonetheless, we need to recall that the charismatic church functioned as well as it did (and how well was that?) not only because of the pressure of the eschaton but also because of the authority of the apostle."[289] There are, as I mentioned earlier, some very poor applications of especially the apostolic gift in evidence in the modern Church. (For example, the idea of leaders being called "Kings"[290] or "Apostles", without the necessary proviso, echoing Jesus, that a "king"

---

apostles. Beyond that the relationship between gift or function and authority is far from clear."

[287]Osmer, *op. cit.*, pp. 27-29.

[288]*Ibid.* These names form the titles of Osmer's four chapters describing the four tasks of Practical Theology.

[289]Bartlett, *op. cit.*, p. 54.

[290]There is a teaching going around in some circles with which I am acquainted, that says leaders are either priests (spiritual leaders) or kings (financial/visionary leaders). Others have taken the title for the senior "apostolic" leader or senior pastor of mega-churches. The title goes together with the treatment of such people as royalty, including thrones on the platform, gold jewellery and bodyguards.

in the context of the New Testament Church is, in fact, the one who is least, who takes a servant's role). Let me repeat it here – if you want to be a king, says Jesus – get into the dust!

Commenting on Paul's self-introduction: "Paul, a servant ... called to be an apostle ..." (Romans 1:1), Robert Mounce writes:

> *Not for a moment did he elevate himself above his assigned position as a servant of God, set apart and called to serve in the interests of the proclamation of the gospel ... What the world calls success has led many gifted leaders gradually to assume a celebrity posture ... It would be well for Christian leaders to begin each day acknowledging before God that they are His servants.*[291]

Looking through the leadership styles window

With the foregoing context and disclaimers in mind, I suggest that the four essential ministry gifts, when seen together with their secular parallels, offer a balanced picture of the spiritual gift of leadership as it operates in the Church at large, and may be implemented practically in local church life. Leadership, although having important common denominators undergirding individual style, is designed to build communities. In the case of the church, the desired effect of good leadership is the founding and development of vibrant communities of faith pursuing effective missional purpose.

Any and every group needs to be facilitated, or led, in four dimensions of group experience, cohesion and achievement, which were well named by Bruce Tuckman as "Forming, Storming, Norming and Performing".[292] To use different terms, every

---

[291]Robert H. Mounce, *Romans* in *The New International Commentary* (Broadman & Holman, 1995), p. 60.
[292]Bruce Tuckman, "Developmental sequence in small groups" in *Psychological Bulletin.* **63** (6): 384–99. doi:10.1037/h0022100. PMID 14314073.

group, including every church, has to be Established, Encouraged, Secured and Informed. In order for these outcomes to be achieved, the four types of leader suggested by Paul, expressed in the historical church and reinforced by modern secular authors, must all be given their place. We will examine them one by one in what follows.

King/apostolic pioneer, planter and builder

Spiritual leaders may lead by the power and influence of their *apostolic/pioneering/building* capacity. This type of leader will be the most assertive in style, putting a hand forth to "take charge", like a king, and employing great vigour and strength of leadership to get the evangelistic job done, churches planted and built, and new barriers conquered. The particular message and work of apostles has to do with challenging unbelievers to believe, so that this gift goes together, in my view, with that of the *evangelist*, in starting any church on the journey to its goal.

> *Ephesians 4 suggests leadership teams expressing varieties of gifts and functions. The order in which Paul presents the gifts of the various leaders may not have been significant in his mind, but in terms of our discussion, that order is noteworthy. The purpose and direction of the church as a missionary people shape apostolic leadership.*[293]

The mention of the word *apostle* raises controversy, both in biblical interpretation and in modern praxis. In discussing the gift of both apostle and prophet (see below), many commentators hold a "cessationist" view, i.e. that apostles became redundant when the canon was completed. Others hold that there have only been 12 apostles, and even that the 11 were premature in appointing

---

Retrieved 2008-11-10. Reprinted with permission in Group Facilitation, Spring 2001.
[293]Guder, *op. cit.*, p. 214.

Matthias after the ascension; instead, they should have waited for Paul to take the place of Judas. According to my reading, the New Testament names more than 11 or 12 apostles (apart from Paul), including Apollos, Priscilla and Aquila (Romans 16:3), as well as Andronicus and Julia (Romans 16:7), while Luke certainly seems to include Barnabas among the number (Acts 14:14). If we were to take a narrow view of apostleship being based on the criterion: "Have I not seen Jesus our Lord?"[294] then there have indeed been no apostles since the first century AD. However, I concur with Gordon Fee, who says:

> *This might be too narrow a view, based strictly on Paul's own personal experience ... Only when "apostle" is used in a non-Pauline sense of "guarantors of the traditions" would the usage be narrowed to the first century.*[295]

My emphasis here, however, is on apostolic *function*, rather than title. I believe, with Alan Roxburgh, that the Church needs to recover its apostolicity, its sense of missionality, as a matter of urgency. "The gift of apostolic leaders is one that creates leaders, like Paul, who are driven by a passion to see the reality of the church as a missional people of God."[296] The term "apostle", says Gordon Fee, "has a sense of function as well as that of office or position. That is, it primarily had to do with some who were 'sent' by Christ to preach the gospel ... and ... those who founded churches as a result of their evangelizing, came to be known as *apostles*, a designation that had inherent in it a sense of position as well".[297]

---

[294]1 Corinthians 9:1.
[295]Fee, *Commentary on First Corinthians* (chapter 9:1–2), p. 397.
[296]Alan Roxburgh, in *Missional Church, op. cit.,* loc 3811.
[297]Fee, *op. cit.,* on 1 Corinthians 1:1, p. 30.

Face: Lion

In the heavenly scene which John saw, the exalted Christ, stepping forward to receive His inheritance, is seen as a slaughtered Lamb, but is called "the Lion of the tribe of Judah" (Revelation 5:5–6). The title refers to the blessing of Jacob over his sons: "Judah is a lion's whelp; from the prey, my son, you have gone up. He crouches down, he stretches out like a lion, like a lioness – who dares rouse him up?"

The lion, in natural habit and habitat, is a territorial animal, which establishes its territory by its strength and hunts its prey by skill. The "alpha male" lion rules his pride and seeks its expansion and wellbeing. He will defend it against external intrusion and internal dilution, and send out its best to make new prides and establish its domain over new territories. The lionesses are the true hunters, often working as a group, running down their prey with great speed, and inviting the pride to the kill, the lead female often waiting until the males and cubs have eaten before eating herself. The eyes of the lion will most often be looking forward, to the scene of the next hunt, new horizons for expansion, and a new place to shelter.

Biblical references to the lion as a symbol cover all the expected metaphorical links, such as strength, courage, conquest and ferocity. Isaiah 31:4 offers a summary:

> For this is what the LORD told me: "Just as a lion or a young lion growls over his objects of prey, – even when a whole band of shepherds is called out against it, it is not alarmed at their shouting or disturbed by their clamor – so the LORD of the Heavenly Armies will come down to do battle on Mount Zion and on its hill."

The lion-type leader is a confident, autocratic and forward-looking leader, seeking new territory to conquer, and healthy and successful progeny. The lion leader does not seek agreement or approval, only opportunity and new horizons. The lion represents the action-oriented, results-driven, apostolic leader.

In Mark's Gospel we discover Jesus as a man of determined, focused action. In describing how Jesus ministered to people, Mark uses the adverb "immediately"[298] more often than the other Gospel writers. He conveys the breathless excitement of an eyewitness reporter as he writes Simon Peter's version of the story of Jesus. His is not a theological treatise or a mystical interpretation of the story. It is the story itself, using the least possible number of words, and beginning the story with the shortest sermon recorded as having been preached by Jesus.[299] Mark's Gospel represents the forward-moving, territory-seeking Son of God coming with power to initiate His Kingdom on earth. The Gospel of a Lion, the king of beasts, on the move with a face like flint[300] and with empire in His eyes.

Role: Parent, builder, beneficent ruler

In the New Testament, there were at least three, if not four, marks or criteria validating apostolic leadership, namely "sentness" or calling; churches being established in new areas; recognition by other apostles; and signs and wonders.[301]

---

[298]"... directly, that is, at once or soon: – anon, as soon as, forthwith, immediately, shortly, straightway", *Strong's Dictionary of Greek Words,* 1890, e-Sword, the online Bible program.

[299]Mark 1:14–15: "Jesus went to Galilee and proclaimed the gospel about the kingdom of God. He said, 'The time is now! The kingdom of God is near! Repent, and keep believing the gospel!'"

[300]Isaiah 50:7.

[301]Bartlett mentions two, with a footnote including a third, in a comment on 2 Corinthians 3:1–2: "The passage nicely shows the twofold nature of Paul's apostolic authority: on the one hand, it derives from Christ, from the Spirit of God; on the other hand, it is validated by the churches Paul has founded." His footnote adds: "Gerd Theissen suggests that three forms of legitimacy were at stake between Paul and some of his 'apostolic' opponents: charismatic legitimacy (the call); traditional legitimacy (rootedness

The first mark is *sentness* or calling (from the understanding of the word *apostolos*, which carries the idea of a delegate or ambassador, implying being sent to foreign places on behalf of the sender). Christ's "sent ones", however, have a particular passion: the gospel is about the Sender. "Above all, in Paul there is devotion to the gospel. The churches exist for the sake of the gospel, and not the other way around."[302] Because of this emphasis, we can easily see the overlap of gifting between the apostle and the evangelist, in that both have a focus on the advancement of the church by the proclamation of the Good News and calling men and women to faith.

In 1 Corinthians 9:1–2, Paul, in defending his apostleship, establishes a second mark or criterion, namely "the establishing of new churches in *new areas* (cf. Romans 15:17–22, especially verse 20)".[303] The Christ who called and "sent" them, and whose calling clothes them "with life-long and church-wide authority over life and doctrine",[304] validates that calling with the fruit of

---

in Palestinian Judaism, or special authorization by an established church); and functional legitimacy (the practical 'workmanship' of the apostle). Paul, as my analysis would also suggest, was stronger in his charismatic and his functional legitimacy than in his 'traditional' legitimacy, and he stresses the call and the fruits of his work. (Gerd Theissen, *The Social Setting of Pauline Christianity: Essays on Corinth,* trans. John H. Schutz (Philadelphia: Fortress Press, 1982) 48–54" (*op. cit.,* p. 30). I believe it is important to reassert the other marks, such as miraculous signs. At a certain level, signs and wonders are markers of *Kingdom* competence, and resulting influence (Luke 11:20). Jesus attracted large crowds when He dealt with their sicknesses and demonic oppressions. They followed Him in numbers having seen that He spoke with authority, that sicknesses were healed by Him, and that demons fled when He spoke (Mark 1:23–39, etc.). This is not the only area in which competence attracts a following. Leaders are to be good at what they advertise. They are to be practitioners of the obedience and effectiveness to which they call others.

[302]Bartlett, *op. cit.,* p. 26.

[303]Fee, *op. cit.,* p. 395, emphasis mine.

[304]Hendriksen, *op. cit.,* p. 196.

apostleship.[305]

Discussing the role of a "missionary", which is the modern but, in my view, slightly weakened synonym for "apostle", Lesslie Newbigin defines their function and fruit:

> *[Paul's] task as a missionary is clear, limited, and – literally – fundamental. He is sent to lay the foundation stone of the church, and that stone is Christ. The result of his work, in other words, will be a community that acknowledges Jesus Christ as the supreme Lord of life. When this community exists, the missionary has done the work for which he was sent.*[306]

> *... I am bound to conclude, therefore, that Roland Allen is right in saying that a missionary's work is done when there has been called into being in any place a living church furnished with the means (Scripture, sacraments, and a ministry linking it with the universal church) by which it may learn and grow in obedience to Christ.*[307]

It seems clear that apostolic leadership has *founding, shaping and linking authority*. This calling and resultant expression of authority has much in common with that of a *king*. Saul, David and Solomon, Israel's first three kings, pioneered and led the creation, structuring, safety and prosperity of the Israelite kingdom or realm. This is the role of those who bring benevolent government to previously chaotic situations.

The metaphor of "king" can be extremely dangerous in a

---

[305] 1 Corinthians 9:2, cf. 2 Corinthians 12:12: "The signs of a true apostle were performed among you with utmost patience, signs and wonders and mighty works."

[306] Lesslie Newbigin, *The Open Secret: An Introduction to the Theology of Missions* (Eerdmans, 1995), Kindle edition, loc 1754.

[307] Newbigin, *op. cit.,* loc 1911, quoting Roland Allen, *Missionary Methods: St. Paul's, or Ours?* (Eerdmans, 1962).

power-hungry environment, and the disclaimers offered by the authors consulted need to be emphasised before I go further. The patriarchal systems prevalent in Greco-Roman society held forth, as Andrew Clarke speculates: "... characteristics of leadership (which) included position ('pride of place') accorded on the basis of honour and wealth, rather than proven leadership skills, administrative ability or other qualifications,"[308] which might have proved tempting for leadership in churches facing situations like that in Corinth. However, Clarke concludes his comments on 1 Corinthians 9: "Paul himself, in contrast to defending his authority, set an example for the believers in laying aside his rights, and he implored his correspondents to do likewise ... he urges the Corinthians to conform to his own pattern of weakness, not of power, and in so doing to follow Christ."[309] As he puts it in 1 Corinthians 4:6–13:

> *I have applied all this to Apollos and myself for your benefit, brothers and sisters, so that you may learn through us the meaning of the saying, "Nothing beyond what is written," so that none of you will be puffed up in favor of one against another. For who sees anything different in you? What do you have that you did not receive? And if you received it, why do you boast as if it were not a gift? Already you have all you want! Already you have become rich! Quite apart from us you have become kings! Indeed, I wish that you had become kings, so that we might be kings with you! For I think that God has exhibited us apostles as last of all, as though sentenced to death, because we have become a spectacle to the world, to angels and to mortals. We are fools for the sake of Christ, but you are wise in Christ. We are weak, but you are strong. You are held in honor, but we in disrepute. To the present hour*

---

[308]Clarke, *op. cit.,* p. 148.
[309]Clarke, *op. cit.,* p. 215.

we are hungry and thirsty, we are poorly clothed and beaten and homeless, and we grow weary from the work of our own hands. When reviled, we bless; when persecuted, we endure; when slandered, we speak kindly. We have become like the rubbish of the world, the dregs of all things, to this very day.

In making his position clear, Paul is asserting that "apostleship is regarded as a ministry of weakness, rather than status and grace"[310] and that, while "leadership in that society was dependent on an integrated power-base … Paul's own example and directives were opposed to such models. The nature of the Christian church and the message of the Christian gospel required a quite different style of leadership".[311] It is, as Max de Pree called it, "leading without power".[312] Analysing the equivalent temptation in the modern church, L. Gregory Jones and Kevin R. Armstrong write:

In a world of make-or-break rankings, mission statements, and business plans, "excellence" is too often interpreted as the capacity to come out ahead, to exercise strength at the expense of weakness – indeed, to leave encumbering weakness behind.[313]

The authors go on to say:

This dimension of resurrecting excellence runs counter to notions of excellence that rely on strength, efficiency, and influence. Christian understandings of excellence must always have at their heart a strong awareness of human frailty, brokenness, and even sin. Resurrecting excellence does not depend on moral perfection, workaholic behavior, or individual

---

[310]Clarke, *op. cit.*, p. 246.

[311]Clarke, *op. cit.*, p. 247.

[312]This phrase forms the title of his excellent book on servant leadership, *Leading Without Power* (Jossey-Bass, 1997).

[313]Jones and Armstrong, *op. cit.*, loc 86.

effectiveness. It depends on the intersection of human creativity with divine creativity and on communities of people who join together in a journey of faithfulness to God's inbreaking kingdom. In contemporary discussions of excellence, we are encouraged to "identify our strengths," "work from our strengths," "build on our strengths." But in Christian life, we cannot work only from our strengths. We must constantly seek to find that place where our weakness intersects with strength — God's strength as well as the strength of the community. Resurrecting excellence calls us to work outside the boundaries of our strengths and interests, to cultivate the whole of who we might become by the power of the Holy Spirit.[314]

The essential quality of a Kingdom leader, whether in the shape of apostle, prophet, pastor or teacher, is always, always, first a servant. The "king" is a humble king, a self-effacing, sacrificial leader, who lives with constant surprise and gratitude that

Christ Jesus our Lord … judged me faithful, appointing me to his service, though formerly I was a blasphemer, persecutor, and insolent opponent. But I received mercy … and the grace of our Lord overflowed for me with the faith and love that are in Christ Jesus. The saying is trustworthy and deserving of full acceptance, that Christ Jesus came into the world to save sinners, of whom I am the foremost.[315]

If we are called to be apostolic leaders, while being true to our calling and vision, and while stepping forward with determination to take people to the goal, we should heed simultaneously the call to a different model of leadership than the culture may tempt us to adopt. The leader of this kind is, to repeat Jim Collins, "a

---

[314]Jones and Armstrong, *op. cit.,* locs 584-589.
[315]1 Timothy 1:12–15 ESV.

paradoxical blend of personal humility and professional will",[316] both self-effacing and yet fiercely ambitious, not for self-aggrandisement, but for the company/group he or she leads to become great. In Matthew 20:25ff., Jesus teaches that, in order to become truly great, you will need to deliberately take the lowest role, and desire to see others, or the group, become great. The essence of the "great" leader is that he or she is a person who is energetically, intentionally and passionately focused on the wellbeing of the group they lead, to their own personal cost. The true leader is only happy when the *group* succeeds, or looks great. This seems to be what Paul is calling for among apostolic leaders, that they may come *first*,[317] but only by putting themselves *last*.[318]

Effect: Establishment and stability

In summary, apostolic leadership is regarded by Paul as catalytic, pioneering, parent-like[319] and foundational. It will have the visible effects suggested by each of these. Churches will be planted where there were none. Foundations of faith and truth that will last for generations will be established. Leaders will be raised up and developed, empowered and set in place. Churches will be networked in an interdependence of existence, mission and ministry. I will elaborate on this in chapter 9, but will note here that the role of a parent has many facets, including praying, modelling, speaking blessing,[320] providing, challenging, guiding, disciplining,[321] and leaving a legacy.[322]

---

[316]Jim Collins, *Good to Great* (Random House, 2001), p. 20.

[317]1 Corinthians12:28.

[318]1 Corinthians 9:9.

[319]1 Corinthians 4:15.

[320]Genesis 26:26–29.

[321]Proverbs 13:24; 22:15; 23:13–14; 29:15, cf. Hebrews 12:7–9.

[322]Thus, says Paul about his role as a father to the Corinthians: "For even if you have ten thousand guardians in your Christian life, you have only one father. For in your life in union with Christ Jesus I have become your father

> *[Paul] insists on his authority as a father, without wishing*
> *to be forced to carry it out in an authoritarian manner ...*
> *where Paul distances himself from the patterns of leadership*
> *in the voluntary associations and Graeco-Roman civic con-*
> *texts, this image of 'father' is not avoided ... but generally not*
> *in order to reinforce a personal **patria potestas**.*[323]

Paul uses the metaphor of father in a specific application here, and refers to his maternal heart over churches elsewhere. These narrow definitions and applications will be covered in more detail in chapter 9. Suffice it to say here that I think fathers are responsible to enable, empower and facilitate the discovery of their children's individual potential and goal achievement. A father is not meant to be a critic so much as a coach. He does not seek to live his life through his children, but facilitates their living their own lives and being the best possible version of themselves. He "calls out" their potentiality.

Paul describes his own passionate commitment as a leader in the letter to the Colossians (1:29), where he speaks of his responsibility to proclaim, to teach, to admonish, to impart wisdom, "so that we may present everyone mature [or fully rounded] in Christ". This, again, is the passion of a spiritual father: to see his children do well themselves, to find that quality that Jesus called "life to the full",[324] to enjoy the Kingdom of God as righteousness, peace and

---

by bringing the Good News to you. I beg you, then, to follow my example. For this purpose I am sending to you Timothy, who is my own dear and faithful son in the Christian life. He will remind you of the principles which I follow in the new life in union with Christ Jesus and which I teach in all the churches everywhere" (1 Corinthians 4:15-17, GNB). Paul's fatherly work involved birthing them in the gospel, guiding them in life, and providing ongoing care for them by connecting them with Timothy and the apostolic team.

[323]Clarke, *op. cit.*, pp. 221-222.
[324]John 10:10.

joy in the Holy Spirit.[325] What we say before God about our children, and what we say to them about their destinies, is lasting and transformational. When apostles have done their work as leaders, the effect on the church and its members will be *advancement, establishing the Church in faith.*

Frequency

A survey of American churches using the Myers-Briggs Temperament Instrument, showed that an SJ temperament, which strongly parallels the apostolic gift, occurs in 35% of US clergy (and 38% of the US population in general).[326] I have a hunch, based on personal contact and a demographic of church planting activity, that this gift occurs far more frequently in Africa, Asia and Latin America than the US statistics reveal.[327]

Leading through presence – priestly personhood

Spiritual leaders may lead by the power and influence of their pastoral personhood. This type of leader is high in care, compassion, mercy and selflessness, and affects a group with a sense of security and empowerment. This is the leader with the face of a *human*, the role of a *priest* and the effect of a *pastor.*

Face: Human

When God creates humanity, the intended purpose, and therefore the characteristics of the being he created, are clarified in the act

---

[325]Romans 14:17.

[326]From a survey conducted among a sample of 250 clergy, cited by Oswald and Kroeger, *op. cit.,* loc 540.

[327]See statistics on church planting and missionary expansion in Steve Addison's book, *Movements that Change the World* (Missional Press, 2009), pp. 125-128. These bear out the fact that, whereas church planting and attendance are in decline in Europe, the UK and even in the USA, the church is still growing rapidly in the majority world.

of creation by God's Word. Therefore, the human is the image (Hebrew *selem*,) or what Scot McKnight[328] calls *eikon*[329] of God (Genesis 1:26–27; 9:6). Aspects of this representative role include being a viceregent or steward but, most importantly, reflecting God's life quality, or what is most often called the "glory" of God (Psalm 8:4). The Hebrew word for "glory" has, as one of its shades of meaning, the idea of "copiousness", an overflow, or "overmuchness"[330] of the life force or power of whichever being is described. Humans are representatives of their Creator, if not in their corporeality, certainly in their relationality, their creativity, and specifically, their capacity for love. The image of God is not only displayed by humanity as strong and in control, but also in humanity as gentle, vulnerable and humble. Even when the *eikon* is cracked, it still carries a treasure: God's life.[331] Though distorted and caked with the mud of our failure, the image of God is still visible in humanity. "The astounding element of being an *Eikon* is not that humans are different from animals and the land and the sky and the stars, but that they, and they alone, *are like God somehow.*"[332] When we fast forward from Genesis to John's

---

[328]Scot McKnight, *A Community Called Atonement* (Abingdon Press, 2007), p. 17, etc.

[329]A transliteration of the Greek word for "image" or "picture".

[330]http://www.thefreedictionary.com.

[331]2 Corinthians 4:3–6. See Eugene Peterson's *Working the Angles: The Shape of Pastoral Integrity* (Eerdmans, 2000), Kindle edition, where he emphasises the pastor's role as a mediator of spiritual formation first and foremost, saying: "For a start, I can cultivate an attitude of awe. I must be prepared to marvel. This face before me, its loveliness scored with stress, is in the image of God" (loc 1790). "... Every meeting with another person is a privilege. In pastoral conversation I have chances that many never get as easily or as frequently – chances to spy out suppressed glory, ignored blessing, forgotten grace. I had better not miss them ... God wants to meet with this person; this person wants, unfocused as the want may be, to meet with God" (loc 1824).

[332]McKnight, *op. cit.,* p. 20.

Gospel, this all comes together in the incarnation of Christ. The epiphanies – revelations of God – in the Old Testament and ultimately in the incarnation (John 1:14–18), reveal a God who is "the Son of man",[333] with His glory veiled behind human flesh, His radiance obscured by blood and tears. God is not ashamed to be seen with human face, to be carried by human frailty. He is not ashamed to be called our God. It is His assumption of human nature that equips Jesus to be our mediating Saviour (John 1:1, 14–18; 1 Timothy 2:5; Hebrews 2:6–9). The one who identifies with us for salvific purpose must first be the son of man before He can be a divine Saviour (Daniel 3:25; Philippians 2:8). Mediation requires identification. The Redeemer is required first to be a Kinsman.[334]

Luke's Gospel portrays a Saviour who is touched by our weakness, who notices the poor, the weak, the marginalised and the broken. Luke, of the four Evangelists, connects Jesus with humanity more than the others. He most often mentions women, and records the stories of Mary and Elizabeth. As a Gentile himself, he most emphatically celebrates the participation of the Gentile roleplayers in the Gospel accounts, from a Syro-Phoenician woman to a Roman Centurion, to Simon of Cyrene. He also uses the most detail in describing the relationship of Jesus with children. In so doing, he calls us as leaders, first of all, to be like Jesus, fellow humans with those we seek to lead. Although I will discuss the teacher's role in more detail later, Moses Aberbach, describing

---

[333]Some older commentators call the "Theophanies" of Genesis 18:1–33; 32:24–25; Joshua 5:14–15; Daniel 3:25, etc., "Christophanies", i.e. appearances of the pre-incarnate "Logos". Thus Matthew Henry, Coffman, etc. But whether they are right or not, the fact is clear enough that there was, in all these cases, an association of human form with God's self-disclosure to Abraham, Jacob and Joshua. Putting these events together with John's statement in John 1:14–18, makes it clearer. When God showed His face, it was in the form of Jesus, the Word made flesh.
[334]Numbers 27:6–11; Ruth 3:9–13; 4:1–14.

Rabbis and their function, says: "The rabbis taught as much by example as by precept. For this reason the disciple needed to take note of his master's daily conversation and habits, as well as his teaching."[335]

Role: Priest

In displaying Jesus with a human face, Luke speaks to us about leadership that identifies with and straddles the divide between the estranged parties, and in this way positions itself to be a *priest*, a bridge, a mediator, representing God to people and people to God. This role depends, more than the others, on the qualification of an exemplary, hospitable and gracious character because, in this case, the person *is* the function. There can be no play-acting, no hiding behind gifting, position or intelligence. To hold that function requires consistency, or integrity.

Integrity means being true to yourself and to God's inner work in you, and living "from the inside out", being the same inside and out. Understanding this requires a working knowledge of the nature of personhood and identity. Walter Wright, quoting Koestenbaum, comments on the importance and nature of identity:

> ... *effective leaders are centered in their souls. They have come to peace with the questions of identity, survival, and meaning. It is this centeredness that makes others listen to what they have to say, that gives them credibility ... Centeredness is what makes people seem powerful, and its absence is what makes people perceive themselves and be perceived by others as ineffective and even impotent ... Centeredness is the source*

---

[335]Moses Aberbach, "Relations between Master and Disciple in the Talmudic Age" in *Essays Presented to the Chief Rabbi Israel Brodie,* Jews' College Publications, New Series, no 3 (Soncino, 1968), p. 318, quoted by Richards and Hoeldtke, *op. cit.,* p. 133.

of authentic faith, belief and realistic self-confidence.[336]

Describing his function as a leader, Paul says: "But by God's grace I am what I am, and His grace shown to me wasn't wasted. Instead, I worked harder than all the others – not I, of course, but God's grace that was with me" (1 Corinthians 15:10). God's grace gave him identity, and with that identity, a leadership gift that he simply needed to allow to express itself. This is the journey of integrity, or character growth. It is "living into the good" of who God has made us by grace, and expressing His grace in the form of gifts with which He has favoured us. You are who God's grace has made you. You do ministry as an expression of that grace in action. That way, no matter how well or how badly you are doing your job as a leader, your identity, your value or worth to God is not affected, either for better or for worse, by pride of life or low self-worth.[337]

Peter Scazzero, in his excellent work, *The Emotionally Healthy Church*, comments as follows:

> *To care means first of all to be present to each other. From experience you know that those who care for you become present to you. When they listen, they listen to you. When they speak, they speak to you. Their presence is a healing presence because they accept you on your terms, and they encourage you to take your own life seriously.*[338]

---

[336]Wright, *op. cit.*, loc 230.

[337]I have written on this in *Learn to Love Yourself.* In it I show the psychological connection between worth and performance, which bedevils especially the baby-boomer generation in the West, and the fact that one of the intended effects of the gospel is meant to be a reversal of this connection, so that we do our work not *in order* to feel valuable, but because we already *are* valuable.

[338]Peter Scazzero, *The Emotionally Healthy Church* (Zondervan, 2003), Kindle edition, loc 2980.

Demonstrating self-control of our own emotions, reactions, sinful urges, etc., is a first qualification for leadership. As I illustrated earlier, leaders need to first lead themselves. We may be wounded healers, but leadership requires that we have at least taken one or two steps ahead of those we lead, on the journey of following Jesus. There is, in some circles, a tendency to encourage pastors to be so "real", so vulnerable, that they may lose their ability to help others with workable counsel. Jones and Armstrong comment at length about this, saying:

> Unfortunately, [Henri] Nouwen's image of the 'wounded healer' has too often been disconnected from the pattern of Christ's dying and rising. And that has allowed people to center themselves in their own wounds – and then return regularly to lick them. The notion of a wounded healer has too often degenerated into a pop-psychology definition of woundedness as a crucial criterion for ordained ministry.[339]

While integrity and authenticity can be attractive and do increase credibility, they may also mitigate against both. The authors quote a young parishioner commenting about his "vulnerable and real" pastor: "You know, mom, the trouble with our new pastor is that he needs us to love him so much that we can't see God anymore."[340] It "is much more difficult to worship God when ordained ministers are so preoccupied with themselves and their own needs that God is relegated to the sidelines. Self-absorbed ministry issues from a pastor's lack of Christian character."[341]

The leader who represents the human face of Christ needs, in an echo of the words of Socrates,[342] to lead him or herself before

---

[339]Jones and Armstrong, *op. cit.,* loc 1178.

[340]*Ibid.,* loc 1182.

[341]*Ibid.,* loc 1189.

[342]Socrates said: *"If a man would move the world, he must first move himself"* (http://www.iwise.com). Much is being written and said in modern-day

attempting to lead others. Richard S. Ascough, in his analysis of the apostle Paul as a leader, quotes Dee Hock's *The Birth of the Chaordic Age*,[343] in which the author writes that the chaordic leader's primary responsibility is to manage his "own integrity, character, ethics, knowledge, wisdom, temperament, words and acts".[344] This is not about whether any of us is a "finished product", but whether we are showing self-leadership. The difference between always being a sinner in need of grace, and a disqualified person is the same as the difference between occasional lapses and habitual, deliberate self-indulgence and character flaws (1 Corinthians 9:26–27). If the default of our lives is sinful self-centredness, rather than grace-filled serving, we will never make it as leaders. If, on the other hand, we choose an attitude of selflessness, the grace of God through us will cover a multitude of errors or lack of skill.

Effect: The security of unconditional love

Jones and Armstrong use three words to describe the key functions of "pastoral leadership", namely to be *interpreters, visionaries* and *reconcilers*.

---

management training circles about the need, before managing others, of first managing oneself. With this the writer of the Proverbs would agree: "*He who is* slow to anger *is* better than the mighty, And he who rules his spirit than he who takes a city" (Proverbs 16:32 NKJV).

[343]Dee Hock, *The Birth of the Chaordic Age* (Berrett-Koehler, 1999), which propounds a view that the organisation of the future will be the embodiment of community based on shared purpose calling to the higher aspirations of people. He goes on to define a new vision of institutional organisation, which he terms "chaordic". A chaordic organisation is "any self-organizing, self-governing, adaptive, non-linear, complex organism, organization, community or system, whether physical, biological or social, the behaviour of which harmoniously combines characteristics of both chaos and order" (Hock, p. 15).

[344]Ascough and Cotton, *op. cit.,* p. 159.

*Interpreters discern carefully the ways of God in leading us from the past to the future; visionaries see their communities and institutions in relation to the abundance of God's grace and the **telos** of God's kingdom, and are willing to exercise authority and power wisely in service of that vision. Yet we also need to cultivate **reconcilers, leaders who draw people together, sustain communities, and minimize the sense in which anyone feels marginalized.**[345]*

The role of the *pastor*, in my view, emphasises the latter concept. It is a "people-focused" function, evidenced by being there for people: accessible, engaged, vulnerable and compassionate; that is to be a person of high "EQ" (Emotional Intelligence).[346] In general, this involves being otherly and compassionate; in ministry terms, it involves preaching God's Word in an accessible, relevant form and applicability; being self-disclosing (within reason) in that application; and being engaged with people in their day-to-day lives by giving counsel and practising pastoral care. In terms of the effects anticipated from this leadership type in Diagram 5, I see the effect of the pastor as the *empowerment in love* of believers in their discipleship and functionality.

Frequency

In the USA, based on Myers-Briggs Temperament Instrument results, it was found that 41% of clergy are of the NF type, which has correlation with the pastor we have just discussed (see Diagram 5). This may be compared to the fact that only 12% of the US population at large are of this type.[347]

---

[345]Jones and Armstrong, *op. cit.,* loc 1629 (emphasis mine).

[346]Goleman, *op. cit.*

[347]From a survey conducted among a sample of 250 clergy, cited by Oswald and Kroeger, *op. cit.,* loc 540.

Leading as a prophetic visionary

Spiritual leaders may lead by the power and influence of their *prophetic vision*. This type of leader is high in inspiration, extroversion and future-orientation, and will raise the level of emotional energy in any gathering, affecting the group with hope and passion. This is the leader with the face of an *eagle*, the role of a *prophet* and the effect of a *visionary*.

In the three places where Paul speaks about gifts (the *charismata* of 1 Corinthians 12; the *prasso* of Romans 12; and the *domata* of Ephesians 4), the prophet (or prophecy) is the only gift mentioned in each list. A special note is necessary here, which I applied earlier to the apostolic gift. Paul sometimes uses the verb *propheteuo*, sometimes the adverb *propheteia*, and sometimes the noun *prophetes*. Many commentators hold the view that both prophecy and prophets, like apostles, ceased after the biblical canon was finalised.[348] John Calvin, like others, believes the prophetic gift was/is "those who were blessed with the unique gift of dealing with Scripture, not only by interpreting it, but also by the wisdom they showed in making it meet the needs of the hour".[349] However, in the three references mentioned, it is recorded as a *gift*, a *function* and an *office*, linked by the verb which is listed as an extraordinary manifestation of the life of the Holy Spirit in the Church.[350] The

---

[348]For example, F. W. Grosheide, in the *New International Commentary* volume *Commentary on the First Epistle to the Corinthians:* "prophets ... only have a task to perform in the first period of the New Testament church" (p. 298).

[349]John Calvin on *1 Corinthians*, p. 271. In his *Commentary on Ephesians* chapter 4, he writes: "I would rather explain it, as in 1 Corinthians 14, to mean outstanding interpreters of prophecies, who, by a unique gift of revelation, applied them to the subjects on hand; but I do not exclude the gift of foretelling, so far as it was connected with teaching" (p. 179).

[350]In expounding this thought, Fee comments: "Paul's understanding – as well as that of the other NT writers – was thoroughly conditioned by his own history in Judaism. The prophet was a person who spoke to God's people un-

leader who exercises a prophetic function is accountable to Scripture for doctrinal correctness, and is subject to judging by other spiritual leaders.[351] However, the proper exercise of the prophetic gift is hugely valuable in leading the church.

I think the issue is not whether "apostles" or "prophets" exist in a formal sense today, but rather what type of leader is represented by these offices, and what role such leaders still play in bringing maturity and wholeness of expression to the Church. Paul in Ephesians speaks of some being given as *"prophets"*, as distinct from the person who, either as occasional *charis* or as more regular *praxis*, offers prophetic encouragement in a group. The difference is one of depth and impact of insight, as well as significance of application thereof. The prophetic or visionary leader sees the "big picture" of what the Church is to become, and facilitates the discernment of direction toward it; they are always calling people to greater heights. He or she gives momentum to the group they lead by moving with determination toward the goal they see; they may even shape the group's thoughts into the direction they have discerned, toward the fulfilment of the vision. This is leadership with the face of the *eagle*.

---

der the inspiration of the Spirit. The 'inspired utterance' came by revelation ... [and] often ... had a futuristic element." In both these senses, I believe it represented more than natural gifting or scholarship, but was a supernatural and extraordinary phenomenon, which is as necessary today as it was then. "The evidence of chapter 14," continues Fee, "suggests that all 'Spirit people' were potentially 'prophets', in the sense that they could prophesy. But this list (i.e. in 1 Corinthians 12:28–29), as well as the similar kind of language in Ephesians 2:20 and 4:11, suggests that for Paul, as for Luke, there were some who, because they regularly functioned in this way, were known as 'prophets'" (Fee, p. 595, 621). Hendriksen concurs, saying: *"Prophets, again in the restricted sense (for in a broader sense every believer is a prophet), are the occasional organs of inspiration ..." (Ephesians 4, op. cit., p. 196).*
[351] 1 Corinthians 14:29.

Face: Eagle

The eagle is the creature among the four around God's throne which represents vision. It is the creature that can soar above the mundane, beyond clouds that obscure, and above the reach of the most determined of enemies. In prophetic literature, God's prophetic anger and urgency are strongly symbolised by the eagle, for example: "Put the trumpet to your lips and give the warning. Be like an eagle over the LORD'S house. The Israelites have broken my agreement. They have not obeyed my law" (Hosea 8:1 ESV, cf. Deuteronomy 28:49).

On the other hand, God is pictured in redemptive care as a mother eagle:

> *Like an eagle stirs its nest, hovering near its young, spreading out his wings to take him and carry him on his pinions, the LORD alone guided him. There was no foreign god with him. He mounted him on a high place above the earth, feeding him from the produce of the field.* (Deuteronomy 32:11–13a)

As the eagle motivates her young to fly, and makes sure they succeed at it, so the prophet works in the Church. As much as the prophet speaks judgment, so she or he also speaks assurance and redemption, or what Paul calls "upbuilding and encouragement and consolation".[352] In the same way, also, the contemporary prophetic leader is responsible for the motivation, inspiration and constant visionary momentum of the local church. As Jones and Armstrong put it: "Visionary leaders have a capacity for the prophetic use of power in both cursing and blessing."[353]

> *Paul teaches us that sharing one's vision requires stamina, commitment and courage. It is not for the tired, somewhat*

---

[352]1 Corinthians 14:3 ESV.
[353]Jones and Armstrong, *op. cit.,* loc 1723.

cynical, detached observer of life ... Too often, our emphasis on what some cynics call 'the vision thing' blinds us to the fundamental need for passionate conviction among leaders ... Leaders without passion may get their way in the short term, but they will not breathe life into the community ... the most effective leaders ... are 'artists' rather than 'technocrats' ... For, as we see in Paul, passion for one's task resides at the heart of transformative leadership wisdom.[354]

Role: Visionary

"Where there is no vision, the people are unrestrained. But blessed is he, the one keeping the law" (Proverbs 29:18 LITV).[355] In this text, the writer plays on the word "vision" (Hebrew *chazon:* sight, dream, revelation, or oracle) to affirm the importance of the primary revelation of Scripture. He makes the point that God's Word has the function of restraining or holding God's people in check, focusing them, stopping their moral and spiritual disintegration. However, I believe the principle is a wider one, namely that the inspired declaration of both the mediate (written) and *immediate* (prophetic, spoken) word from the Lord is the key guiding, containing and ordering force of the community of faith. A visionary leader sees more than "a mental portrait of a preferable future";[356] he or she sees what is next on the way to reaching that destination. The prophetic leader is someone who most clearly sees or discerns what Frederick Marais called "a shorter list of things to do",[357] and who has their ear to the ground to hear what the Spirit is saying to the church right now.

---

[354]Ascough and Cotton, *op. cit.,* pp. 35-36.

[355]See Diagram 1, p. 44.

[356]Barna, *op. cit.,* p. 47.

[357]A phrase coined by David Allen and expanded on in his book *Getting Things Done* (Penguin, 2001), used by Dr Marais in lectures delivered during my M.Th. coursework.

> *How is that gift of vision cultivated among pastoral lead-*
> *ers? The secular literature on leadership often describes the*
> *importance of 'casting a vision,' 'articulating a vision,' and*
> *then mobilizing people around that vision. Such emphases*
> *are important in moving people beyond mere management*
> *to envisioning what might be possible ... visionary leaders*
> *involve the whole community in the Christian practice of*
> *discernment, helping them imagine possibilities and then*
> *take faithful risks that they might otherwise be unwilling to*
> *take.*[358]

The prophetic leader, then, is someone who, while they may receive vision by revelation, whether occasionally or regularly, or
cultivating it corporately by a discernment process, is able to help
in the translation of that vision into strategies and goals, which
are designed to move the group they lead toward something. It is
my experience, though, that often visionaries are not detail-aware,
and that they will need to rely on the administrative analysts to
do that part. That said, it remains true that "[l]eaders have visions
that make a difference, empowering visions that offer hope for
tomorrow and shape behaviors today".[359]

Effect: Future-orientation and passion

Vision, as I discussed in chapter 2, is made up of a blend of *calling, purpose* and *values*. A clear sense of calling from God provides
a sense of purpose, in the emotional and motivational sense of
resolve, commitment, focus or compulsion. Purpose is determination or motivation, as well as an ability to keep the end in view.
Values define the "Why?" of a course of action, together with the
"What?" and "Where?". Together, these three factors of calling,
purpose and values condense into a clear sense of what he or she

---

[358]Jones and Armstrong, *op. cit.,* loc 1694.
[359]Wright, *op. cit.,* loc 1069.

is to do, with which "target" group (a people or peer group, a nation, or a city), and to what end result. When this has happened, the vision will motivate and stir the leader's heart with unusual and sustainable passion and compassion.

Paul, after a Macedonian man appeared to him in a night-time vision, was immediately captured with a sense of purpose toward that place and people group. So will anyone be who receives a vision from God. As Luke describes it: "As soon as Paul had this vision, we got ready to leave for Macedonia ..." (Acts 16:10). Paul's later testimony about this describes a sense of compulsion, when he says: "And so, King Agrippa, I did [literally, "could"] not disobey the vision I had from heaven" (Acts 26:19 GNT). He was drawn into obedience by the power of vision.

In addition, the visionary leader needs to be a person who understands and is able to articulate values, and keep everyone on track concerning those values. Values are the ingredients of vision that give it moral weight, or meaning. Without meaning, all vision or task achievement is hollow, and may ultimately be damaging to all participants.

> *[Abraham] looked forward to the city which has foundations, whose builder and maker is God ... These all died in faith, not having received what was promised, but having seen it and greeted it from afar, and having acknowledged that they were strangers and exiles on the earth. For people who speak thus make it clear that they are seeking a homeland. If they had been thinking of that land from which they had gone out, they would have had opportunity to return. But as it is, they desire a better country, that is, a heavenly one. Therefore God is not ashamed to be called their God, for he has prepared for them a city.* (Hebrews 11:10–16)

Abraham saw a city with heavenly origins, shape and significance. He, and the people who followed him, would not stop in their search, or settle for less than the vision they had seen. If they had not seen that vision, they would have stopped short of it, or quit and returned home when the going got tough. The job of the prophetic leader is to paint the visionary picture, so that those who follow can "see" it through their eyes, hear its song in their ears, and believe it is there because of the picture their words paint. The vision of the heavenly city Abraham painted for them was so powerful as to change their entire frame of reference! They did not even think of the place they had left. Their imagination had been captivated by something they saw, and "greeted from afar". The job of the leader is not only to receive vision, but also to "cast" it; that is, to articulate it, communicate it, refine it, and to engage the senses of those he leads, so that they can smell its fragrance, thrill at its colours, feel its warmth on their faces, and enjoy its textures.

I said earlier, when I talked about vision as a necessary ingredient of any leader's role, that the leader needs to be an effective, inspiring, non-stop facilitator and *communicator* of vision. If that is vital for all leaders, it is even more so for the leader who specialises in being a visionary in style and effect. The leader who can communicate a uniting word of visionary power can motivate a group beyond itself, almost without limit.

The five elements of effective visionary (prophetic) comunication, in my view, are *persuasion, inspiration, desire, internalisation* and *visualisation*. People will have absorbed vision only when they are persuaded it is true, when they want what it promises, when they believe that they can have or achieve it, and when it is repeated so often that it is part of their belief system. What this calls for from the "prophetic" leader is creativity, poetic feel, humour and the involvement of as many senses as possible in communicating. The result is the *influence* about which I wrote in chapter 1.

"Prophetic" leadership is thus an intangible, but real power that radiates from an individual and causes a response of curiosity, attention, attraction and, ultimately, a loyal following on the part of others. It is manifest through oratory skill as well as the resulting motivation of the group toward its strategic objectives for Christ's sake.

The work of the visionary leader involves constantly matching suggested action to vision attainment. While preaching, they will constantly show how the action they are calling people to, will lead to the achievement of the vision in a specific, measurable way. Similarly, when problems arise, they will link remedy to vision. Well-articulated vision attracts to the task resources of every kind, whether people, money, or anything else. A good visionary leader will show people how every small job in the organisation relates to the big picture. He or she will help them celebrate their achievement of any milestone reached, making everyone aware of it and applauding those responsible. The prophets are also entertainers and expressives. They are the "party animals" among leaders, who are naturally able to keep the "fun factor" high! At the same time, the visionary leader needs to keep in mind constantly that the job of a leader is to give away his or her job! A visionary leader, like any leader, is like the mother eagle, who stirs up the nest to make the chicks uncomfortable so that they prefer flying to nesting, but also watches how they do in flight and is ready to catch them should they fall. In this respect, a true visionary leader is someone who ensures that vision has been "passed on" effectively.

In terms of Diagram 5 (page 224), the effect on church members of the prophet-type leader is *encouragement*. He or she will instil fresh *hope* as they face obstacles on their discipleship journey.

Frequency

The Myers-Briggs study of clergy in the USA showed that the SP temperament type, which correlates with the prophet as a leader type, is represented in only 8% of the US clergy, compared to

38% of the American population in general.[360]

Leading with truth and wisdom – teacher and sage

Spiritual leaders may lead by the power and influence of the information and wisdom they give (the teacher). This type of leader is usually quiet, introverted or impersonal, often preferring the company of books to that of people. They often show a quiet passion for the truth, are linear and logical in their thinking, and are unemotional except when the truth is threatened. They may manifest these character traits either as administrators and organisers, or as teachers and developers of doctrine, and will affect the group with the stability of solid information. This is the leader with the face of an *ox*, the role of a *sage* and the effect of *stabilising people in truth*.

Face: Ox

In Scriptural usage, the ox is often a symbol of hard, determined work. Solomon says: "Where there are no oxen, the feeding trough is clean, but profits come through the strength of the ox" (Proverbs 14:4). Paul uses an Old Testament text to affirm the right of ministers to be remunerated for their work: "For the scripture says, 'You shall not muzzle an ox while it is treading out the grain', and 'The labourer [especially the teacher] deserves to be paid'" (1 Timothy 5:18, referencing Deuteronomy 25:4). Both these texts are speaking about the relationship of providing nourishment (the process of ploughing, sowing the seed, watering and harvesting the wheat, and then grinding or milling it to flour) to the strength and patient work of the ox. Bread is often used in Scripture as a symbol of God's Word. The ox is a symbol of strength, hard work and leadership in the form of the systematic teaching of systematic truth.

Teachers have several traits in common with oxen: they are

---

[360]Oswald and Kroeger, *op. cit.,* loc 540.

strong, steady and stubborn, and the nature of their work is to take the yoke on their necks, and then put one foot in front of the other in a "long obedience in the same direction",[361] in order to pull a plough, or to walk repeatedly around and around to turn the mill wheel, occasionally stopping for water and licking up some of the grain it is grinding. The work of an ox reminds me of the word God gave Isaiah: "For it is: 'Do this and do that, do this and do that, Line upon line, line upon line, a little here, a little there.'"[362] Isaiah is quoting, in a sarcastic way, a poem used by the teachers of the law to keep children and adults faithful to Scripture: "*tsav tsav, tsav tsav, kauv kauv, kauv kauv, zehayr, zehayr*". Teachers build doctrinal truth that way: line by line, precept upon precept, adding text to text, letting the Bible interpret itself. For the ox, the focus is short and low, rather than long and high; the goal is grain and bread, and the joy is in the quality of the meal. In similar fashion, the focus of the teacher of the Word is the text itself, and the detail contained in what is in front of him or her. The outcome the teacher pursues is not fame for him or herself as much as spiritual nourishment and resulting growth for the recipients of the teaching.

Another application of the dogged, single-minded and systematic way of the ox is the administrative leader, whose focus and role is the implementation of plans and strategies to achieve goals. They have an ability to co-ordinate people and programs, often without being noticed. Yet this dimension of leadership is what makes the difference between vision and empty idealism. The overall leader may not be a detail person, and may not be administratively efficient. If that is so, she will need to have someone alongside who is.

---

[361] The title of a book by Eugene Peterson describing discipleship (IVP, 1980).
[362] Isaiah 28:10.

Role: Sage

Jones and Armstrong point out that "a central means by which we pattern our lives in Christ, and discover the overwhelming grace of being embraced by God, is by attending to the treasures of the gospel that sustain us over time".[363] The type of leader who deals in truth (the teacher), has a particular love for the Word of God, and its systematic teaching, as an end in itself. Thiselton states: "Teachers exercise rational reflection on goals, content, and methods of communication."[364] He later adds: "Teachers more typically perform speech acts of *transmitting* or *handing on* and *explaining*."[365]

As we saw in discussing the temperament types that fit into the four quadrants,[366] those of the NT temperament type "desire to comprehend, explain, predict and control ... and also tend to pursue perfection and see stupidity and incompetence as the worst possible faults".[367] When Paul speaks about the process of transformation, he makes it clear that it occurs "by the renewing of your minds", which in turn can produce the ability to "discern what is the will of God" and makes possible behaviours that are "good and acceptable and perfect".[368] The truth that renews the mind is God's truth, which is engraved on the minds and hearts of God's new covenant people by the indwelling Spirit,[369] and when lived,

---

[363]Jones and Armstrong, *op. cit.,* loc 1748.

[364]Thiselton, *op. cit.,* p. 213.

[365]*Ibid.,* p. 214.

[366]Diagram 5, pp. 224.

[367]C. P. Michael and Marie C. Morrisey, *Prayer and Temperament* (The Open Door Inc., 1997), p. 80.

[368]Romans 12:2.

[369]Hebrews 8:10–11: "This is the covenant that I will make with the house of Israel after those days, says the Lord: I will put my laws in their minds, and write them on their hearts, and I will be their God, and they shall be my people. And they shall not teach one another or say to each other, 'Know the Lord,' for they shall all know me, from the least of them to the greatest."

becomes the lifestyle of wisdom. When the apostle John describes the new covenant, he relates it to an "anointing that teaches":

> *I write these things to you concerning those who would deceive you. As for you, the anointing that you received from him abides in you, and so you do not need anyone to teach you. But as his anointing teaches you about all things, and is true and is not a lie, and just as it has taught you, abide in him.* (1 John 2:26–27)

Union with Christ[370] fulfils the New Covenant promise of new life, empowerment and transforming revelation. The indwelling "Christ in me"[371] brings with Him "power, and love, and a sound mind".[372]

The spiritual teacher is, in John's stated view, neither an inventor nor an originator of truth, but an "unwrapper" of truth that already exists, not only in the Body of Christ universal, but also within each believer. The anointing (i.e. the Holy Spirit) instils truth, like a light bulb that is lit up, but wrapped in the masking tape of old, entrenched paradigms and taught concepts. A teacher

---

[370]Miroslav Volf, writing in *Free of Charge* says: "Luther believed that Christ – or rather, God in Christ – is the source of gifts and the model for human giving. He made one more crucial step in describing the relation between God's giving and ours. Christ, he believed, is also the agent of our giving. Our giving is, as it were, an echo of his. That's where the idea of the 'indwelling Christ' comes in. The apostle Paul wrote, 'I have been crucified with Christ; and it is no longer I who live, but it is Christ who lives in me. And the life I now live in the flesh I live by faith in the Son of God, who loved me and gave himself for me' (Galatians 2:19–20). Believers' lives are paradoxically both their own ('the life I now live') and not their own ('it is no longer I who live'), but rather Christ's ('it is Christ who lives in me'). It is not just that Christ sends the goods to flow into us; Christ makes the goods flow from us as well, truly indwelling, motivating, and acting through us. That's Luther's point when he made what seems like a strange claim, namely that a Christian is a 'Christ' to others" (loc 723).

[371]Galatians 2:20.

[372]2 Timothy 1:7.

has the task of unwrapping the light bulb, revealing more and more of the light of God's truth which abides within the believer. A leader with a teaching gift, John is saying, must maintain a certain humility, while insisting on a hearing for the hard-won truth he or she has stewarded to clarity in his or her own mind. When a teacher teaches, believers will often be seen to nod, as though they instinctively know what is being taught. Jones and Armstrong write:

> *Conscious learning becomes unconscious knowledge, and you cannot say precisely how … And thus an imagination that is at its heart a "seeing in depth" turns out to be an imagination full of creativity – an imagination that sees what is "not yet" and begins to create it. The practice of the moral life, meanwhile, is not so much about being creative or clever as it is about taking the right things for granted.*[373]

Explaining the Pentecostal worldview, James K. A. Smith writes as follows:

> *While the pentecostal believer might not be able to elucidate this tacit understanding in theologemes, she's nonetheless right when she emphasizes, "I know that I know that I know." This is a knowledge, an "affective understanding," that is on a register prior to propositional articulation.*[374]

Notwithstanding the cogency of Smith's confident point, we must note that the early Pentecostals put together the above texts to mean that believers did not need teaching, and that truth would spontaneously arise when it was needed. People would be led to Christ, prayed over for the baptism of the Holy Spirit, and sent out

---

[373]Jones and Armstrong, *op. cit.,* locs 1584–1608.
[374]James K. A. Smith, *Thinking in Tongues* (Eerdmans, 2010), Kindle edition, loc 706.

as preachers within a week.[375] What is forgotten in this model is that, while the seeds of transformation, giftedness and even truth do indeed come to us "by grace through faith", the link between grace and competence is stewardship (1 Peter 4:10). God gives us the tools, but those who use them to serve will care for and sharpen them, and grow into maturity of service by studying, submitting to other leaders, and keeping integrity with the Church and its truth. A teacher must be a student, firstly and continuously,[376] if they are to please God with their serving. They "must cultivate a sense of the office and of the education and competence needed to flourish in service to the Christian community".[377]

As Paul admonished Timothy, in preparation for being a teacher:

> *Do your best to present yourself to God as one approved by him, a worker who has no need to be ashamed, rightly explaining the word of truth.* (2 Timothy 2:15)

However, the study, and resulting delivery, of truth need not be dry and lifeless. Jones and Armstrong recognise that "seeking insight into Christ's mind is not simply a matter of cognitive reasoning".[378] The damage done to the Church in the long term by modernism and rationalism, has been to overemphasise

---

[375]Also included in the rationale for this were texts such as Luke 12:12; John 14:26 and Acts 1:8. The ministry of John G. Lake (who came from Zion, Illinois) in South Africa in the early 1900s, has been linked to the rise of the Zion Christian Church (ZCC), the largest of the African Indigenous (or Independent) Churches, which has a curious blend of Pentecostalism, Catholicism and animism. A lack of teaching of sound Christian doctrine, despite strong Christian faith-roots, has led to these syncretistic distortions. Walter Hollenweger's *The Pentecostals* (Augsburg Press, 1972), pp. 120–122, concurs with the above as a sequence of events and causal connection.

[376]"The reading and study that preaching requires is not preparation for ministry ... it *is* ministry" (Jones and Armstrong, *op. cit.,* loc 1366).

[377]Jones and Armstrong, *op. cit.,* loc 1090.

[378]Jones and Armstrong, *op. cit.,* loc 286.

> *... the "learned clergy" model, [in which] education seems to displace a concern with either calling and spiritual formation or office and holiness. Indeed, one of the criticisms of the "professional" model of clergy is that it is preoccupied with "book learning" rather than calling and relationship with God ... Like any vocation, intellectual work can be done well or poorly; it can form or deform. And it is important that the education and formation of clergy offer a spacious vision for a critical, lively, and generous-spirited intellectual life as an integral feature of the pastoral vocation ... Our image depends on the recognition that "learning" involves the shaping of our hearts as well as our minds and hands and feet, the cultivation of a way of life that is affective, cognitive, disciplined, and integrally connected to action.*[379]

Additionally, one of the prime ways truth, and the defining wisdom that holds a group together, is passed on, is by the art of story. Max de Pree urges leaders to "identify and elevate the tribal storytellers in the organization who will keep the past visible, the values illuminated, and the future alive".[380] Jones and Armstrong elaborate:

> *As teachers and storytellers who bridge the gap between systematic theology and religious narrative, pastoral leaders must be attentive to both what we have to say (Scripture) and how we say it (interpretation). We have an opportunity to interpret the word in a way that enriches the imagination, finds universal themes in particulars, and invites the world to consider ways of living together under the gospel of the crucified and risen Christ.*[381]

---

[379]Jones and Armstrong, *op. cit.,* locs 1425-1440.
[380]Quoted by Wright, *op. cit.,* loc 1983.
[381]Jones and Armstrong, *op. cit.,* loc 1837.

Effect: Truth and wisdom

Wisdom is applied truth. It translates truth into rules of engagement with the world, and transforms lives. This raises the need for more than information to characterise the teaching ministry. It also requires insight and application. The role of the teacher, like that of the Rabbi, is to be an agent of discernment or wisdom.

> *Christians who are described as "knowing what to say" or "being in the right place at the right time" are likely people who remain attentive to God and holy Scripture, who cultivate wisdom and knowledge through careful study, and who engage regularly in Christian practices and friendships that open our eyes and ears to the presence of God in and for the world.*[382]

> *... Christians are called to be people for whom the language of Scripture becomes a "second first language", so that we read the world, and our lives, through the lens of Scripture. We do so by learning these practices together and, especially as we are being initiated into Christian faith, by apprenticing ourselves to those who are wise. Christian life involves lifelong learning.*[383]

The ox-type leader, then, is to be both a teacher and a sage. In the modern Western Church, this has often evolved into a professionalising of the "pastoral counsellor" role, with many pastors majoring in psychology and various forms of psychotherapy. Counselling itself becomes extremely technical and pseudo-medical and, as proponents of biblical counselling will point out, is often at the expense of the courage simply to put counsellees in mind of God's truth.[384] There is a need for balance here because, as Eugene

---

[382]Jones and Armstrong, *op. cit.,* loc 715.

[383]Jones and Armstrong, *op. cit.,* locs 1463–1473.

[384]See Jay Adams, *op. cit.,* where he uses as the basis of his Nouthetic approach Paul's previously quoted mandate in Colossians 1:28 (see also Colos-

Peterson points out: "We can never know just how Christ will be formed in another. If we should mistakenly do our work in the dogmatic schoolmaster style of Dr Cradock, we well deserve the epitaph 'miserable comforter'."[385] Pastors are to be reflectors (St Ambrose called them "mirrors") of truth, and work with truth as artists rather than artisans. In introducing the urgent need for pastors who are spiritual directors (another name for sages?), Peterson elaborates:

> *Spiritual direction takes place when two people agree to give their full attention to what God is doing in one (or both) of their lives and seek to respond in faith ... three convictions underpin these meetings: (1) God is always doing something: an active grace is shaping this life into a mature salvation; (2) responding to God is not sheer guesswork: the Christian community has acquired* **wisdom through the centuries that provides guidance;** *(3) each soul is unique:* **no wisdom can simply be applied without discerning** *the particulars of this life, this situation.*[386]

I believe that the answer is not either/or, but both/and. Wisdom is discerned in the communion between pastor and parishioner, in the light of God's truth and the larger community of faith. The difference between the "teaching pastor" and a psychotherapist is both in the truth that underpins the counsel given, and in the gentle but insistent way in which it is offered. I therefore see the effect of the teacher on members of the church as that of *establishment in the knowledge and practice of truth.*

---

sians 3:16). In these texts, Paul uses the word *noutheteo* (translated "admonish" in several translations) to describe a part of the responsibility of leaders toward growing Christians. It literally translates "to put in mind". Adams advocates this as a counter to the non-directive counselling approach of secular models.

[385] Peterson, *Working the Angles, op. cit.,* loc 1773.

[386] Peterson, *op. cit.,* locs 1426-1428 (emphasis mine).

Frequency

The Myers-Briggs temperament type that correlates with the teacher style of leader, is characterised as the NT (iNtuitive Thinker) type. In the US, only 12% of the population, and a mere 16% of the clergy, have this temperament type.[387] In my work with leaders all over Africa, when I ask the question: "What do you (church leaders) need most for your churches?" I will hear most frequently the answer "teaching and training". Again, it requires more scientific research, but initial impressions suggest that this is the African Church's greatest need.

It is important to emphasise the fact that there is no one style of leadership that is ideal for every church. As we will see in the next chapter, each of them is critical at various stages of a church's life, and giving space to the "square peg" to operate when there is a "square hole" is one of the tasks of discerning leadership. Although Paul is discussing a different category of gift in 1 Corinthians 12:18–21, 27, I think the principles he teaches are applicable to every ministry "level" or function in the church, as he urges each member to value all the others, and to love the person God has made them to be, rather than constantly wanting to emulate someone else:

> *But our bodies have many parts, and God has put each part just where He wants it. How strange a body would be if it had only one part! Yes, there are many parts, but only one body. The eye can never say to the hand, "I don't need you." The head can't say to the feet, "I don't need you." All of you together are Christ's body, and each of you is a part of it.* (NLT)

---

[387]Oswald and Kroeger, *op. cit.*

CHAPTER 8

Process Leadership

"Coming together is a beginning, staying together is progress, and working together is success." **Henry Ford**

I wrote earlier about the different styles of leadership, and the fact that a mark of the spiritual gift of leadership is that it maintains momentum toward the achievement of the group's goal(s). We are going to explore the lessons contained in the Book of Nehemiah, and see how our direct application, or indirect facilitation, of different styles of leadership is the key to maintaining momentum in the organisation. It is the responsibility of the leader to see that this happens. Therefore, leadership is not just about vision, or influence, or even just empowering, but also about strategy and its implementation. Leaders, as we have seen, have been given authority by God, through the group itself, in exchange for benefit received. The continuation of that authority will depend on continued benefit which, in turn, requires that things are not only taught, but also done; not just prayed for, but also practically experienced. Keep in mind that the Kingdom leader is always responsible to exercise this leadership in the way of a servant. Nonetheless, it is to be *given*, not just talked about.

The difference between management and leadership is visionary momentum. It is what gives the group its cohesive reason for existence. Leaders are responsible to cultivate a going-places atmosphere in the group they lead. The level of need for momentum will vary, depending on the nature of the group. For example, a family, a "kinship" group, a relational or a support-oriented group will not need as much momentum as a mission group, an army regiment or a sales department. Nevertheless, some sense of directional energy will usually be needed. How you engender it will be determined by your style, or gift mix. However, you will need to ensure that tasks are accomplished, goals reached and, ultimately, the group's destiny is realised. As we saw in the area of creating community, you do not need to do it all, but you do need to see that someone does.

Not only does the nature of the group require different styles of leadership, the phases through which every group goes also call for adaptation of leadership styles. The New Testament writers use a range of metaphors for the church, each of which highlights elements of group life. For example, as we saw at the close of the last chapter, the Church is a *body*.[388] This calls for flexibility, interdependence and functionality of the parts. The Church is also called a *temple*,[389] which requires stability, strength and design. It is referred to as a *flock*,[390] which involves caring, feeding, protection and productivity. In another text, it is called a *family* or household,[391] where the emphasis is on relationships, love and permanence of commitment. Another metaphor for the Church

---

[388] 1 Corinthians 12.
[389] Ephesians 2:20–22; 1 Peter 2:5ff.
[390] Matthew 26:31; Acts 20:28; 1 Peter 5:2–4.
[391] Galatians 6:10; Ephesians 2:19.

is an *army*,[392] with requirements of order, training, efficiency and militant preparedness. Elsewhere, the Church is referred to as a *bride*,[393] which speaks of perfected beauty, radiance and covenantal grace. Each of these aspects of being the Church calls for a different kind of leadership. Thus:

- A body needs a brain;
- A temple needs a builder;
- A flock needs a shepherd;
- A family needs parents; and
- An army needs a general.

Think about it: Some of these are, in fact, mutually exclusive, and we should beware of stretching any metaphor too far. The other danger is of mixing metaphors. For example, to use an army officer's style of communication and interaction in a family could damage the family members. Conversely, if an army officer were too "fatherly" in a war zone, he or she would lose the authority needed to lead a platoon in battle conditions. The gentle style of a shepherd is not as organised as a builder needs to be. Style needs to be matched to context.

Every church will go through the stages of being primarily a family, later a body, then perhaps a flock and an army. The wise leader will know which stage is current, and how to match their leadership to the stage in question. In reality, these stages are not clear-cut, but somewhat concurrent and overlapping, requiring the leader to wear different hats, often in quick succession. Sometimes the leader has to lead a family in one meeting, then move, in an hour's time, to another meeting where the hat he wears is that of a builder. Forgetting which hat is current can lead to cognitive dissonance, affecting everyone in the room. This is what I mean

---

[392] 2 Timothy 2:3–4; Ephesians 6:11–18.
[393] Ephesians 5:25–27; Revelation 19:7–8.

when I use the term "process leadership". The group is not static, but in process. The same is true for your leadership gift.

For the rest of this chapter, we are going to study how the spiritual gift of leadership goes through a process of growth in each person to whom it is given. You may be able to identify such growth in yourself, if you have been a leader for some time. If you took one of the tests designed to identify your spiritual gift(s) (e.g. "Network"[394] or the Houts Questionaire[395]) early in your ministry, and then took another some years later, you might have two different assessments of your gift mix. This is an indication that your gifts grow with you; that you adjust your leadership style to the situation in which you are leading; and that God equips you in context. Avoid the temptation to put yourself in a box. Think of leadership "outside the box", and exercise faith in the Giver of the gifts, not in the gifts themselves. In addition, you may need to be thinking of situations that call for a leadership style that you may never express yourself, but that you can see in others who form part of your team. In this case, you will delegate or defer to them at certain stages of the group's life. Ask Him to give you what the people need, and be faithful to give away what He entrusts to you.

Four possible approaches to leadership

For centuries, churches have been defined by, among other things, their leadership structure and style. Denominations use names like Episcopal, Congregational, Presbyterian and Charismatic to tell us how they are led: by a Bishop, the members, a Council

---

[394]Course in spiritual gifts – *Network: What You Do Best in the Body of Christ* by the Willow Creek Association.

[395]*Houts Inventory of Spiritual Gifts* by Richard F. Houts, written from a Baptist perspective, tests for 16 non-sign gifts. It was later adapted by C. Peter Wagner for his courses at the Fuller Institute of Church Growth, *Wagner-Modified Houts Questionnaire* at http://experiencetherock.com/mp3/message/2009/broken/spir_gift_sur.PDF.

of elders, or a gifted pastor respectively. Leadership consulting organisations use models to identify styles of leadership, such as those listed in the previous chapter. Building on the leadership styles analysed in that chapter, let us observe the fact that, apart from public styles such as apostolic, prophetic, pastoral and didactic, there are also approaches to leadership itself that will be different according to several factors. Through the observation of any church, management or other organisation, we can identify at least four approaches to leadership. Other models which analyse leadership use different language for these styles:

- *Autocratic:* Leadership as power, by authority, top-down. Tasks are primary.
- *Democratic:* Leadership as serving, by permission, bottom-up. Relationships are primary.
- *Visionary:* Leadership as directional, from the front. Momentum is primary.
- *Empowerer:* Leadership as people development, side by side. Participation is primary.

We may learn something about ourselves by looking more closely at these four styles that operate within the church context. John Wimber identified the first three of them, and my friend Mark Manley[396] has added the fourth. I am grateful to both of them for the ideas, and for permission to use them here. The diagram below shows them in graphic form. The little triangle inside the large one indicates the place of the leader, and the arrows show the direction of authority exercised.

---

[396] *The LeaderSHIP* (Mark Manley Associates, 2007).

Diagram 6: Four Leadership Approaches

The first three are well used to illustrate common styles of leadership in the traditional contexts that employ them most often. The fourth was suggested by Dr. Mark Manley, illustrating what groups such as the Quakers and Vineyard churches may envision:

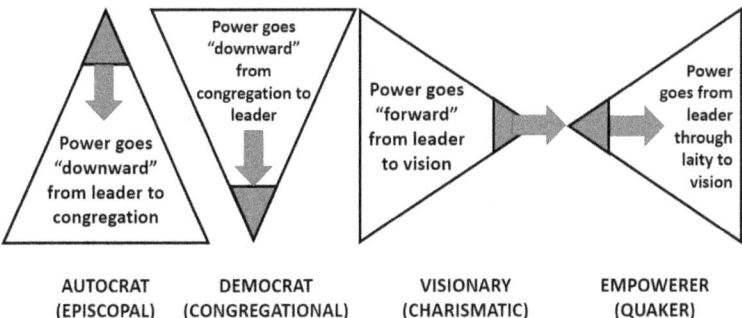

| AUTOCRAT (EPISCOPAL) | DEMOCRAT (CONGREGATIONAL) | VISIONARY (CHARISMATIC) | EMPOWERER (QUAKER) |

You will see that the autocratic leader focuses authority on his people. He requires them to listen and obey, achieve his goals for him, and he maintains law and order. If there is a problem, he will "pull rank" to get compliance. He runs a tight ship!

The democratic leader has the authority and the weight of the people coming down on him. He holds everyone and everything up. The leader is told by the group what he is to do, how and by when. Not only instructions, but also the very position and right to lead, are subject to a vote, whether by simple or two-thirds majority.

The visionary leader uses her authority to focus on a goal or direction. She leads "from the front", toward the group's agreed outcomes, and "carries" the people with her on the strength of the vision. This type of leadership requires a high component of enthusiasm, or charismatic inspiration.

The empowering leader also focuses a group toward a goal or vision, but the authority flows through the people themselves. The leader is not content merely with the achievement of the vision; it is equally important that people get to participate, find, use and grow their gifts in such achievement. The leader's job in this model is to give away his job.

The other thing to note is that social style and gifting usually go hand in hand. With very few exceptions, I have seen that the way a person is comfortable to lead will depend on how best they function socially in leader mode.[397] Our motivational gifts, as I mentioned in chapter 1, create a "poise", a way of being, and a comfort zone.

Authors such as Dr Ichak Adizes[398] have proposed that there is no such thing as the "complete" leader and that this makes the ideal, the function and the management of teams of leaders all the more important. My "process leadership" model posits the idea that every organisation grows through a typical "bell curve" with different stages. If the pattern is just allowed to unfold, history shows that the curve will flatten, then turn downward and, ultimately, the organisation will die. What prevents this pattern is a leadership model that understands the need for constant renewal and reinvention, thus creating a repeating bell curve instead of one that flatlines, declines and dies, if the right type of leadership is applied (see Diagram 7).

Adizes' version of this model identifies the four stages as Courtship, Infancy, Dramatic Growth and Adolescence. His four categories of leader are the Producer, Administrator, Entrepreneur and Integrator. He shows how, at each transition between the stages, the application of specific leadership skills can make the transition positive and smooth, while the absence or neglect of those skills can paralyse the system and lead to its stagnation and eventual death. The following diagram illustrates this process. The vertical axis represents growth, and the horizontal axis, time:

---

[397] A good example of the exception clause in this regard is the upsurge of books and articles about strong leaders who are introverts. Their social style is not "up front" at all, but when leading, they become much more assertive.
[398] Ichak Adizes, *Corporate Lifecycles: How and Why Corporations Grow and Die and What to Do About It* (Prentice Hall, 1989).

Diagram 7: The Organisational Growth Curve

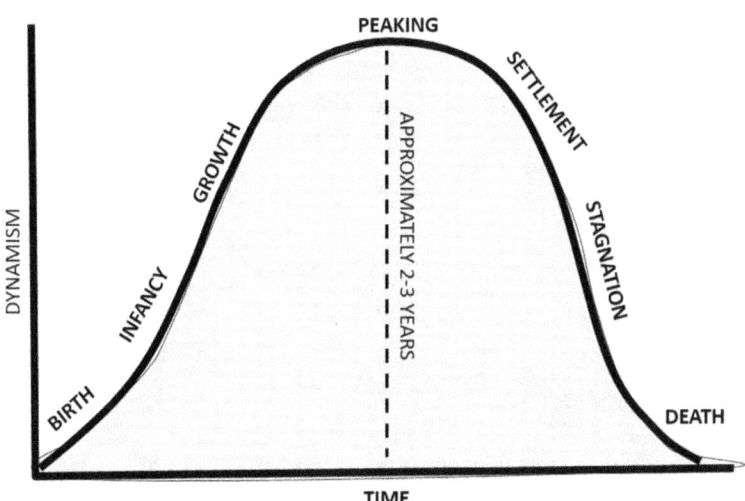

The peak of this curve, which typically would be reached in two to five years, represents the process of an organisation's birth, growth and peaking. The "downhill" half of the curve represents settlement, followed by potential stagnation and death. In Adizes' model, instead of the bell curve declining after the first two-year cycle, it may be "reinspired" for the next phase to begin as we see in Diagram 8.

Diagram 8: The Pattern of Organisational Renewal

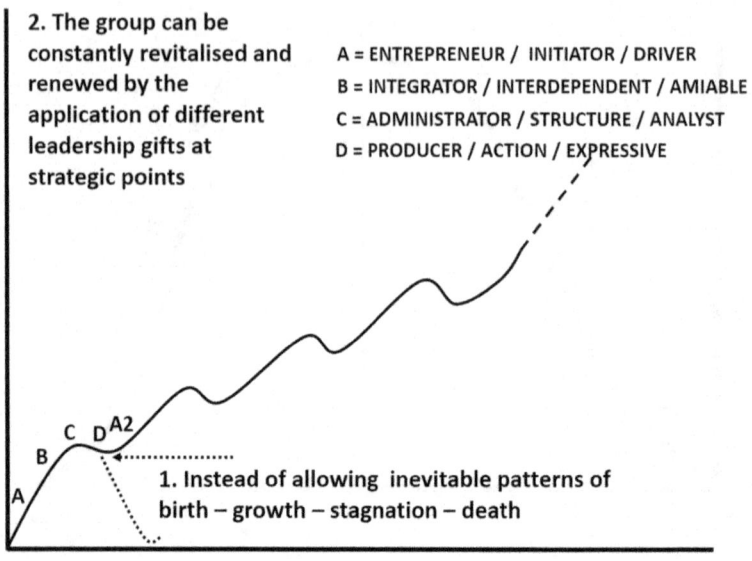

2. The group can be constantly revitalised and renewed by the application of different leadership gifts at strategic points

A = ENTREPRENEUR / INITIATOR / DRIVER
B = INTEGRATOR / INTERDEPENDENT / AMIABLE
C = ADMINISTRATOR / STRUCTURE / ANALYST
D = PRODUCER / ACTION / EXPRESSIVE

1. Instead of allowing inevitable patterns of birth – growth – stagnation – death

It is evident in the life of any group that it experiences phases of initiative (A), growth (B), consolidation (C) and decline (D). This is followed by either closure (death) or new initiative (A2), and so on. Each cycle lasts roughly two years. Diagram 8 shows a typical pattern of organisational life over about 10 years, with the peaks of the diagrammatic mountain range being separated by two-year gaps.[399]

Instead of Adizes' leadership labels, I will use below the four styles of which I spoke earlier, namely Catalyst, Democrat, Empowerer and Visionary, or apostolic, pastoral, teaching and prophetic respectively. The leadership style that takes and stimulates initiative (A) is that of the Catalyst. The growth phase (B) requires a democratic style of leader to bring cohesion and community. When consolidation (C) occurs, the empowering style is called for to develop systems and enable every person to feel that he or she

---

[399] Adizes, *op. cit.*

adds value. When the group goes into decline (D), the visionary leader can lift its mood with fresh perspective and inspiration, until the catalytic leader arises once again to direct the group into a new phase with fresh initiative. That is a rough outline of how process leadership works, although it is not always as neat as I suggest; the initiatives of the Lord may always intervene and confound (or compound) our best-laid plans!

Provided that new initiative is applied by an appropriately gifted leader each time the group goes into decline, there can be continued "reinvention", fresh momentum and growth. Without such leadership, the group will plateau, and probably slowly decline and die. Some groups I have seen, have died without ever facing the fact of their demise! They exist in name, and even continue to conduct "business", but without growing, achieving anything or experiencing real purpose or joy. They are, in fact, fossils, petrified trees, or corpses that have not fallen over yet!

On the other hand, effective deployment of focused, envisioning leadership can massage new life into groups on the edge of extinction. In the words of John Maxwell: "Everything rises and falls on leadership."[400] What is important is that the particular style of leadership applied, matches the phase or need of the group. For this to happen, the leader will need either to grow into the new style, or to defer to another leader who can supply it. Both of these possibilities exist for the person exercising the spiritual gift of leadership, because the gift resides in the person. If you are operating under God's direction, you may possibly receive new ability, new focus, and new skills, as new challenges arise. However, sometimes (and, I suspect, more often), the answer lies not in you, but in someone to whom God will direct you. When Barnabas saw the challenges of leading the Antioch church, he went and recruited Saul, and deferred to his gift mix for the new season of

---

[400]Maxwell, *op. cit.*

the church's life. Barnabas was the primary leader at that stage, but he recognised that God was directing him to build a team.[401]

As mentioned, there are very few "complete leaders", only individuals who embody one or other combination of charisma and praxis that contributes to the life and growth of the church. The church, however, needs all these types or forms of leader to operate within it for its full formation and maturity. Usually, gifts are noticed by their effect on a group. The effect of the spiritual gift of leadership, applied through a team of translocal leaders on a group of people, will be a constant and repeated sense of security, excitement, momentum and purpose on the way to achieving a goal.

Within local churches in the NT, there seems to have been considerable flexibility in terms of leadership and structure (see the seemingly interchangeable use of "elder", "bishop" and "pastor" in a single verse of Acts),[402] but Paul assumed that the churches to which he wrote needed to acknowledge some clear authority, namely his own (or, in the case of Corinth, that of him and Apollos). As Bartlett puts it: "There was a strong stress on the interdependence of all Christians and the inter-relatedness of all forms of ministry."[403] All forms of ministry, including apostleship, were seen above all as servant ministries, and all existed for the sake of the gospel and for the upbuilding of the church. There were both local (elders) and trans-local (Ephesians 4:11 level) leaders in most churches, the latter coming and going as team leaders like

---

[401]Acts 11:22–26.

[402]Acts 20:28, where Paul, speaking to the assembled "elders" (verse 17) of the Ephesian church, says to them: "Pay attention to yourselves and to the entire flock over which the Holy Spirit has made you overseers to be shepherds of God's church, which he acquired with his own blood." Peter uses the same words interchangeably in 1 Peter 5:1–3.

[403]Bartlett, *op. cit.,* p. 54.

Paul sent and summoned them.[404] Apostles and prophets seemed to work in a co-ordinating as well as a foundation-laying role, to keep the leadership "wheel" turning, according to the need of the individual church concerned.

Diagram 9: Identifying Your Style

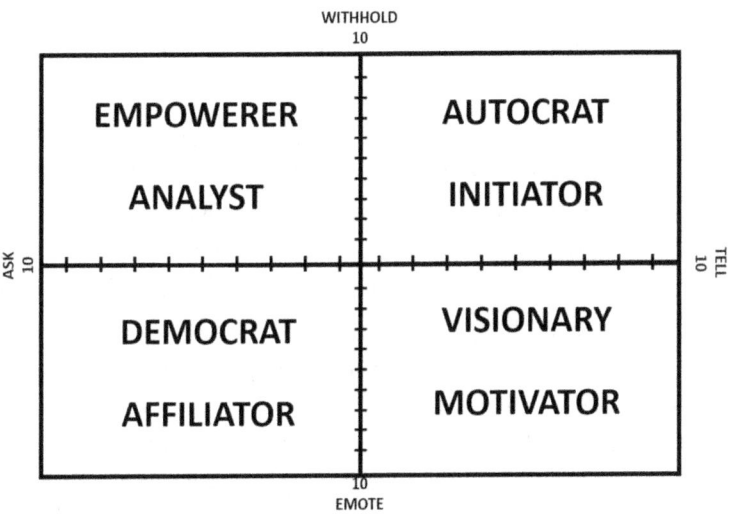

On the above diagram, the place where the axes cross is point "zero", where you would be least likely to, or "never", operate. The two outer points of each axis represent the "high", most likely or "always" mode of operating. On the horizontal axis, answer this question: When you are leading a group, and want to get someone to do something, do you usually and naturally tend to *ask*, or rather to *tell* them, to do it? Make a cross on the line where you most often "fit". Then, on the vertical axis, answer this question: In the context of leading the group, when you are feeling something strongly, do you tend to *emote* (show your feelings publicly),

---

[404]Examples abound in Paul's letters, e.g. read 1 Corinthians 16:11–12; Philippians 2:19–29; 2 Timothy 4:11.

or *withhold* (keep them to yourself)? Make a cross on the axis indicating where and how you usually operate.

You should now have two crosses on the diagram. If you join one to the other by the most direct route, it would fall into one of the four quadrants of the diagram. Which one are you in? Do you agree with the description it offers about you, your style of leadership and comfort zone? More especially, does your spouse, and do your colleagues, agree with it? It is not a comprehensive way to assess your style, but is, at least, a preliminary one. Nor should you see it as a "prison" or a type-casting mechanism. It indicates how you spontaneously and instinctively come across to others in a group setting, especially when you lead. However, you might be aware that this instinctive way of operating has changed over your time in leadership. Mine certainly has, and I have often seen growth and change happen in other leaders, moving their style from one quadrant to another as they have matured and/or as the context required.

We are all people in process, human "becomings" rather than a finished product. We are growing – in grace, in faith, in maturity and in confidence. The more we do so, the more flexibility we can show in our leadership role. Our strengths overcome our weaknesses, rather than vice versa. Instead of remaining in our comfort zone, we take risks with new ways of leading. Those who follow us will comment on this, saying things like, "You have more authority now" or "Something has happened to you." Bearing a different fruit in people's lives inspires greater risk-taking and visionary drive.

For a biblical example of this, you can read the story of David from 1 Samuel 16 to 2 Samuel 7, as the psalmist-shepherd boy becomes the military champion, the king's servant, the general, the civic organiser, the king-in-exile, and the king. He always remained, first and foremost, a worshipper, desiring nothing more than being in God's presence, but he rose to the challenge presented by challenges his people experienced: sometimes being autocratic; at other times being a pastoral, fatherly figure; sometimes an inspirer and sometimes an empowerer of others. We could discern a similar evolution in the lives of many biblical leaders. In the remainder of the chapter, we will study one of them more closely.

Nehemiah – process leadership in action

The Book of Nehemiah is probably the most often quoted text for the illustration of godly principles of leadership. Nehemiah seems to model faultless leadership attitudes as well as skills, to the point of being an almost messianic figure in the history of Israel. His passion and vision provide a great framework for Christian leaders to understand their sense of calling, and his successful organisational skills and patterns of implementation are excellent models for leaders in any sphere of operation. I want to examine his application of process leadership, matching the gift style he used to the need of the people in the moment. We will look at the Book in overview, and highlight some of the principles I have mentioned. Please read the following with the Book of Nehemiah open, so that you can follow the biblical context.

1. Motivations for leadership (chapter 1)

Unselfishness

Nehemiah's motivations for involvement in Israel's crisis are seen to be unselfish and sacrificial (verse 4). This involves a genuine ability to forego his own comforts, and to find joy in sacrificially serving the purposes of God and the needs of others. It is this servant attitude that is the prerequisite for leadership and, as we saw in Chapter 3, it is where Kingdom leadership begins.

Compassion

To experience compassion or empathy is to feel the hurt and shame of others (verse 4). It literally means to get into their skin, to be immersed in their feelings, and feel what Bill Hybels calls a "holy discontent", which is the identification with God in terms of His heart for them. Nehemiah experienced this regarding the land of Israel, the city of Jerusalem, and the Jewish people who still lived there. Their hurt and, in fact, God's hurt, was his hurt. For the Christian leader, this is based on the Word and Spirit of God. We would be crushed if we bore the pain of others without the initiative of the Lord. However, when we receive His love poured out into our hearts by the Holy Spirit, it enables us to bear the load of true compassion without being destroyed by it. It is a necessary price for the Kingdom leader to pay.

Identification

Nehemiah accepted the responsibility for the sin and brokenness of Israel (verses 6, 7). Stronger than empathy, identification means not only to feel, but also to own responsibility with the pain of broken people. This is what Jim Collins meant when he spoke about "the window and the mirror" approach of the leader.[405] As leaders, we are not only co-responsible with those we lead; in the spirit of the expression, "as goes the leader, so go the people". In addition, we are often the cause of their pain, because there is a spiritual law of reaping what we sow (Galatians 6:7–9). In a sense, as an early mentor of mine taught me, a leader sows and later reaps, his character into the spiritual climate of the group he leads. You and I, as leaders, are the seed we plant. John Wimber famously once answered the question: "How can I grow my church?" with

---

[405]See my exposition of this on page 99.

the words: "First decide: How many more people like you do you want?" The leader who shows a true, humble spirit of servanthood will accept that, when the people are not doing well, he is to identify with them in their pain.

Faith

This encompasses the tone of determination required in the person who would give leadership in God's Kingdom (verses 4–5, 11). It involves expectancy, a spirit of optimism and hope that we, with God, can make a difference. Your prayers have effect in heaven. Leadership gets results. Spiritual leadership expects God to do something about the problem through us. Notice that true faith is willing to be the answer to its own prayer! It does not "pass the buck" of responsibility, but accepts that the Lord works through sharing responsibility with faith-filled people.

2. Nehemiah as a visionary leader (chapter 2)

Vision, as we saw earlier, is the key to a leader's ignition. Let us examine the elements of visionary focus that ignited Nehemiah:

Goal-directed

His vision was specific enough so that he could plan ahead, set a time, and go and ask precisely for what he needed to fulfil his goal (verses 6–8). Where his faith had stimulated a dream and a mission, his gifting translated these into a set of goals.

Real goals are "SMART": Stretching, Measurable, Attainable, Recorded and Time-related. They put us in a state of internal commitment and accountability. The visionary leader will be motivated by deadlines, the "bottom line" and the anticipation of achievement. She will see the end from the beginning, and start, work and live, with the end in view. Goal direction is not the same as daydreaming. There were specific plans in Nehemiah's mind. He knew the route he needed to take, the names of those whose help he would ask for, and the materials he needed, before he started. Visionary leadership plans from the inside out, and from the bottom up.

Dependent on God

I have noticed that some leaders, operating by the "secular" approach to vision, have ended up making a god of the vision itself. Nehemiah was careful to acknowledge that God was the provider of both the vision and the favour needed to achieve it (verse 8b). Other leaders fear goal setting because it seems to exclude faith, Spirit-directedness or dependence on God. However, the two principles need not be mutually exclusive. Good planning does not exclude God, nor does God operate apart from good principles of management or stewardship. He is a God of planning, yet planning must always be held lightly, and be held before the Lord for confirmation, direction and course correction.[406] Nehemiah was, no doubt, aware of God's Word with regard to the king (Proverbs 21:1). His goals and planning were not independent of God's Word, but rather took their cue from that Word. The same should be true of any godly leader. It is not a matter of either planning *or* being dependent on God, but rather planning *while* being dependent on God. Depend on Him to give you the goals; depend on Him for the plan to pursue the goals; and depend on Him for the strength and wisdom to complete the goals.

---

[406]I enjoy *The Living Bible's* translation of Proverbs 24:3–4: "Any enterprise is built by wise planning, becomes strong through good sense, and profits wonderfully by keeping abreast of the facts." Keeping abreast of facts includes constant checking with the Lord of the plan!

Anticipates opposition

Every vision includes a healthy facing of the "what-ifs", or potential obstacles, and plans a range of possible responses to them (verse 10). Opposition on earth reflects conflict in the heavenly realm. It does not signal defeat or loss, but is rather, in my opinion, God's vote of confidence in the outcome. God will not allow any test His children cannot pass.[407] Rather, He allows the tests that will demonstrate our capacity to succeed by His grace, and grow us up. Equally, a victory is won in prayer in heavenly places before it is manifested on earth (Matthew 16:19; Ephesians 6:12). Leaders know that "there is more going on than is going on", that there is a constant spiritual dimension to our work, and will engage in the vital practice of prayer alongside planning and hard work.

Faces and identifies the problem

Nehemiah demonstrates a willingness, as should any leader, to see the "worst" of the bad news, and to descend to the depths of the situation (verses 12–15). Vision and goal setting involve knowing the starting point, no matter how bleak. In Joel 2:17, the prophet exhorts the priests to arrange themselves "between the vestibule [gate] and the altar", i.e. to engage with the people, to become aware of their pain, their sin and their need. A true leader is in touch, so that he may answer the questions people are asking, not only those of his own design. This is a difficult thing for a leader who is a natural optimist; it is a growth requirement for us to learn the difference between optimism and denialism.

These, then, are the elements that make up vision. A true insight into God and His plans, the enemies we face, the plight

---

[407] 1 Corinthians 10:13.

of the people and our own inadequacy without God, as well as our adequacy by His grace. The example of Isaiah (Isaiah 6:1–8), which we explored earlier (pages 55 to 57), applies here as well.

3. Nehemiah as an empowering leader (chapter 2 continued and chapter 3)

This aspect of leadership highlights the leader's role as trainer/ equipper (Ephesians 4:11–13). It contains the elements of *Identifying, Recruiting, Training, Deploying, Monitoring* and *Nurturing*.[408] We will look at this in Nehemiah's story as he works to empower people. It occurs early in the Book because, as we will see, he anticipates the need for this style of leadership early in the process, before he even engages in doing the job.

Identify and Recruit

He knew his helpers by name (chapter 3; 7:7) and by faith, he saw their potential (2:16). Nehemiah had not yet told them, but as a matter of principle, he anticipated delegating work to others. He knew "who would be doing the work". Jesus spent all night in prayer before choosing the 12 (Luke 6:12–13) and, like Nehemiah, called followers into what they would become, not because they were that person already. He saw the potential of a Simon who would become a Peter, and of other unrefined fishermen who would become "fishers of men", and called them into a work that would change them while it moved toward its fulfilment. Leaders are able to select, prayerfully, the right people to fit the mission profile, and confidently call them to it. The army of God is populated by

---

[408]An outline on leadership development first cited by Todd Hunter of Vineyard USA in 1986, quoting John Wimber's Church Planters' Profile in "Expanding the Kingdom Now".

conscripts, not volunteers (Acts 13:2–3).

Train

The language of the empowering leader is: "Come ... let us" (verse 17). Nehemiah let them own the job as theirs. It is the element of "let us" rather than "you must" that creates "self-starters" and "self-sustainers". He trains them as the job grows, according to the skills required at that moment. The proof of empowering leadership is people taking ownership of the job at hand, and growing with it as they go.

Deploy

The empowering leader casts vision, and then looks for an "echo" in those she is to lead. And she is a wise leader who gives people work according to what was in their heart to do anyway. A motivational climate is created when people can see a correlation between their personal vision and that of the leader (and thus the organisation). Therefore, the leader remains the catalyst for what she wants done, but has only succeeded when others take responsibility for it (verse 18).

Monitor

The enemy sends discouragement (2:19–20), questioning the vision. The empowering leader needs to monitor the emotional climate of the group, and model optimism, faith and courage in the face of the enemy. The enemies of Nehemiah sought to intimidate him with what they believed the king had said. His reply was to confess his faith in God, deny their authority and access, and get to work! He monitored the work practically, so that they knew when they were half-way, because he knew what the final goal was (4:6). A leader needs to be courageous, so that encouragement is a part of the impact he or she has on followers. Monitoring also involved a measure of conflict resolution or "relationship maintenance" (5:1–13). One of the primary functions of leadership involves encouraging people to maintain peaceful, loving and honest relationships with one another.

Nurture

Nehemiah constantly fed his people with both material and spiritual resources. He took personal responsibility for their protection and maintenance. Chapter 5 is a reflection of his selflessness (putting himself last in line for food) and generosity (feeding his fellow leaders and visiting dignitaries at his own cost). He maintained optimism by encouragement (4:14, 19–20) and a regular practice of intercession for the work and the workers (4:4–5, 9).

4. Nehemiah as a democratic leader (chapter 3)

This is the leadership dimension that operates with people and relationships as the highest value. The giving leader is a "people person". As we saw earlier, identifying, recruiting, training, deploying, monitoring and nurturing are vital leadership activities. They give people value, and the group a sense of community, belonging or warmth. Although we may see it in some chapters of Nehemiah more than others, he constantly refers to people and their interests, concerns and wellbeing. Here are some of the most striking examples of this essential characteristic of the truly people-orientated leader as exemplified in Nehemiah:

- We have already referred to the "Come ... let us" principle he employed in 2:17, to which the empowered people replied: "Let us arise and build" (2:18). True delegation brings a willing response.
- The whole of chapter 3 shows his heart to empower the

people, including young and old, men and women.

- He gives them credit when they finish a task, looking through his "window" and saying: "The people had a mind to work" (4:6). The democratic leader does not need to take the credit – he passes it on to the people.

- He constantly modelled what he expected of others, taking no special privileges as a leader (4:23; 5:14–16), and saying that this was because "the servitude was heavy on this people" (5:18–19 RSV). The democratic leader is an example, and seeks to lighten the load of people.

- He enrolled them by name, and detail, to secure their birthright in the nation of the covenant (chapter 7). The democratic leader fights for the rights of others.

- He united them in observance of their responsibility before God (8:1), and in responding appropriately to God's victory through them. He is a leader who cares that people should enjoy the right emotional climate in their faith, teaching them and engaging Ezra and others to do the same, so that the people would recover the joy of the Lord (8:9–10, 17). This chapter epitomises Nehemiah's democratic leader heart. He wants people not only to participate, but also to have a good time doing so!

- He has them cast lots (one man, one vote) on important issues like: "Who may live in Jerusalem?" (11:2). The democratic leader will know when to take his own counsel, and when to involve others in the decision.

- He throws a megaparty to celebrate the final victory of the people (12:36–47). Nehemiah was a leader who knew both how to work hard with his followers, *and* how to have fun with them!

5. Nehemiah as an "autocratic"[409] leader (chapter 5)

I am aware that the concept of autocratic leadership can be viewed very negatively. When I use the word here (in quotes) I mean clear, self-confident decisiveness. I mean that kind of leadership that sometimes has to make a judgment call, not bullying, unaccountable dictatorship for the sake of power. Is autocratic leadership ever necessary? If so, when? We saw Nehemiah taking the initiative for the job at hand in chapter 2, where he asks the king to "send me to Judah to rebuild the city where my ancestors are buried" (2:5 NLT). He becomes a catalytic leader when he realises that "he who gets the burden, gets the job"! He would have to act on the sense of burden, because it would not leave him in any other way. Vision does not happen automatically; it needs a person willing to steward it, to do what is necessary though no one else goes with him. This is the peculiar courage and determination of the catalytic, or autocratic, leader.

In chapter 5, we see Nehemiah resorting to a very directional model of leadership in the re-establishing of the community. In violation of the Law, Jews in the newly resettled Jerusalem were exacting interest on loans from fellow Jews. It is evident that, when the values expressed in the Word or work of God are at risk, or being violated, the leader needs to "take counsel with himself" (5:7) and "tell" rather than "ask". He will be required to make "judgment calls" on things, as Nehemiah does in this chapter. In chapter 6, he is called upon to do the same, when faced with intimidation and the suggestion of compromise by his enemies. Through quiet affirmation of truth and refusal to engage

---

[409] I use the word to describe the quality of self-starting, entrepreneurial leadership that is seen in pioneers or barrier-breakers. I am aware that the word has negative connotations, in the sense of dictatorial, unaccountable leadership. It is possible to affirm the former aspects while being careful not to affirm the latter. That is why I put the word in quotation marks here.

in game-playing, he demonstrates a firm example of confident, "autocratic" leadership.

Chapter 13 is full of examples of intense, confrontational authority in action, as Nehemiah throws Tobiah's possessions out of the temple room he had occupied (verses 7–8), gives very directional orders regarding implementation of the Law (verses 9–11), even beats and later pulls out the hair of offenders (verses 20–25), and fires wrongly appointed workers (verse 28). Not a job for the sensitive! Moreover, it is not to be resorted to quickly or easily, but only when the issues of unrighteousness concerned are objectively crystal clear, in those extreme situations of threat to the values of the group, such as the one Nehemiah faced. A New Testament equivalent can be seen in the actions taken and instructions given by Paul in 1 Corinthians 5:1–5 (the condoning of incest); 1 Timothy 1:19–20 (blatant sin by leaders) and 2 Corinthians 13:1–11 (unnamed but blatant sin in the church).

Thus, what we call "autocratic" leadership is necessary at the start of something, or when the vision is under attack, being compromised, sinned against or suffering neglect. Be careful of too much use of this style of leadership. You may find that authority is like soap: the more you use it, the less of it you have!

Application

The Wheel of Leadership

The model on which I am basing this is a wheel. Picture, if you will, the leadership window (page 224) being made into a circle.[410] More specifically, a wheel. Not a modern one with a hub cap or mag rims, but an old-fashioned one (a horse-drawn-cart wheel) with spokes.

---

[410]I first saw this "rounding" of the window proposed by Mark Manley in "The LeaderSHIP" (*op. cit.*).

Diagram 10: The Wheel of Leadership

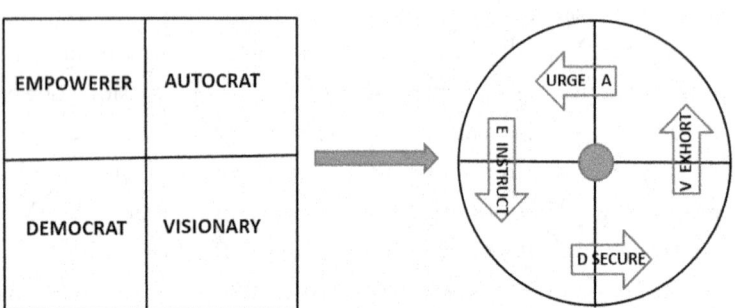

In this wheel there are four quadrants (**A**utocrat, **E**mpowerer, **D**emocrat, **V**isionary). The wheel has the following components:

- The axle hub is the values every leader holds, and that gives momentum and cohesion to what leaders do.
- The wheel rim is what puts the leader and her gift in contact with the context – the world of people and their circumstances.
- The spokes are the means of support and tension connecting the hub to the axle, holding the leader to the context, and making the values relevant. As the axle turns, the spoke will apply the tension and momentum from the axle to the road.

In leadership terms, each style of leadership is given momentum by applying the unique gift of the leader, through her grace, faith and action. To return for a moment to Paul in Romans 12, we saw earlier that he "urges" (Greek *parakaleo*) people, by the grace given to him, to surrender to the service of Christ, then "calls" (Greek *lego*) them to think, and later to act, in accordance with the grace given to them. The grace by which he saw the centrality of the Lordship of Christ led to a compelling, passionate call to Christians to use their gifts in His service. In summary, each leadership gift will be driven and come across to the context with the following dynamic:

1. The apostolic/evangelistic (autocratic) leader will *urge* people to believe and follow. He says: I bring this good news, therefore I beseech you – be reconciled to God.
2. The analytical/teaching (empowering) leader will quietly *instruct* people to order their thoughts according to God's Word. He says: I understand this truth; let me help you see what I see in this text.
3. The pastoral (democratic) leader will empathetically *secure* people into community. She will say: I care about your wellbeing and growth together with us – let me embrace you into this family.
4. The prophetic (visionary) leader will *exhort* people to greater passion and excitement. He says: This is what the Lord says: don't settle for being comfortable – get up, cheer up, buck up!

As the leader exercises her gift, the wheel of community turns and makes progress through this age toward "the age to come"; the Kingdom of God advances in and through the community's life and practices, from spirit, to mind, to body, to community, to world.

The discernment questions for the overall leader of a church (if there is one), or the team involved, in every stage of a church's life, are the following:

- How is our community doing?
- What do we need now?
- How should we be responding?
- What steps need to be taken so that we move toward our stated vision?
- What kind of gift mix needs to be prominent?

- Who should be "taking point" at the moment?

In planning a church's preaching schedule, short-term or annual program or curriculum, the focus should not only be on the subject matter, but also on the leadership style necessary. Remembering Itchak Adizes' model of the organisational growth curve, the work of the church's leadership is to maintain momentum through all the stages, from birth to ageing, then rebirth or renewal to new growth, and out of decline into resurrection life, over and over again.

For example, as a new community is encountered as God sends the church on mission, a founding (apostolic, evangelistic or catalytic) leader (usually with a team) will gather a group, or plant a church; soon after a pastoral (democratic) leader will need to make a crowd into a community; later the members will need to be taught (empowering leader) to understand and function; still later, they will have to be exhorted (visionary leader) to new energy and renewed effort, so that the wheel turns again from those already there to those not yet there, and the church evangelises, reproduces itself, and so on.

However, the process leadership model does not follow a predictable sequence in Nehemiah's case; nor will it do so in yours. You will find the needs of the group calling for styles from Catalyst to Empowerer, to Visionary, to Democrat and back again, without warning. As we saw in Nehemiah's case, he not only adapted as necessary to the style called for by the context, but also deferred to others to complement what he could do. Ezra was clearly the stronger teacher, so Nehemiah got him to explain the meaning of God's Word (chapter 8). We saw earlier how Barnabas went to fetch Saul when teaching was required in the Antioch church (Acts 11). Is the church you are leading in need of some emphasis for which you are not gifted? Defer to someone else on the team for a season, and "dial down" your own role for a while. This does not mean abdicating your leadership; it comes through the doorway of your deferment, and shows that for you, leadership is not an ego trip, but a function of servanthood. God will raise and defend your authority as long as you serve with a pure heart.

So, we return to where we started. Leadership is mysterious and supra-rational and, at the same time, definable and rational. You, as a leader, will need to depend on grace and to ask God for the wisdom and ability to respond to the needs of those you lead. My friend, Brian Anderson, pastor of the North Phoenix VCF in Arizona, taught us pastors in the early days of the Vineyard movement's formation to ask the Lord to send in the gifts needed for every stage of the church's growth. You will always lack the necessary wisdom, always lack resources, always be inadequate. But God has no lack. He is willing to supply the wisdom (James 1:5), the workers (Matthew 9:38), and the adequacy of gifting (2 Corinthians 2:15–16; 3:5). He will lead you into fruitful partnerships and enable you to network with those of His choosing for you. Remain open to growth. It occurs through facing barriers and challenges, and calling on the grace and power of the Lord of leadership.

CHAPTER 9

Leadership as Fathering: Potentiality

"A great mentor has a knack for making us think we are better than we think we are. They force us to have a good opinion of ourselves, let us know they believe in us. They make us get more out of ourselves, and once we learn how good we really are, we never settle for anything less than our very best."
The Prometheus Foundation

In what follows, I am going to focus on a leadership trait that is, by definition, gender-specific in origin, if not in application. Although I will also discuss "mothering" at the end of the chapter, the bulk of it will focus on fathering. I think the concept speaks to some specific ways in which leaders are to relate to their followers. This does not mean only males can do this. "Fathering" refers to a specific orientation and way of being involved and doing things. We have many examples of women expressing this – often better than men – just as "mothering" can be done by men. Paul describes his specific way of doing this for the Thessalonian church:

... we were gentle among you, like a nursing mother tenderly

caring for her own children. We cared so deeply for you that we were determined to share with you not only the gospel of God but our very lives. That is how dear you were to us.
(1 Thessalonians 2:6–8)

However, because the word "father" is gender-specific, please excuse my political incorrectness in this chapter. In the interests of consistency of grammar, I will use only male pronouns from here on.

God and fatherhood

God is quite enigmatically described by Paul in Ephesians as "the Father, from whom every family in heaven and on earth is named" (Ephesians 3:14–15). I understand this text to be holding the Father-nature of God up as a model, and saying, in other words, that every human family should receive the power of that nature to motivate and mould it. In specifically naming the Father, furthermore, Paul is speaking to fathers everywhere as those primarily responsible for the family they form. He is saying, in effect: "Don't call it family if it's not like this. If you take the name, then live the game."

Without wishing to impose too narrow a typecasting here, I do think that each member in the mom and dad parenting team brings their unique gift to the task of raising children. It seems to be true that men and women differ in their predispositions. In a generalised, though not exclusive sense, whereas the psychosocial role of mothers is to provide a sense of "here and now" (responsibility in the present) for her children, the role of fathers is to call their children to focus on "there and then" (hope for the future).[411] A father challenges his children to develop them-

---

[411]This is even demonstrable in biochemical terms. The function of testosterone is future-focused, goal-oriented and task-driven, whereas oestrogen is the hormone that motivates women toward a nest-creating, security-enhancing and being-oriented mode. The fact is that all men and women

selves on the way to achievement as much as to the achievements themselves. Ideally, the father's role is to affirm what he sees the child could become. The father will give himself to the growth of his sons and daughters, not to make *himself* look good, but to promote *them*. Fathering is not a merely psychological, emotional and practical exercise in raising, and passing something on to, our children. It is powerful and spiritual in effect. What we say before God about our children, and what we say to them about their destinies, is lasting and transformational.

I want to emphasise again that parental effect is not limited to gender, in that women as well as men can fulfil either role, but will usually need to be stretched into one or other role based on both individual physiological and psycho-social factors, while the other may come more naturally. With that disclaimer in mind, though, I think, in general, that fathers enable, empower and facilitate the discovery of their children's individual potential and goal achievement.

A father is not meant to be a critic so much as a coach. He does not seek to live his life through his children, but facilitates their living their own lives and being the best possible version of themselves. This is what fathers are uniquely given to do – to give their children the loving acceptance and confidence that "you're safe here", and then to inspire a sense of future, of faith to live up to the name you carry, and achieve a significant life.

The model of God as Father, of course, does not stand alone, because the God of the Bible is Trinity. The Father is interdependent with the Son and the Spirit, intertwined in a dance, the *perichoresis*, a word used by the early Church Fathers to describe the Trinity.[412] This term was first used by Gregory of Nazianzus,

---

have both of these hormones in different, but gender-loaded proportions. See the article by Dr Steven F. Hotze, "Testosterone" at http://www.aehf. com/articles/Testosterone.htm.

[412]"John of Damascus and the Perichoresis", an article by Rev. Angus

and later by John of Damascus, and best expresses Trinity as interpenetration and interdependence. It is a picture of both eternal embrace and joyful dance, of differentness and co-equality that is always blurred, because the interpenetration of the Three Persons is so complete, and yet is gloriously diverse, because each is also highlighted and celebrated as unique. Daniel Migliore puts it: "The three of the Trinity 'indwell' and pervade each other; … 'encircle' each other … or to use still another metaphor … 'make room' for each other, are incomparably hospitable to each other."[413] And, in a sense, the nature of one is the nature of all. Because God is Father, there are characteristics of fatherliness about God as Son and God as Holy Spirit.

The Christian is called to be embraced by and to enter this dance of loving fellowship with the divine. And, in being embraced, the Christian also participates in, and imbibes that love. That is why John can say: "God is love, and whoever abides in love abides in God, and God abides in him" (1 John 4:16). God is love, and when God is in you, and you are in Him, He cannot help Himself – He will pour His love through you – you will love!

But God's love also cannot be contained. Therefore, mission is the inevitable overflowing of divine life, overcoming every obstacle with His love, saturating all enmity with a presence of goodness that will not be denied. The eschatological goal of God's self-manifestation in the world is that "the earth will be covered with the knowledge of the glory of the Lord, as the waters cover the sea" (Habakkuk 2:4). Thus, the local church gathers around His presence with the rightful response of worship, and then goes

---

Stewart (slightly modified from an article first published in the *British Reformed Journal*). In the article, he draws mostly from "John of Damascus, Exposition of the Orthodox Faith", trans. S. D. F. Salmond, in *The Nicene and Post-Nicene Fathers,* second series, eds. Philip Schaff and Henry Wace, vol. 9 (Eerdmans, repr. 1989).

[413]Migliore, *op. cit.*, pp. 78–79 (loc 1740).

into all the world with the equally inevitable, automatic, spontaneous response of mission. We know Him so that we may make Him known. We receive His blessing so that we may be a blessing to every family on the earth. This is not legalism, or a duty, but a natural response to the Triune God whose presence has engaged us. He cannot help Himself, but will always be love. And He cannot contain Himself – God insists on being love to those beyond our walls, on scattering hope to the hopeless by the stories of those He has infected with hope.

If God is your Dad, you will leak love! This is the nature of God, and therefore, specifically, of God as Father. It is love, expressed in community and mission. God invites us as believers (and therefore, as leaders), into the dance, to be fathered into a sense of self-acceptance and love, and then launched into the living of a significant life.

Keep this in mind as we speak about fathering, and of leadership as an expression of it.

What fathers do

Fathering, like God's fathering of us, is a qualitative thing, operating between individuals who feel drawn into a relationship that comes about by one of two dynamics, namely birth or adoption. Both are used in the New Testament, without value distinction. So Paul, when insisting on his place as a father to the Corinthian church, says, in the NKJV: "For in Christ Jesus I have begotten you through the gospel" (1 Corinthians 4:15), he means that he gave them life, or was responsible for their existence, through his proclamation of the gospel in that city (Acts 18:1–8). Conception is the main way of becoming a father, at least biologically. On the other hand, countless people have testified (in natural, social terms) that an adoptive father was more of a father to them than their biological father had been. The Bible also has much to say about the principle of adoption where, by the choice of the parent, a child can enter all the rights and privileges of "sonship". Paul refers to Onesimus as someone he "fathered" (Philemon 10, probably by conversion), while it seems clear that Timothy had been a Christian for some time before Paul "adopted" him. Yet both were regarded by Paul as his sons "in the Lord".[414]

No matter which dynamic applies, when the relationship has thus begun, the "father" has responsibilities, which I want to discuss in this chapter. The role of a parent has many facets, including providing, modelling, blessing,[415] securing, challenging, guiding, disciplining,[416] and leaving a legacy.[417] The outcome of all of these will be arrival at an appointed destiny.

My father passed away at the age of 85, after suffering an aortic aneurysm. As I spent time with him in the hospital, prayed with him and watched his struggles, it was a time to think about what he had been for me as a father, and my thoughts naturally turned to what that means in general for leadership. I will unashamedly

---

[414]"Adoption" also refers to one of the practices of the Graeco-Roman world, where a father would take his son to the public forum of the city's fathers, and legally declare him as his son. It was a rite of passage by which the son, now "adopted", would have legal and material rights in his father's domain and on his father's behalf.

[415]Genesis 26:26–29.

[416]Proverbs 13:24; 22:15; 23:13–14; 29:15, cf. Hebrews 12:7–9.

[417]Thus, says Paul about his role as a father to the Corinthians: "For even if you have ten thousand guardians in your Christian life, you have only one father. For in your life in union with Christ Jesus I have become your father by bringing the Good News to you. I beg you, then, to follow my example. For this purpose I am sending to you Timothy, who is my own dear and faithful son in the Christian life. He will remind you of the principles which I follow in the new life in union with Christ Jesus and which I teach in all the churches everywhere" (1 Corinthians 4:15–17 GNB). Paul's fatherly work involved birthing them in the gospel, guiding them in life, and providing ongoing care for them by connecting them with Timothy and the apostolic team.

apply some of the lessons of his life and practice as a dad in what follows, while being very conscious that not all who read this would have had the privilege I had, of an ideal father, who loved us and showed it, said it and lived it without fail, for my entire life with him. I hope that you can enter my story and learn from it, rather than being embarrassed or hurt if you cannot share in every aspect of it. Leaders are meant to offer a level of "fathering" to those they lead. But the concept is in danger of being over-stated and becoming abusive, or at least controlling. I think the way some people apply it is, in fact, the very antithesis of being a father.

Providing

A father is a *generous provider*. One of the most noticeable things about my dad was his generosity of spirit. He was constantly thinking about other people. Even in the life-and-death struggle I watched him go through at the end of his life, he was asking about the wellbeing of my family, was concerned that my mother should not travel to and fro between home and hospital as much as she was, and was anxious that we express our gratitude to the doctors and nursing staff for their care of him. He was always known as a man who would "give you the shirt off his back". This kind of material generosity begins with a generous spirit. It is a spirit that seeks to provide what the children require, and to see to it that they have more, enjoy more, and do better than the father himself did as a child. The father will work hard to provide and protect his children, literally to the point of laying down his life for them. He will endure personal discomfort and self-denial, without be-grudging it to his children. I have sometimes heard leaders speak with disparagement, impatience, even contempt about those they lead. In contrast to this, the true father will believe the best of his "children", and work, as Paul did, with all the energy with which

God inspires him, to present them complete in Christ (Colossians 1:29; 2:1).

Securing

Giving security is another father-function. Someone has called it "anchoring". It speaks of the security of love, as well as protection, and the knowledge that there is someone who will fix my broken stuff. I remember the sense of awed realisation about this striking me for the first time as a five-year-old boy, when our beloved dog disappeared. I was distraught, crying in my bed for Simba. I went to my parents' room, and cried out my fears and sadness to my dad. He wasn't a "born again" Christian at the time, and I don't know if he operated on faith, or a hunch, or was just lucky, but he told a frightened little boy: "He'll come back – don't worry! Pray for him, and you'll see – he'll be home tomorrow!" The next day Simba dragged himself home – injured, bleeding, and bedraggled, but home safe. I thought my dad was a miracle man! And, in all honesty, I never doubted throughout my childhood that my dad could fix anything!

It may be quite a responsibility to put on a father, but the principle is important. Fathers owe their children the security of knowing they are loved, that someone other than themselves is attentive, involved and caring. The most securing thing fathers can offer is their availability. We have experienced the pain and dysfunction of what has been called the "fatherless generation"[418] over 40 years. Research in the USA revealed that the average child got 45 *seconds* of his father's focused, personal attention every day. I read of a pastor many years ago who wrote in his diary one

---

[418]A generation which has grown up, mostly in urban environments, with fathers being either physically or emotionally absent. In South Africa, the generation of black children from 1950 to 1990 had their fathers living and working in cities far from home, being forbidden by apartheid laws from relocating with their families.

particular day: "Took Jim fishing today – a day wasted!" While eight-year-old Jim wrote in his diary on the same day: "Dad took me fishing today – the best day I ever had!" What a sad reflection of the value clash between father and son! They operated with completely different units of emotional currency. Many can testify similarly of how men have failed as fathers to supply this simple gift of themselves to their children.

The securing role of a father has the effect of creating a warm, relational environment in the family. When I visit churches, I can often tell before the service starts if the pastor is a father-leader by how warm and engaging the members are – to one another and to strangers. This is not the job of the pastor alone, but this is a major area that illustrates the principle: "As goes the leader, so go the followers!" We need to keep in mind that cultivating a warm, relational environment is part of the job of leaders. It has to do with giving people security, with ensuring that how they feel while making the journey is as important to us as getting them to the destination.

My dad was always the "life and soul" of every family gathering, welcoming people, being a generous and gracious host, making them feel at home, making them laugh, and have a good time. I guess it's one thing I have managed to catch from him, and is part of my social DNA, as my friends will attest. I have made it a part of how I lead churches and any other group. It may not always come naturally to everyone, but I believe, as we saw in chapter 4 on "Character", that a warm, hospitable, open-hearted nature is part of a leader's essential equipment, and is a valid way to measure the presence of the spiritual gift of leadership. As a leader, the question is: "Are you available? Involved? Attentive?" Unless you are, you will not be able to "father" anyone.

Modelling

Fathering involves *modelling*, or *mentoring*. A child learns more in its first two years than in the rest of its life put together. Most of that learning will be by observing its parental models. There are times when the same-sex parent is more influential, and others when the opposite-sex parent is. However, what we as leaders may learn from this is that we influence far more by what we *do* than we *think* – and perhaps much more than by our profound teachings. I believe the structuring and formalising of "mentoring" relationships can be overdone, and made artificial. The most effective mentoring relationships I have involve spontaneous get-togethers for a meal, a cup of coffee, to watch a rugby game, as well as sharing ministry experiences and structured training appointments. We mentor people by having them share our lives, watching us at work, at play, at home, in crisis and at our best. Thus, it is a self-limiting role. Jesus had three close "mentees" among the 12, who saw him at His most vulnerable, intimate moments, such as the raising of Jairus' daughter,[419] the Transfiguration on the mount,[420] and Gethsemane.[421] We may be able to have a similar number of people, or perhaps up to a maximum of six, close enough to us to share our lives at any given time. It is, however, part of the responsibility of the leader to be sufficiently in touch with those he seeks to influence, to be able to be a model of the lifestyle and ministry values for which he stands. Thus, says Paul about is role as a father to the Corinthians:

> *For even if you have ten thousand guardians in your Christian life, you have only one father. For in your life in union with Christ Jesus I have become your father by bringing the Good News to you. I beg you, then, to **follow my example**.*

---

[419] Mark 5:37ff.
[420] Mark 9:2.
[421] Mark 14:33.

> *For this purpose I am sending to you Timothy, who is my own*
> *dear and faithful son in the Christian life. He will remind*
> *you of the principles which I follow in the new life in union*
> *with Christ Jesus and which I teach in all the churches eve-*
> *rywhere.* (1 Corinthians 4:15–17 GNB, emphasis mine)

What Paul was saying about Timothy was that he was a reliable witness, able to model effectively what Paul had modelled to him. The fathering he had given his adopted son had been successful!

Disciplining

Perhaps the most distasteful role the father plays is that of *bringing discipline* to his children. Scripture is clear on the subject of the need for discipline, and its association not with hatred, but with love (Proverbs 13:24; 22:15; 23:13–14; 29:15). And, famously, God is represented as loving us as sons too much to leave us without discipline:

> *God is treating you as sons. Is there a son whom his father*
> *does not discipline? Now if you are without any discipline,*
> *in which all sons share, then you are illegitimate and not*
> *his sons. Furthermore, we had earthly fathers who used to*
> *discipline us, and we respected them for it. We should even*
> *more submit to the Father of our spirits and live, shouldn't*
> *we?* (Hebrews 12:7–9)

I have had to do the unpopular job of calling leaders into line, reprimanding them before others, and applying some level of disciplinary boundaries. As a parent of our own children, I tried to learn the difference between punishment and restorative discipline. It has to do with motive and desired results. Am I doing this because of concern for my reputation or image? And what do I see as the desired outcome – pain inflicted for its own sake? Ridding myself of a problem? Restoring my children to righteousness or helping them to establish a boundary of good behaviour for their life? In ministry contexts, this has sometimes succeeded and sometimes failed. It has always been heartbreaking to have to do it, regardless of outcome. But it is, nonetheless, a requirement for responsible fathering. True, godly discipline is only present when the consequences affect the father as much as they affect the "child".

In a movement like the Vineyard, where we value "adult-to-adult" relationships,[422] discipline can be a dirty word. Certainly, it is difficult to apply without compromising the stated value. Discipline needs to take the value of the person seriously, thus presenting the dilemma faced by parents as their children move into adolescence and young adulthood. When our children reached adolescence, we had to adjust the style of discipline to their newfound maturity. We would no longer apply corporal means of punishment. They had more choice about things like curfews, attending church, parties, etc., but we discussed boundaries of behaviour, values they would uphold in the home and outside it, and consequences for serious violations. It was when the first violation occurred, and consequences had to be applied, that I learned, with considerable pain, that "parenthood is not a popularity contest". I have had to repeat that phrase to myself many times since, in modified form: "Leadership, likewise, is not a popularity contest!"

Parents of emerging adults have to balance the task of maintaining good order in their homes, while respecting and encouraging their children's dignity and responsibility. This means communication, allowing choice, and operating on the basis that choices

---

[422]Based on the concepts of Transactional Analysis defined and expounded by Eric Berne in his book, *Games People Play: The Basic Handbook of Transactional Analysis* (Penguin, 1975), where he shows that every interaction between two humans involves each operating either as a child, a parent or an adult over against the other.

carry consequences, and that love requires freeing the person to choose, but also to take responsibility for the consequences. As a leader of leaders, this translates into the mutual agreement, ahead of time, of "father" and "children", to the values and biblical norms to which we will be accountable, and to the way we will be dealt with if we violate them. But, if you choose to exercise the spiritual gift of leadership as a "father" of those you lead, you need to be willing to apply these agreed processes without fear or favour.

Calling forth potential

Long before any books were written on the subject, my dad understood that success for any individual is a matter of identifying, pursuing and achieving one's personal goals. I am the middle of three sons born to my parents. But I was different to either of them with regard to physical development and skills. A late developer, short for my age, and not a sprinter, as both my brothers were. I will always remember him talking with me about this, and bringing home to me the implication that I should think not in terms of what *they* were achieving, but what *I* wanted to achieve. He encouraged us all in this, in terms of academics, sport and, ultimately, career choices. A phrase he would use often was: "It does not matter what you do, as long as it is something *you* want to do and that makes you happy." What he was doing as a father-leader, was helping me discover my own potential, and pursue it. He knew that this had to do with dreams, desires and goals, and that the goals imposed on one by others, either implicitly or explicitly, would not satisfy anyone, even if they were achieved. I hear in this the echoes of the apostle Paul, describing the church as a body with different parts, and encouraging each one to find her specific function and to be the best at that that she could be:

> *I want you to think about how all this makes you more significant, not less. A body isn't just a single part blown up*

into something huge. It's all the different-but-similar parts arranged and functioning together. If Foot said, "I'm not elegant like Hand, embellished with rings; I guess I don't belong to this body," would that make it so? If Ear said, "I'm not beautiful like Eye, limpid and expressive; I don't deserve a place on the head," would you want to remove it from the body? If the body was all eye, how could it hear? If all ear, how could it smell? As it is, we see that God has carefully placed each part of the body right where he wanted it.
(1 Corinthians 12:14–18 MSG)

Paul also says elsewhere: "When they measure themselves by themselves and compare themselves to themselves, they show how foolish they are" (2 Corinthians 10:12). Thus, a father is someone who enables, empowers and facilitates the discovery of his children's individual potential and goal achievement. He is not a critic, he is a coach. He does not seek to live his life through his children, he facilitates their living their own lives and being the best possible version of themselves. This is particularly important when a leader is responsible not only for individuals, but also for an organisation or an institution that he is leading. The subtle danger of using individuals to accomplish corporate goals is a constant one that a servant leader must avoid. This sense of empowering generosity must be the constant counterbalance to that other leadership character trait we have discussed before, namely vision. Vision that ignores the human factor becomes the abuse of authority or leadership. We need, as leaders, to constantly remember that we lead and are responsible for *people*, not just what they can achieve. A person is not merely a function or a packet of gifts, but a valued individual. God values us not for what we do, but for who we are, and a leader who forgets this may achieve goals through the organisation he leads, but will be responsible for the human casualties, the loss of spiritual and emotional wellbeing, and even the bitterness with God that might result.

So, we are to lead as those who will have to give an account. The standard of accountability measurement to which the gospel of the Kingdom constantly points, is how we treated people, not so much the results we gained in treating them that way. Thus, the well-known passage in Matthew 25 reminds us that Jesus will not ask if we healed the sick so much as if we cared for them. Not: "Did you liberate prisoners?" but: "Did you visit them?" (Matthew 25:36). What is at stake is the issue, not of fixing the problem so much as giving people dignity in our attempts to minister to them. It is important, then, for us to remind ourselves as leaders of that "Wheel of Life" I referred to in chapter 4, as a way to think not only of ourselves, but also of the people we lead. Caring about the whole person; their family life, their intellectual life, their emotions and their spiritual integrity, is a most important way for a leader to measure her effectiveness. It is the way of the father-leader.

Of course, we want the job done, and done well. But, to paraphrase another text and apply it in this context: "What does it profit a leader, if he gains the whole world of achievement, but loses the soul of even one person he has led in that achievement?" Paul describes his own passionate commitment as a leader in the letter to the Colossians (1:29), where he speaks of his responsibility to proclaim, to teach, to admonish, to impart wisdom, "so that we may present everyone mature [or fully rounded] in Christ". This, again, is the passion of a spiritual father: to see his children do well within themselves, to find that quality that Jesus called "abundant life",[423] to enjoy the Kingdom of God as righteousness, peace and joy in the Holy Spirit.[424] Achievement of goals needs to be a by-product of the quality of Kingdom life that is suggested

---

[423]John 10:10.
[424]Romans 14:17.

by texts like these. A leader who is a true father to those he leads, will desire nothing less than this for them.

Challenging

A father plays a unique role in instilling idealism in his children. Where mothers provide a sense of "here and now" (responsibility in the present), fathers call their children to focus on "there and then" (hope for the future). A father challenges his children to develop themselves on the way to achievement as much as to the achievements themselves. He does this, not by criticising or scolding, but by expressing the affirming faith of what he sees the child could become. One couple I have mentored for 20 years said the thing that drew them into the relationship was that "you believed in us"!

As I said earlier in this chapter, I was something of a late developer as a teenager. When I talked through with my dad my goal to attain selection for a provincial cricket team in my Grade 11 year, he was an eager supporter and encourager. He also happened to be the coach of our cricket team. However, as a 160 cm, chunky, not very athletic (but fairly accurate!) off-spin bowler,[425] I did not gain selection at the end of that year. I was devastated and discouraged, feeling like a failure, especially in a family of sporting achievers. I will always remember my father's encouragement that devastating evening. He said: "My boy, selection for the team is not the main goal. Your development is. You have the ability, but you are not strong enough yet for it. When you are ready, selection will come." I made the team the next year. I was stronger, more emotionally mature, and better at the game than I had been the year before, and saw the wisdom of my dad's words.

I believe that the same principle is true with regard to spiritual

---

[425]With apologies to readers from non-cricket playing cultures! It's like a pitcher in baseball.

gifting. God, as a Father, loves us too much to allow us simply to achieve external goals, even for ministry, when our character and relationship with Him are not strong enough to sustain it. Promotion in the sense of ministry growth happens along with the growth of our Christlikeness, in the ideal scenario. One of the tragedies of life and ministry is seeing someone whose ministry or skill outstrips their spiritual health or maturity. A true father wants his children to be able to carry their success on developed shoulders.

Leaving a legacy

Many years ago, someone told me that the true mark of leadership is not seen while you are busy leading, but only after you have departed the scene. It is seen in the footprints you leave in the lives of people who can no longer see you. In this sense, Jesus Christ was a unique leader: If you look at the number of people who were loyal to Him or His teaching at the end of His life, He was a seeming failure. Those He personally chose as the bearers of His flame, abandoned Him. They hid away from the very people who had put Him to death, in a seemingly craven attempt at self-preservation and the betrayal of the principles to which they had been called. It is only after the Holy Spirit was poured out upon them that they seemed to remember what those principles were, and committed themselves to living and, indeed, dying for the things that Jesus had taught them while He was with them. Two thousand years later, His footprints are clear for anyone who wants to follow them, because the legacy He left was taken up, first by the apostles and, subsequently, by generation after generation of those who have received the same legacy. Jesus Christ changed the world *after* He left it, far more than He did in His short life here. He did so through a legacy left in the lives of about 120 people.

There are many other stories, less dramatic than this one, but illustrating the same principle. A true leader leads, not only for his immediate followers, but for the next generation and the generations after that. In this sense, the leader, as a true father, is able to defer compensation in the pursuit of a better future for those he will impact through his leadership.

A legacy is only as valuable as the passion with which it is claimed. That passion is the result of the personal loyalty that the heirs thereof feel for the person who has left it to them. In other words, the spiritual father motivates his children to want the legacy he leaves for them, by the quality of his life and the intrinsic values by which he lives.

There is an old story, which may be true or mythical, but which illustrates this point: A wealthy Christian man had a son who was living a prodigal life. The son wanted nothing more passionately than a particular sports car which cost a large amount of money. On his twenty-first birthday, his father called him into his study and said, "I have your birthday present here." He presented him with a Bible and said: "Read it, for it contains the source of your joy." The son screamed out in rage: "A *Bible!* You have all this money, and you know what I have always wanted! And you give me a *Bible* for my birthday! You can keep your Bible!" He threw it down and stormed out, continuing to live his decadent life. The father went to his son's bedroom and placed the Bible on his dresser with the card saying: "Read it, for it contains the source of your joy." Some years went by and the son, like the prodigal of Luke 15, came to himself. Returning to his father's home late one night, he went to the bedroom that had been his from years before. Finding the Bible on the dresser, he opened it. An envelope fell out from between its pages and he opened it. It contained a note and a key. The note said simply: "Here is the key to that Ferrari you always wanted. It is paid for in full and awaits you at the showroom." His avoidance of his father's gift, caused by his personal estrangement from his father, had cost him years of the joy he thought was so important to him. In order to embrace the legacy left by a leader, we will need to embrace a personal love for and allegiance to the leader himself.

Thus, the father-leader will seek sons and daughters, not to make himself look good, but to promote them. In fact, it is probably incorrect to speak of "seeking" sons and daughters. What I have seen is rather that they find their fathers, if they are not "born from their loins", so to speak. I have had several young leaders say, over the years: "I want you to be my spiritual father," or words to that effect. It is an experience that has often fascinated me, and sometimes even alarmed me. It is almost as if the child adopts the father, rather than the other way around. It puts a sense of responsibility on the chosen parent. It seems to operate at different levels, but I have experienced it in many places, and also found that it cannot be organised, imposed or "faked".

Blessing

Finally, fathers *pass on blessing* to their children. We began with the story of Isaac blessing Jacob. The story illustrates some interesting spiritual dynamics, namely: that we may confer blessing by our words spoken in faith; that the words have effect, even when the recipient does not "deserve" the blessing; and that words have eternal effect (cannot be rescinded). Fathering is not a merely psychological, emotional and practical exercise in raising and passing something on to our children. It is powerful and spiritual in effect. What we say before God about our children, and what we say to them about their destinies, will endure long after we are no longer there. What it leaves me with is both fear and excitement. As a leader, I pray regularly for those I lead. I ask God to bless them, sometimes with new gifts, with wisdom and strength, with endurance and fortitude, or with grace to do the right thing. I also seek to respond to any promptings I may feel, to speak to them, pass on a message, Scripture or encouraging word, and initiate contact in the form of an appointment, a visit, etc.

The clear implication is that one of the more wonderful ways we lead, is by our intercessions for people, in private and in public. When they are with us, and when they are absent. Paul was a man of prayer for those for whom God had given him responsibility:

> *I bow my knees before the Father of our Lord Jesus Christ, from whom every family in heaven and on earth receives its name. I pray that he would give you, according to his glorious riches, strength in your inner being and power through his Spirit, and that Christ would make his home in your hearts through faith. Then, having been rooted and grounded in love, you will be able to understand, along with all the saints, what is wide, long, high, and deep – that is, you will know the love of Christ, which goes far beyond knowledge, and will be filled with all the fullness of God.* (Ephesians 3:14–19)

> *To Timothy, my dear child. May grace, mercy, and peace from God the Father and Christ Jesus our Lord be yours! I constantly thank my God – whom I serve with a clear conscience, as my ancestors did – when I remember you in my prayers night and day, recalling your tears and longing to see you so that I can be filled with joy.* (2 Timothy 1:2–4)

The spiritual gift of leadership, especially in this vital dimension of fathering, is an essentially spiritual exercise. It involves faith toward God, faith about people and their potential, and faith that our prayers make a difference. We may, like Jacob, and like other earthly fathers and mothers, sometimes not see the fruition of our faith. We may even lose hope while children go "walkabout" from the very things we have sought to pass on to them. But true fathers will persevere, and desire nothing more than that their children do better than they did.

Mothers in Israel

It is here that "mothering" manifests its own unique ways of being a source of blessing to children. Mothers share many of the traits I have attributed to fathers and, additionally, have some unique features to offer. It is mothers who give birth to their children, and only mothers can offer themselves to a baby as the source of physical nurture. They balance the disciplines that fathers sometimes have to mete out, with the comfort and reassurance of unconditional love. It is mothers who make practical what fathers often only dream about. Where men are idealists, women are realists. Where fathers can easily reduce their children to extensions of their name, their "honour", and even their ambitions, mothers are more concerned for the wellbeing of the child herself. The prayers of a mother are the stuff of legend, not without the corroboration of many true stories.

Paul's application of the mother image to his own role as a leader, speaks of being "affectionately desirous" of the Thessalonians, and willing to give (impart) himself even to the point of giving his own soul, as does a nursing mother, for their wellbeing and growth.[426] Where fathers give their vision and ideals, mothers give their lives.

I said at the chapter's beginning, that both roles, while being derived from the gender-specific functions and styles of natural fathers and mothers, may be exercised in the sphere of spiritual leadership by either men or women. As men, we need to learn from the maternal virtues displayed by women, and which reflect some unique elements of God's nature. Women need to understand that leadership requires growth and change of them, in ways they may see coming naturally (and sometimes bringing

---

[426] 1 Thessalonians 2:7–8 KJV: "… we were willing to have imparted unto you, not the gospel of God only, but also our own souls, because ye were dear unto us."

irritation) to and through the men in their lives. This is not to call for a kind of "unisex" approach in leaders. Rather, I believe each gender, and what is expressed as being feminine and maternal, as well as masculine and paternal, needs the other, and needs to show humility and adaptability in the style we bring to leadership.

As spiritual "parents", then, we are called in our leadership role to apply these traits to the way we care, pray, work, and lay down our lives for our followers. Whether by spiritual birth or adoption, when we become parents, we are responsible to love, nurture, bless and challenge those we lead. Not to become a slightly younger version of ourselves, but the best version of themselves that they can be. Not to match us, but to outstrip us, outrun us and outdo us. To take the legacy we have left them, and multiply it for their children, and their children's children.

CONCLUSION

I began this book with "the end in mind".[427] The "end", in terms of Ephesians 4:11–16, is a church operating as loving community, growing in quality as well as quantity, because of the raising, training, empowerment and release of its members "to do the work of ministry".[428] I also set out to establish the fact that the church's leaders are, in large part, pursuing the wrong vision, and reaching the wrong outcomes, in terms of their personal influence, their ministry styles and their churches. The marks of "success" are external, such as size of church (numbers of attendees), income, buildings, activities offered, and "professions of faith". The goal of many leaders is self-centred: to become famous, prominent, and to establish and promote "my ministry". Discipleship and formation of church members is not a prominent goal or outcome in most cases – except for external observance of religious practice and ethical rules – and this is partly due to the way leaders lead. The achievement of this goal, therefore, calls for a paradigm shift among leaders, to acknowledge: "The responsibility of leaders is not to manage the church. Whatever titles we give leaders in

---

[427]A phrase used by Stephen Covey, *op. cit.,* p. 96.
[428]Ephesians 4:16 NLT: "As each part does its own special work, it helps the other parts grow, so that the whole body is healthy and growing and full of love."

churches today, and whatever roles they play, their common mission is an equipping, shepherding one."[429]

I believe that the notion of leadership itself, and its continued and vital place as one of the "motivational gifts" listed in Romans 12, is established in both biblical and modern practice. The fascinating parallels between biblical word-pictures and modern, secular theories give sufficient basis for me to work with and seek relevant applications for them in the modern church. There are sufficiently strong grounds for defining leadership as purposeful and goal-focused, to be able to say that leadership is missional, in that it has to do with someone stepping to the front with the intention of taking a group to a goal.

The missional church, writes Craig van Gelder, is to be "the sign, foretaste, firstfruits, and agent of the reign of God that Jesus announced and inaugurated".[430] For this to be the case, it needs to have faith, hope, love and truth; its leadership needs to be apostolic, prophetic, pastoral and instructive. Leaders, according to Ephesians 4:12, are to "work themselves out of a job" by doing what Jesus commissioned them to do, i.e. to make disciples. The healthy church, the truly missional church, then, will be evidenced by "maximum mobilisation" of its laity.

In my experience, the roles and types of leaders operating in many places where churches are being planted and grown, are very different. Instead of apostolic leaders being servant-kings, many are dictatorial, operating by entitlement, and exercising the harsh rulership about which Jesus is so scathing. Prophets, similarly, are self-focused, insisting on being called the "Man of God" and believing that they alone are God's "Oracle". Instead of compassionate pastors, many churches are led by haughty and inaccessible lords over their flocks, who operate above accountability or

---

[429]Richards and Hoeldtke, *op. cit.,* p. 92.

[430]Craig van Gelder, in *Missional Church, op. cit.,* p 76.

correction, and believe that they own "their" people.

The overall effect of these models is an undervalued, under-trained, overcontrolled and dependent laity. There is insufficient focus on making disciples, so that the church is experiencing in missional terms what Dallas Willard called "the Great Omission".[431] Many pastoral leaders are "lone rangers", operating as a law unto themselves, non-accountable and independent. Even pastors' fraternals are not really places of accountability, but of posturing and seeking a platform. I do not advocate that there be no clear leader, or that the church be ruled by committee. Rather, I believe churches should be led by a pastoral leader, with and through a team, which "distributes leadership", in an interdependent relationship with the pastor, who is the team leader.[432] I believe that, in the Church in general, the need for greater interdependence, team involvement and ecumenical co-operation is urgent.

On the other hand, every leader, like every local church, is only a small piece of the ministry jigsaw puzzle which reveals what Christ is like. Pastoral leaders need to understand their limitations, and that those limitations invite us to "comprehend *with all the saints* what *is* the width and length and depth and height, and to know the love of Christ which passes knowledge; that [the Church] may be filled with all the fullness of God".[433] This also raises the question of inter-church co-operation. If the ideal of church members being brought to maturity by the operation of

---

[431]Dallas Willard, *The Great Omission: Reclaiming Jesus' Essential Teachings on Discipleship* (HarperOne, 2006). His thesis in this book suggests that, whereas the last command Jesus gave the church before he ascended to heaven was the Great Commission, the call for Christians to make disciples of all the nations, we have responded by making Christians, not disciples. This has been the church's Great Omission.

[432]Wright, *op. cit.*, loc 956. He later continues: "A gifted leader is also needed to serve the team: to see that the mission is pursued, the people are cared for, and the decisions are made" (loc 976).

[433]Ephesians 3:18–19 NKJV, emphasis mine.

all four leadership types is to be accomplished, the issue, for most churches, will be the scarcity of available ministry. Multi-staff teams are rare: the average church is small and is fortunate if it can adequately support just one pastor. Alan Roxburgh offers a recommendation for what John Wimber and others have called "multi-congregational churches",[434] which is a model very easily implemented in urban contexts, given attitudes of humility and unity between leaders in that context:

> *One potentially fruitful way of understanding this plurality is to pursue leadership as a team function in any particular geographic area. Hence the particular community would not be seen as a relatively independent unit with its own, **solus pastor** leadership. Instead, a team of leaders, each bringing unique gifts, would function within a number of connected congregations, equipping and empowering them as a missional people for a particular area.*[435]

Whether in one single congregation, or in an urban environment, as Roxburgh suggests, I would recommend that leaders work in teams with a balanced variety of gifts, giving those gifts not only for one congregation, but also for the whole Body of Christ to benefit. This applies within denominations, where the price of reaching the missional goal of the church is that pastors forego the *solus pastor* model, and instead see themselves as part of the ministry team for "the church in their city". However, beyond such parochial models, what is needed is a robust, trusting ecumenism, with ministry being offered across lines of denomination, seeking Kingdom alliances.

The church can gain much in terms of its missional integrity, credibility and momentum, from the surrender of personal

---

[434]John Wimber seminar, *Church Planting: God's Heart for Expansion* (Vineyard Ministries International, 1985).
[435]*Missional Church, op. cit.,* p. 215.

agendas, in the true spirit of servanthood, and an obedience to the call to unity implicit in the high-priestly prayer of Jesus:

I do not pray for these alone, but also for those who will believe in Me through their word; that they all may be one, as You, Father, are in Me, and I in You; that they also may be one in Us, that the world may believe that You sent Me. And the glory which You gave Me I have given them, that they may be one just as We are one: I in them, and You in Me; that they may be made perfect in one, and that the world may know that You have sent Me, and have loved them as You have loved Me. (John 17:20–23 NKJV)

It is such radical missionality, expressed in radical unity of spirit, purpose and lifestyle, that will make our witness credible and the Church's destiny achievable. A missional church, being a sign, agent and foretaste of the Kingdom of God, has the characteristics described in Psalm 84:5–7:

Happy are those whose strength is in you,
in whose heart are the highways to Zion.
As they go through the valley of Baca
they make it a place of springs;
the early rain also covers it with pools.
They go from strength to strength;
the God of gods will be seen in Zion.

If it is true that the church goes as its leaders go, then leaders will need to take on board all the terms of their calling, to be, become and do leadership as:

L = Life quality
E = Envisioning
A = Attraction
D = Dividend
E = Empowering
R = Relationality
S = Servanthood
H = Hustle
I = Implementation
P = Potentiality

REFERENCES

Major works consulted

Allen, Joseph J., *The Ministry of the Church: The Image of Pastoral Care* (New York: St. Vladimir's Seminary Press, 1986)

Ascough, Richard S. and Cotton, Charles A., *Passionate Visionary* (Peabody, MA: Hendrickson Publishers, Inc., 2006)

Barrett, Lois Y., et al., *Treasure in Clay Jars: Patterns in Missional Faithfulness* (Grand Rapids, MI: Wm. B. Eerdmans Publishing Co., 2004)

Bartlett, David Lyon, *Ministry in the New Testament* (Minneapolis, MN: Augsburg Fortress Publishing Co., 1993)

Clarke, Andrew D., *Serve the Community of the Church: Christians as Leaders and Ministers* (Grand Rapids, MI: Wm. B. Eerdmans Publishing Co., 2000)

Guder, Darrell L., ed., *Missional Church: A Vision for the Sending of the Church in North America* in *The Gospel and Our Culture* series (Grand Rapids: Wm. B. Eerdmans Publishing Co., 1998), Kindle edition

Jones, L. Gregory and Armstrong, Kevin R., *Resurrecting Excellence: Shaping Faithful Christian Ministry* in *Pulpit & Pew* series (Grand Rapids, MI: Wm. B. Eerdmans Publishing Co., 2006), Kindle edition

Wright, Walter C., *Relational Leadership: A Biblical Model for Influence and Service* (Colorado Springs, CO: Paternoster Press, 2009), Kindle edition

Other sources consulted

Books

Adams, Jay E., *Pastoral Counselling* (Grand Rapids, MI: Baker Book House, 1975)
Pastoral Leadership (Grand Rapids, MI: Baker Book House, 1976)

Addison, Steve, *Movements that Change the World* (Smyrna, DE: Missional Press, 2009)

Adizes, Ichak Kalderon, *Management/Mismanagement Styles: How to Identify a Style and What to Do about It* (Santa Barbara, CA: The Adizes Institute Publishing, 2004)
The Ideal Executive: Why You Cannot Be One and What to Do About It (Santa Barbara, CA: The Adizes Institute Publishing, 2004)
Corporate Lifecycles: How and Why Corporations Grow and Die and What to Do About It (Englewood Cliffs, NJ: Prentice-Hall, 1988)

Allen, David, *Getting Things Done* (New York: Penguin Books, 2001)

Allen, Roland, *Missionary Methods: St. Paul's or Ours?* (Grand Rapids, MI: Wm. B. Eerdmans Publishing Co., 1962)
The Spontaneous Expansion of the Church (Grand Rapids, MI: Wm. B. Eerdmans Publishing Co., 1960)

Armour, Michael C. and Browning, Don, *Systems-Sensitive Leadership* (Joplin, MO: College Press Publishing Company, 2000)

Banks, Robert and Ledbetter, Bernice M., *Reviewing Leadership* (Grand Rapids, MI: Baker Academic, 2004)

Barna, George, *Leaders on Leadership* (Ventura, CA: Regal Books, 1997)

Berkouwer, G. C., *Holy Scripture* in *Studies in Dogmatics* series (Grand Rapids, MI: Wm. B. Eerdmans Publishing Co., 1982)

Berne, Eric, *Games People Play: The Basic Handbook of Transactional Analysis* (New York: Penguin, 1975)

Billings, J. Todd, *Union with Christ: Reframing Theology and Ministry for the Church* (Grand Rapids, MI: Baker Academic, 2011)

Black, Malcolm, *The Pursuit of Apostolic Christianity* (Johannesburg: South African Theological Seminary Press, 2009)

Black, Matthew, ed., *Peake's Commentary on the Bible* (London: Thomas Nelson and Sons, 1967)

Brooks, M., Stark J. and Caverhill, S., *Your Leadership Legacy* (San Francisco, CA: Berrett-Koehler Publishers, Inc., 2004)

Bruce, F. F., *The Epistles to the Colossians, to Philemon, and to the Ephesians* (Grand Rapids, MI: Wm. B. Eerdmans Publishing Co., 1984)

Romans: An Introduction and Commentary in *The Tyndale New Testament Commentaries* series (Intervarsity Press, 1974)

Burridge, Richard A., *Four Gospels, One Jesus?* (Grand Rapids, MI: Wm. B. Eerdmans Publishing Co., 1994)

Calvin, John, *Calvin's Commentaries: The Epistles of Paul the Apostle to the Corinthians,* trans. John W. Fraser (Grand Rapids, MI: Wm. B. Eerdmans Publishing Co., 1960)

Calvin's Commentaries: The Epistles of Paul the Apostle to the Romans and to the Thessalonians, trans. MacKenzie Ross (Grand Rapids, MI: Wm. B. Eerdmans Publishing Co., 1973)

Calvin's Commentaries: The Epistles of Paul the Apostle to the Galatians, Ephesians, Philippians and Colossians, trans. T. H. L. Parker (Grand Rapids, MI: Wm. B. Eerdmans Publishing Co., 1965)

Carson, D. A. and Moo, Douglas J., *An Introduction to the New Testament* (Grand Rapids, MI: Zondervan, 2005)

Clinton, Robert J., *The Making of a Leader* (Grand Rapids, MI: NavPress, 2005)

Collins, Jim, *Good to Great* (New York: Random House, 2001)

The Concise Oxford Dictionary (Oxford: Clarendon Press, 1990)

Conzelmann, Hans, *I Corinthians*, trans. James W. Leitch (Philadelphia, PA: Augsburg Fortress Press, 1988)

Cornwall, Judson, *Profiles of a Leader* (Plainfield, NJ: Logos International, 1980)

Covey, Stephen R., *The 7 Habits of Highly Effective People* (New York: Fireside, 1990)

De Pree, Max, *Leadership Is an Art* (New York: Dell Publishers, 1989)

Leading without Power (San Francisco, CA: Jossey-Bass, Inc., Publishers, 1997)

Douglas, J. D., ed., *The New Bible Dictionary* (London: Intervarsity Fellowship, 1967)

Ellis, Joe S., *The Church on Purpose* (Cincinatti, OH: Standard Publishing, 1982)

Farmer, William, ed., *The International Bible Commentary* (Collegeville, MN: The Liturgical Press, 1998)

Fee, Gordon D., *The First Epistle to the Corinthians* (Grand Rapids, MI: Wm. B. Eerdmans Publishing Co., 1987)

Fowl, Stephen E., *Philippians* in *Two Horizons New Testament Commentary* series (Grand Rapids, MI: Wm. B. Eerdmans Publishing Co., 2005)

France, R. T., *Jesus and the Old Testament: His Application of Old Testament Passages to Himself and His Mission* (Vancouver: Regent College Publishing, 1998)

Frankl, Viktor E., *Man's Search for Meaning* (Boston, MA: Beacon Press, 1959).

Gee, Donald, *Concerning Spiritual Gifts* (Springfield, MI: Gospel Publishing House, 1972)

Gibbs, Eddie, *Leadership Next* (Nottingham: Inter-varsity Press, 2005)

Giuliani, Rudolph W. and Kurson, Ken, *Leadership* (London: Little, Brown, 2002)

Goleman, Daniel, *Emotional Intelligence: Why It Can Matter More Than IQ* (London: Bantam Publishing Co., 1995)

Grenz, Stanley J., *Theology for the Community of God* (Grand Rapids, MI: Wm. B. Eerdmans Publishing Co., 2000)

Grosheide, F. W., *Commentary on the First Epistle to the Corinthians* (Grand Rapids, MI: Wm. B. Eerdmans Publishing Co., 1972)

Gundry, Robert H., *Commentary on Ephesians* (Grand Rapids, MI: Baker Academic, 2011)

Guthrie, Donald, *New Testament Introduction* (Leicester: Apollos/ IVP, 1990)

Hays, Richard B., *First Corinthians* (Louisville, KY: John Knox Press, 1997)

Hendriksen, William, *A Commentary on the Epistle to the Philippians* (London: The Banner of Truth Trust, 1963)
Ephesians in *New Testament Commentary* series (Edinburgh: Banner of Truth Trust, 1972)

Hirsch, Alan, *The Forgotten Ways: Reactivating the Missional Church* (Ada, MI: Brazos, 2006)

Hock, Dee, *Birth of the Chaordic Age* (San Francisco, CA: Berrett-Koehler Publishers, Inc., 1999)

Hodge, Charles, *A Commentary on Romans* (London: The Banner of Truth Trust, 1972)

Hodges, Melvin L., *The Indigenous Church* (Springfield, MI: Gospel Publishing House, 1999)

Hollenweger, W.J., *The Pentecostals* (Minneapolis, MN: Augsburg

Publishing House, 1972)

Hughes, Selwyn, *Discovering Your Place in the Body of Christ* (London: Marshall Pickering, 1982)

Hybels, Bill, *Courageous Leadership* (Grand Rapids, MI: Zondervan, 2002)

Who You Are When No One's Looking (London: IVP, 1987)

Jacobsen, Eric O., *The Three Tasks of Leadership* (Grand Rapids MI: Wm. B. Eerdmans Publishing Co., 2009)

Keirsey, David and Bates, Marilyn, *Please Understand Me II* (Del Mar, CA: Prometheus Nemesis, 1984), Kindle edition

Khoza, Reuel J., *Attuned Leadership – African Humanism as Compass* (Johannesburg: Penguin Books, 2011)

Kraft, Dave, *Leaders Who Last* (Wheaton, IL: Crossway, 2010)

Manley, Mark, *The LeaderSHIP* (Johannesburg: Mark Manley Associates, 2007)

Manning, Tony, *Discovering the Essence of Leadership* (Cape Town: Zebra Press, 2002)

Marshall, I. Howard, *Ephesians* in *Eerdmans Commentary on the Bible,* ed. James D. G. Dunn (Grand Rapids, MI: Wm. B. Eerdmans Publishing Co., 2003)

Maslow, A., *Motivation and Personality* (New York: Harper, 1954)

Maxwell, John C., *The 21 Irrefutable Laws of Leadership* (Nashville, TN: Thomas Nelson, Inc., 1998)

McKnight, Scot, *A Community Called Atonement* (Nashville, TN: Abingdon Press, 2007)

Michael, Chester P. and Norrisey, Marie C., *Prayer and Temperament* (Charlottesville, VA: The Open Door Inc., 1997)

Migliore, Daniel L., *Faith Seeking Understanding: An Introduction to Christian Theology,* 2nd ed (Grand Rapids, MI: Wm. B. Eerdmans Publishing Co., 2004)

Mitchell, Costa, *Learn to Love Yourself* (Cape Town: Vineyard International Publishing, 1991)

Moo, Douglas J., *The Epistle to the Romans* (Grand Rapids, MI: Wm. B. Eerdmans Publishing Co., 1996)

Morris, Leon, *The First Epistle of Paul to the Corinthians: An Introduction and Commentary* (London: The Tyndale Press, 1958)

Mounce, Robert H., *Romans* in *The New International Commentary* (Nashville: Broadman & Holman Publishing, 1995)

Müller, Jac. J., *The Epistles of Paul to the Philippians and to Philemon* in *The New International Commentary on the New Testament* (Grand Rapids, MI: Wm. B. Eerdmans Publishing Co., 1980)

Murray, John, *The Epistle to the Romans* (Grand Rapids, MI: Wm. B. Eerdmans Publishing Co., 1968)

Nathan, Rich and Kim, Insoo, *Both-And: Living the Christ-Centered Life in an Either-Or World* (New York: IVP, 2013)

Newbigin, Lesslie, *The Open Secret: An Introduction to the Theology of Mission* (Grand Rapids, MI: Wm. B. Eerdmans Publishing Co., 1995), Kindle edition

Nouwen, Henry, *In the Name of Jesus* (New York: The Crossroad Publishing Company, 1989)

Osmer, Richard R. *Practical Theology: An Introduction* (Grand Rapids, MI: Wm. B. Eerdmans Publishing Co., 2008)

Oswald, Roy M. and Kroeger, Otto, *Personality Type and Religious Leadership* (Herndon, VA: Alban Institute, 1988), Kindle edition

Oswalt, John, *The Book of Isaiah 40-66* in *New International Commentary on the Old Testament* (Grand Rapids, MI: Wm. B. Eerdmans Publishing Co., 1998)

Peterson, Eugene H., *Working the Angles: The Shape of Pastoral Integrity* (Grand Rapids, MI: Wm. B. Eerdmans Publishing Co., 2000), Kindle edition

Pilpel, Robert H., *To the Honour of the Fleet* (London: Chaucer Press, 1979)

Piper, John, *Brothers, We are Not Professionals* (Nashville, TN: Broadman & Holman Publishers, 2002)

Richards, Lawrence O. and Hoeldtke, C., *A Theology of Church Leadership* (Grand Rapids, MI: Zondervan Publishing House, 1981)

Richardson, Peter Tufts, *Four Spiritualities* (Palo Alto, CA: Davies-Black Publishing, 1996)

Roberts, J. H., *Die Brief aan die Efesiërs* (Goodwood: NG Kerk-Uitgewers, 1983)

Robertson, Archibald and Plummer, Alfred, *A Critical and Exegetical Commentary on the First Epistle of St Paul to the Corinthians* (Edinburgh: T&T Clark, 1911)

Roxburgh, Alan and Regele, Mike, *Crossing the Bridge: Church Leadership in a Time of Change* (Santa Margarita, CA: Percept Group, 2000)

Rudge, Peter F., *Management in the Church* (London: McGraw Hill, 1976)

Ruiz, Jesus Asurmendi, *Ezekiel* in *International Bible Commentary*, ed. William Farmer (Collegeville, MN: The Liturgical Press, 1998)

Rush, Myron, *Management: A Biblical Approach* (Wheaton, IL: Victor Books, 1983)

Sanday, William and Headlam, Arthur C., *A Critical and Exegetical Commentary on the Epistle to the Romans* (Edinburgh: T&T Clark, 1895)

Sanders, J. Oswald, *Dynamic Spiritual Leadership: Leading Like Paul* (Grand Rapids, MI: Discovery House Publishers, 1999)

Scazzero, Peter, *Emotionally Healthy Spirituality* (Nashville, TN: Thomas Nelson, 2006)

The Emotionally Healthy Church (Grand Rapids, MI: Zondervan, 2003)

Schwarz, Christian A., *The 3 Colors of Ministry* (Alberton:

Churchwise, 2001)

Schweizer, Eduard, *Church Order in the New Testament* (Eugene, OR: Wipf & Stock, 2006)

Shearman, David, *The Unstoppable Church* (Tonbridge: Sovereign World Ltd, 1995)

Simpson, E. K. and Bruce, F. F., *The Epistles to the Ephesians and the Colossians* (Grand Rapids, MI: Wm. B. Eerdmans Publishing Co., 1957)

Smith, James K. A., *Thinking in Tongues* (Grand Rapids, MI: Wm. B. Eerdmans Publishing Co., 2010)

Springer, Kevin and Wimber, John, *Riding the Third Wave: What Comes After Renewal?* (New York: Harper Collins Publishers, 1987)

Tenney, Merrill C., ed., *The Zondervan Pictorial Encyclopedia of the Bible* (Grand Rapids, MI: Zondervan Publishers, 1976)

Thiessen, Henry Clarence, *Lectures in Systematic Theology* (Grand Rapids, MI: Wm. B. Eerdmans Publishing Co., 1990)

Thiselton, Anthony, *1 Corinthians: A Shorter Exegetical & Pastoral Commentary* (Grand Rapids, MI: Wm. B. Eerdmans Publishing Co., 2006)

Towner, Philip H. *The Expository Commentary to the New Testament* (Nottingham: IVP, 1994)

Van Engen, Charles, *God's Missionary People: Rethinking the Purpose of the Local Church* (Grand Rapids, MI: Baker Book House, 1991)

Vine's Expository Dictionary of New Testament Words (Macdonald, undated)

Volf, Miroslav, *Exclusion and Embrace* (Nashville, TN: Abingdon Press, 1996)

Free of Charge: Giving and Forgiving in a Culture Stripped of Grace (Grand Rapids, MI: Zondervan, 2009)

Wagner, C. Peter, *Discover Your Spiritual Gifts* (Ventura, CA:

Regal Books, 2012)

Walker, Williston, *A History of the Christian Church* (Edinburgh: T&T Clark Ltd, 1976)

Willard, Dallas, *The Great Omission: Reclaiming Jesus' Essential Teachings on Discipleship* (San Francisco, CA: HarperOne, 2006)

Wilson Learning Corporation, *Managing Interpersonal Relationships* (Eden Prairie, MN: Wilson Learning, 1979)

Wimber, John and Kevin Springer, *Power Healing* (New York: HarperCollins Publishing, 1991)

Woolfe, Lorin, *The Bible on Leadership* (New York: American Management Association, 2002)

Wright, Christopher J. H., *The Mission of God's People: A Biblical Theology of the Church's Mission* (Grand Rapids, MI: Zondervan, 2010)

Articles, seminars and websites

Burger, Coenie, *Die Predikantsamp,* five articles on the website academic.sun.ac.za, publ 2004

Catholic view on Gospel writers: www.catholicresources.org/Art/Evangelists_symbols.htm

Hotze, Steven F., "Testosterone" on http://www.aehf.com/articles/Testosterone.htm

Lindsey, F. Duane, "The Call of the Servant in Isaiah 42:1-9" in *BIBLIOTHECA SACRA* 139 (553) (Jan. 1982): (Dallas Theological Seminary; 1982)

Mother Teresa quote: http://www.iloveindia.com/indian-heroes/mother-teresa/quote.html

Nel, Christo, *VISA to the HILT Workshop in PEAK Leadership Seminar* (© The Village Leadership Consulting, 2012)

Schweitzer, Albert, "Happiness", on www.cybernation.com quotation centre

Socrates quotation: http://www.iwise.com

Stewart, Angus, "John of Damascus and the Perichoresis" in *British Reformed Journal,* www.christianstudylibrary.org

Webster, Noah, *Webster's 1928 Dictionary of American English,* E-Sword edition, www.e-Sword.com

Wimber, John R., *Church Planting: God's Heart for Expansion* seminar (Anaheim: Vineyard Ministries International, 1986)

Winston, Bruce E. and Ryan, Barry, "Servant Leadership is more Global than Western" in *International Journal of Leadership Studies,* Vol. 3 Iss. 2, 2008, pp. 212-222 © 2008 School of Global Leadership & Entrepreneurship, Regent University ISSN 1554-3145, www.regent.edu/ijls